Watching
the
Watchdog

Bloggers as the Fifth Estate

Other Books of Interest from
MARQUETTE BOOKS

Jami Fullerton and Alice Kendrick, *Advertising's War on Terrorism: The Story of the Shared Values Initiative* (2006). ISBN: 0-922993-43-2 (cloth); 0-922993-44-0 (paperback)

Mitchell Land and Bill W. Hornaday, *Contemporary Media Ethics: A Practical Guide for Students, Scholars and Professionals* (2006). ISBN: 0-922993-41-6 (cloth); 0-922993-42-4 (paperback)

Joey Reagan, *Applied Research Methods for Mass Communicators* (2006). ISBN: 0-922993-45-9

Ralph D. Berenger (ed.), *Cybermedia Go to War: Role of Alternative Media During the 2003 Iraq War* (2006). ISBN: 0-922993-24-6

David Demers, *Dictionary of Mass Communication: A Guide for Students, Scholars and Professionals* (2005). ISBN: 0-922993-35-1 (cloth); 0-922993-25-4 (paperback)

John C. Merrill, Ralph D. Berenger and Charles J. Merrill, *Media Musings: Interviews with Great Thinkers* (2004). ISBN: 0-922993-15-7

Ralph D. Berenger (ed.), *Global Media Go to War: Role of Entertainment and News During the 2003 Iraq War* (2004). ISBN: 0-922993-10-6

Melvin L. DeFleur and Margaret H. DeFleur, *Learning to Hate Americans: How U.S. Media Shape Negative Attitudes Among Teenagers in Twelve Countries* (2003). ISBN: 0-922993-05-X

David Demers (ed.), *Terrorism, Globalization and Mass Communication: Papers Presented at the 2002 Center for Global Media Studies Conference* (2003). ISBN: 0-922993-04-1

Watching
the
Watchdog

Bloggers as the Fifth Estate

Stephen D. Cooper

Marquette Books
Spokane, Washington

Library of Congress Cataloging-in-Publication Data

Cooper, Stephen D, 1950-
Watching the watchdog : bloggers as the fifth estate / Stephen D. Cooper.
p. cm.
Includes bibliographical references and index.
ISBN-13: 978-0-922993-47-5 (pbk. : alk. paper)
ISBN-10: 0-922993-47-5 (pbk. : alk. paper)
ISBN-13: 978-0-922993-46-8 (hardcover : alk. paper)
ISBN-10: 0-922993-46-7 (hardcover : alk. paper)
1. Online journalism--United States. 2. Blogs--Political aspects--United
States. 3. United States--Politics and government--Blogs. 4. Mass media--
Political aspects--United States. 5. Political participation--Technological
innovations--United States. 6. Mass media--United States--Objectivity.
I. Title.
PN4784.O62.C665 2006
302.23'1--dc22
2006018047

Marquette Books
3107 East 62nd Avenue
Spokane, Washington 99223
509-443-7057 (voice) / 509-448-2191 (fax)
books@marquettebooks.org / www.MarquetteBooks.org

Dedication

This book is dedicated to all of you out there in pajamas, banging away on your keyboards in the living room. Whatever the merits or deficiencies of your individual contributions, we're all better off with the blogosphere in the mix.

Table of Contents

Foreword

Watching the Watchdog: Bloggers as the Fifth Estate is a small book that packs a punch far larger than its size would suggest. The blogosphere — that murky universe in which blogs exist — is a relatively new phenomenon, and unfortunately it is also a poorly understood one. Within this universe, however, exist blogs and bloggers. Both of these terms are bantered about, but often with little consensus on their meanings. I paraphrase here, but a blog is a single Web site, focused on self-publishing documents written by one individual or perhaps a small group. Those who write blogs are called bloggers. Cooper's book recognizes both the nature of blogs and the general lack of knowledge about how they work; he does a remarkable job of making sense of the writings of bloggers, focusing on those acting as critics of the mainstream media in America.

This later point is the focus of this book. Cooper examines that group of bloggers which arose specifically to monitor the actions of the mainstream media. As an example of their powerful public presence, consider the controversy surrounding Dan Rather's use of certain documents describing President Bush's National Guard service. Their exposure as forgeries came not though the mainstream media, but through the insightful critique of bloggers. The power of bloggers is great, according to Cooper, and thus compels us to take a closer look at who they are and how they operate.

The main contribution of this book is that it helps the reader to better understand the value of blog content as that content specifically relates to the public discussion of various events and issues. Thus Cooper's book helps us to better understand the very real contribution of bloggers to the process of democratic deliberation. This is a distinct and major contribution.

What I particularly appreciate about this book is how Cooper examines blogging as a phenomenon, instead of examining it from a specific political point of view. Bloggers come in all political persuasions, are a diversified group, and offer alternative points of view for consideration. Cooper allows this important truth into his examination. He illuminates the working of the blogosphere in all its heterogenous glory, focusing on bloggers as they exist, not on how he wishes them to be. The concern is with the grass roots actions the media criticism of bloggers represents, not on whether or not their criticism fits into a particular political niche.

I feel that this book makes a solid contribution to the literature about new communication technology in several ways. As an overarching consideration, look for how Cooper makes sense of this complex, rapidly evolving, almost anarchical area of the Internet: the blogosphere. Within this sphere, he illuminates those bloggers acting as media critics and demonstrates their influence in the public sphere. Specifically, he helps to better flesh out our understanding of the actions of media bloggers by demonstrating how their writings have grown into four distinct genres: critiques of news accuracy, critiques of news framing, critiques of news agenda-setting, and critiques of journalistic practices.

Cooper's knowledge is impressive, but shared in a way that invites, rather than puts off, participation. His central thesis is provocative, and one that will undoubtedly generate further discussion: that blogs, taken collectively, are evolving into a legitimate social institution.

Jim A. Kuypers
Virginia Polytechnic Institute and State University

Acknowledgments

Even when only one performer is listed on the program, a work like this is hardly a solo recital. Sincere thanks are due, in no particular order of appearance, to:

Gwen Brown of Radford University, who put the arm on me to write a National Communication Association panel presentation back in 2003 — which ultimately led to this book.

Paul Siegel of the University of Hartford, who said to me after the panel, "You know you've got a book there, don't you?" No, Paul, I didn't — not until you burst open the lid on my imagination.

The TRWC crew, for encouraging me to think outside the box. You know who you are.

Carolyn Capelli, my trusty research assistant on this project, for truly savvy go-fer work.

David Demers, the honch at Marquette Books, for (1) giving this thing the green light, and (2) coming up with the fantastic cover art. Inquiring minds want to know: how many Milk Bones did it take to get those dogs to pose for the picture?

The faculty and staff of the Department of Communication Studies at Marshall University, for their collegiality. I couldn't ask for a better home.

Bert Gross, my department chair, for showing me an appearance of the word *bloggers* in an unlikely place: a book he was reading about the Adams/Jefferson presidential campaign! When a contemporary historian refers to early American pamphleteers as bloggers, it's a good indicator the concept has gone mainstream — even if the reference is ahistorical.

Ken Chase of Wheaton College, for sharing an obscure Habermas translation. **Susan Gilpin**, my newest colleague at Marshall, for putting a translation of Alexy in my hands.

Monica Brooks of the Marshall University library, for reminding me that librarians are people who know how to find stuff, and **Floyd Csir**, also of the library, for the author photo.

Sandy Hamon, for believing in me.

Lou Pullano, Frank Paoni, and Bob Edelson — my bosses in one of my prior lives — for encouraging me in my graduate studies.

And thanks to **God**, from whom all blessings flow — including the opportunity to write this book.

Stephen D. Cooper
Marshall University
Spring 2006

Introduction

A mixed metaphor seemed appropriate for the title of this book on weblogs. Perhaps this is because the blogosphere, as an emergent social object, is genuinely new — and one of the time-honored ways of making sense of something new is to liken it to something familiar.

The metaphor of watchdog has long been popular as short hand for the structural role of the free press in a representative democracy. Should government officers fail in their responsibility to exercise power on behalf of the general public, that watchdog would alert the citizens at large to their malfeasance. In itself, the metaphor draws on the canine traits humans seem to enjoy the most: loyalty, courage, and strength. So, as a check on the power of the legislative and executive branches of government, the press has for some time enjoyed — if not always merited — a privileged place among our social institutions, and a warm fuzzy metaphor to symbolize it.

But what of that watchdog's leash? If the people need a watchdog to make sure the institution of government does not abuse the power they have granted it, would there not be a need for a comparable check on the press, as a social institution with power in its own right? A number of works have pointed, directly (e.g., Goldberg, 2003) or indirectly (e.g., Lichter, Rothman, Lichter, 1990), at problems with the press's influence on public discourse, or at indications that the mainstream press sometimes acts more in self-interest than in the public interest.

The mainstream press exercises no direct regulatory control over the socio-political system, yet is thought to act as a watchdog for the public because of its surveillance of other institutions and exposure of their operations to public scrutiny. So, too, do blogs lack direct control over the activities of the mainstream press, yet many of them monitor the mainstream press in the same way. In both cases the watchdog function is performed in the open marketplace of ideas. In both cases the watchdog's bite is the threat of diminished credibility, manifest as lost votes for politicians and as reduced consumption of their media products for the mainstream press.

While the editorial staff of mainstream news outlets have the power to spike stories (i.e., cancel their publication) or to generate headline coverage, bloggers do not. But bloggers do have the power to identify factual inaccuracies in mainstream reporting, second-guess the news judgment of mainstream editors, argue for different interpretations of facts than those offered in mainstream stories, or draw attention to stories they feel have been insufficiently covered.

As has been the case with talk radio, some observers have objected to what they see as an ideological tilt in the blogosphere. It is important to note, at the outset, that this particular question is irrelevant to this work. This book is not intended as either an endorsement or a criticism of the ideological or political views of any bloggers. Moreover, it is obvious upon only a casual observation that bloggers, as a cohort, are extraordinarily heterogeneous with regard to their ideology and politics. Instead, this work is intended as an exploration of the distinct types of media criticism which have evolved in the blogosphere, and it does make the argument that the blogosphere, as an emergent social object in itself, is a constructive addition to the media mix.

So if Edmund Burke was onto a fundamental insight when he said the press was, in a practical sense, the Fourth Estate of the legislature (Carlyle, 1993, p. 141), we might now be seeing the emergence of a Fifth Estate in our social system, a watcher of the watchdog. In one sentence, the thesis of this little book is that the blogosphere is in the process of maturing into a full-fledged social institution, albeit a non-traditional one: emergent, self-organizing, and self-regulating.

Some degree of imprecision has crept into the term blog lately, as one might expect in a living language such as English. Definitions and usage reciprocally influence each other, in the sense that the pre-existing meaning of a term conditions its use in giving expression to a thought, but simultaneously the meaning is defined by its use in the expression. It is not hard to see from that how a term's meaning might drift over time. Moreover, it is to be expected that the terminology for an emerging social object will evolve as our understanding of that object — hopefully — is refined.

For our purposes here, we will take the term blog to denote a Web site with the primary purpose of self-publishing documents, which are made individually accessible by hyperlink and displayed in reverse chronological order (Blog, n.d.). We will exclude group discussion sites such as *Free Republic* or *Democratic Underground*, since the content of these sites consist primarily of running commentary and interaction by a large number of individuals. Blogs, for our purposes, are sites on which the primary content is authored by no more than a small group of individuals. While there may or may not be comments threads on a blog, the format is a collection of time-sequenced documents produced by a particular blogger or, in the case of a group blog, a small number of bloggers..

The universe of blogs — named the blogosphere by fiction writer Bill Quick (I Propose a Name, 2001) — includes a great number of sites devoted to personal stories, journaling, hobbies, or other topics not normally thought to be of widespread public interest. No doubt these personal blogs are quite rewarding for both their authors and readers, and would be a worthy subject for study as a form of computer-mediated interpersonal communication on a global scale. Other blogs are devoted to the author's ruminations about the events and public issues of the day, along the lines of opinion magazines. Some amount of this content consists of free-form, bare-knuckle commentary on politics and political actors. In all fairness, much of it strikes this author as either emotional venting or some sort of group bonding ritual; on the other hand, some of it can offer genuine insights into the political machinations or policy issues of the time. These blogs are also of interest and frequently offer a great deal to the reader, but they are not the central focus of this work, either.

As well as the distinction can be drawn, this little book will restrict itself to critical blogging about news products created by what many now refer to as the mainstream media (MSM). As it turns out, there is a great deal to cover in that corner of the blogosphere alone.

CHAPTER 1

Bloggers as Media Critics

Distinct genres of news media criticism have already emerged in the blogosphere. There are also good indications that collaboratively-authored or highly interactive genres will develop, since web pages use HTML and hypertext is built into that language. There are suggestions of this interactivity already in individual blog posts which use hyperlinks to other bloggers, and in the incorporation of readers' e-mails into the posts to which they are responding. Moreover, the diaries pages on *Red State* (http://www.redstate.com) and *Daily Kos* (http://www.dailykos.com) appear to be early forms of collaborative and interactive generation of media criticism in blogs.

In addition to criticism of the mainstream media *per se*, some blogs have begun to offer alternative reporting or news analyses of their own. At the time of this writing, there are a number of online news portals with roots in the blogosphere. They include *memeorandum* (http://www.memeorandum.com), *The Huffington Post* (http://www.huffingtonpost.com), *Pajamas Media* (http://pajamasmedia.com), and *Power Line News* (http://www.powerlineblognews.com).

Often a single blog post will be a self-contained critique of a news story in the traditional media or of a trend or pattern across several pieces of reporting. Sometimes, though, the critique takes the form of a series of posts, over a time period ranging from a few days to a month or longer. The individual entries may be relatively short, but when pieced together contain a comprehensive exploration of some question or topic. It is common practice, in this kind of serialized critique, to indicate the running theme in the header of the post. This form of criticism is analogous to the mainstream journalism practice of a reporter "following" a story.

As young as the blogosphere is, we can start to perceive a typology of media criticism found in it. In the broadest terms, some is criticism of particular news stories, and some is criticism of news coverage in general. Four major types of media criticism have already become staples of the blogosphere, and we can distinguish variants of each of the four types.

While placing real-world phenomena into some sort of typology is a time-honored scholarly routine, tradition alone is not the reason for doing so here. If blogs are evolving into a legitimate social institution — the essential thesis of this book — then it will be helpful to have an analytical framework with which to weigh the value of the media criticism available in the blogosphere. In other words, our purpose here is not just to describe the emergence of a new variety of computer-mediated communication, as a historical curiosity, but to thoughtfully consider how that material relates to earlier forms of mass communication and earlier scholarly analysis of mass communication effects, with an eye toward its impact on the public sphere. Moreover, that a workable typology can be constructed from the large quantity of media criticism blogging is, in itself, an indicator of the blogosphere's maturation into a social institution.

Along that line, we can identify accuracy, framing, agenda-setting/gatekeeping, and journalistic practices as distinct genres of media criticism in the blogosphere, each with their own variants. Blog criticism of accuracy concerns factual evidence mentioned in reporting. Framing concerns the interpretations or meanings of facts and events. Agenda-setting/gatekeeping concerns the newsworthiness or importance of particular events and issues. Criticism of journalistic practices concerns the working methods of professional journalists and news outlets.

In tabular form, the typology would look like this:

Accuracy
    Fact-checking Descriptions
    Fidelity of Quotations
    Authenticity of Documents
    Interpretation of Statistics or Scientific Studies
    Trustworthiness of Memes

Framing
    Disputing the Frame
    Reframing a Set of Facts
    Contextualizing

Agenda-Setting/Gatekeeping
    Questioning the News Judgment
    Setting an Alternative Agenda

Journalistic Practices
    Newsgathering
    Writing and Editing
    Error Correction

While blog posts sometimes are pure examples of one of these types of criticism, there is often a mixture of several in the same post. Again, the intent here is to begin to develop an analytical framework within which to consider the value of the blog content to the public discussion of issues and events. The informal and highly personal writing style of many bloggers might obscure the quality of their insights to readers more accustomed to the third person voice standard in the mainstream media; so, too, might a reader be put off by the occasional bluntness of the language or the facetious, sometimes self-deprecating, names given to the sites. This typology will hopefully make the substance more accessible, and a reasoned assessment of its quality more convenient. Implicit here is the notion that different criteria apply to different varieties of media criticism; for instance, one's expectations for quality in a critique of framing — primarily a matter of interpretation of facts — ought not be identical to the expectations for quality in a critique of accuracy — primarily a matter of verification of facts.

That we can discern distinct genres of blog criticism is a good indicator of the blogosphere's maturation into a social object of consequence. Critical blog posts have accumulated and gradually delineated various types of criticism, while those emerging types have provided a pre-existing form in which critical bloggers can create new content. This is to say that each critical blog post utilizes its respective genre (as a cultural resource upon which to draw) while it simultaneously recreates the genre (maintains, modifies, or develops it). The name structuration (Giddens, 1984, p. xxxi) has been given to this sort of process by which social system features emerge, evolve and persist.

The following chapters describe the genres and their variants, and give examples. The examples are not in any way intended to take a position on the issues they concern. They are intended to illustrate the distinct types of criticism, and to provide insights into the interactions among bloggers, their readers, and mainstream journalists. The merit of particular examples of media criticism is left to the reader, as is the substance of the controversies to which they relate; to that end, the examples include lists of URLs in the endnotes. The key point here is that the blogosphere, as an emergent social object, is clearly a vehicle for legitimate media criticism; the examples are provided to demonstrate that point.

CHAPTER 2

Accuracy

Acommon form of media criticism appearing on blogs consists of challenging the factual accuracy of reporting by the mainstream media. Accuracy is a core ethical tenet of responsible journalism (Cooper, 2006a), and is addressed at the beginning of the ethics code written by the major professional association of reporters (Society of Professional Journalists, 1996).

> Journalists should test the accuracy of information from all sources and exercise care to avoid inadvertent error.

Near the end of the SPJ's ethics code is a tenet describing proper conduct in the event of a factual error in the reporting.

> Journalists should admit mistakes and correct them promptly.

Fact checking has long been common practice in the mainstream media; news organizations employ staff who verify factual statements in copy filed by reporters, before the copy is distributed to the public. What is new, with the emergence of blogs, is the fact-checking done by people outside the news organizations. Bloggers are not bound by the organizational routines and conventions of establishment journalists and, except for journalists who also blog, have not been acculturated into the conventional viewpoints shared by news professionals; in effect, they bring a "fresh set of eyes" to news copy, and thus may point out errors which professional journalists might overlook out of a mild case of groupthink.

This is not necessarily to impute bad intent or negligence to mainstream journalists, but rather to note that professional news workers can make mistakes in the hurry and time pressures of the contemporary news cycle, or may be unduly influenced by the conventional understandings of events and issues among their peers. While it is reasonable to believe that some number of mainstream journalists have, on occasion, exhibited some degree of malice toward particular public figures, it seems more likely that the majority of factual errors in news coverage occur as a result of the shared viewpoints among news professionals, a conformity which may even verge on orthodoxy in some newsrooms. When purported facts are consistent with a shared interpretation of an event, situation, or issue, those purported facts may get far less scrutiny than they should; put another way, their consistency with elite opinion may cause factual errors to be considered presumptively accurate statements.

Neither is this to imply that bloggers are operating on purer motives than mainstream journalists, or are necessarily more scrupulous or more skilled in their fact checking! Here, we are simply noting that bloggers often point out what they see as deficiencies in the factual accuracy of mainstream media reporting, and that the viewpoints of these journalistic outsiders can be of value to the reasoned and constructive public discussion of issues and events. On many occasions the critique of the bloggers has turned out to be well-founded; the major news outlets have issued corrections or at least published rowbacks (i.e., run substantially different updates on stories without forthrightly acknowledging the inaccuracies in their earlier coverage). Less often, the bloggers' challenges to the factual accuracy of mainstream outlets' reporting have led to genuine scandals in media circles; that is to say, the bloggers identified significant professional misconduct on the part of journalists, reporting later acknowledged as substandard by their peers. It is worthwhile to examine a few examples of this type of criticism of factual accuracy, in the blogosphere.

Fact-Checking Descriptions

A good deal of news copy consists of accounts of events. The consumers of this copy trust news outlets to accurately describe places, actions, and statements which they cannot observe directly for themselves. Because mainstream news outlets frequently rely on wire copy or each others' reporting of facts, the consistency of these accounts across mainstream outlets does not, in itself, guarantee their accuracy; in actuality, the practice of repackaging other outlets' descriptions tends to spread a factual error when one occurs early in the news cycle. Often, bloggers will question the accuracy of these descriptions, drawing on eyewitness accounts from outside the journalistic establishment to do so. Often, the factual detail is of significant consequence, regarding the interpretation of the event.

An interesting example of this type of media criticism involved an Associated Press story about a campaign speech in Wisconsin, in September 2004, by President George W. Bush. In the initial version of the AP story (Audience Boos, 2004), the crowd was reported to have booed when Bush mentioned former President Bill Clinton's hospitalization for a heart ailment; the story added the comment, "Bush did nothing to stop them" (AP Changes "Boos" to "Ooohs", 2004). The accuracy of this account was quickly challenged by Brian Mosely on a blog called *Swimming Through the Spin* (AP Bias Strikes Again, 2004). Mosely, a journalist himself, had noticed comments posted on the conservative discussion site, *Free Republic*, by people who had listened to the speech live; they insisted there had been no booing, and were incensed by the inaccuracy of the reporting. The AP first issued a revised version of the story (Bush Offers Best Wishes for Clinton, 2004) without noting the correction — a rowback — deleting the references to the crowd's boos and Bush's inaction and changing the headline, and on the following day a formal retraction stating there was no booing (AP Retracts "Boo" Story, 2004).

Power Line, a more prominent group blog, picked up on the controversy and traced the widespread dissemination of the factual inaccuracy, even after the retraction had been issued (The Associated Press Makes It Up, 2004). Two following posts described their query to the reporter bylined on the story, concerning the basis for his description of the crowd booing (Let's Open a Dialogue, 2004; Waiting for Mr. Hayes, 2004). The *Power Line* blogger, John Hinderaker, also queried another reporter who had drawn on the first AP story for his own writing, and relayed that reporter's answer to an e-mail from a *Power Line* reader (We Hear From Mr. Borenstein, 2004). Of interest here is the way this reporter relied on the original

AP story, and thus unwittingly disseminated a factual inaccuracy:

> As a science correspondent, I was writing, from Washington, a story on the Clinton surgery and heart problem. I was sent an insert about Kerry mentioning the Clinton surgery and tried to balance it with something taken from AP on Bush mentioning it ... . I was in error not mentioning AP's contribution and in using what was later retracted by AP. When Knight Ridder learned of AP's retraction, we sent out a similar correction ... .

This incident illustrates a number of features of fact-checking in the blogosphere. The accuracy of a mainstream reporter's summary account of an event was challenged by members of the general public, based on their own perceptions of a live telecast of the event. Their complaint about the accuracy of a wire story originated on a Web site designed as a discussion forum, where it was noticed by a blogger who then created a post around it and added more material, including the text of the original wire story and subsequent revision. Another blogger, with a larger audience, elaborated the criticism by adding personal correspondence to the thread and tracking distribution of the factual inaccuracy through the mainstream media. This sort of collaborative, interactive media criticism is a new element in the news media mix, introduced by the emergence of the blogosphere.[1]

Patterico is the pseudonym of Patrick Frey, a criminal prosecutor in California. His critique of a *Los Angeles Times* editorial on the retirement of Supreme Court Justice Sandra Day O'Connor (O'Connor Leaves ... , 2005) is a straightforward example of fact-checking by bloggers. The post on *Patterico's Pontifications* (*L.A. Times* Needs a New Fact-checker, 2005) began by quoting the lede of the editorial (emphasis in the blog post).

> One fact sums up Justice Sandra Day O'Connor's pivotal role on the Supreme Court and the enormity of her resignation — she alone was in the majority of every one of the court's 13 5-4 decisions this last term.

Frey pointed out that the *Times* editorial was built around an assertion which was factually inaccurate in two respects; there were more split decisions than 13 during that term, and O'Connor was in the minority in quite a number of them. As evidence he linked to five Supreme Court decisions during the term in which O'Connor had dissented.

> Justice O'Connor dissented from the decision in *Granholm v. Heald,* a 5-4 decision regarding interstate shipments of wine. The majority consisted of Justices Kennedy, Scalia, Souter, Ginsburg, and Breyer.

> Justice O'Connor dissented from the decision in *Kelo v. City of New London,* a 5-4 decision relating to eminent domain. The majority consisted of Justices Stevens, Kennedy, Souter, Ginsburg, and Breyer.

> Justice O'Connor dissented from the decision in *Roper v. Simmons,* a 5-4 decision striking down the death penalty for juveniles. The majority consisted of Justices Kennedy, Stevens, Souter, Ginsburg, and Breyer.

> Justice O'Connor dissented from the decision in *Medellin v. Dretke,* a 5-4 decision that refused to consider a death row prisoner's claim under the Vienna Convention. The opinion was a per curiam decision; Justice O'Connor's dissent was joined by Justices Stevens, Souter, and Breyer.

> Justice O'Connor dissented from Part I of the decision in *U.S. v. Booker,* a 5-4 decision holding that the Federal Sentencing Guidelines are unconstitutional unless they are treated as merely advisory in nature. The majority in Part I of Booker consisted of Justices Stevens, Scalia, Souter, Thomas, and Ginsburg.

We should note that the factual inaccuracy Frey pointed out was not a small background detail in the *Times* op-ed. The idea that O'Connor represented a consensus voice on the Court was central to the op-ed's argument that her replacement should be similar in judicial philosophy. Five days after the publication of the op-ed, the *Times* issued the following correction (O'Connor Leaves ... Correction Appended, 2005):

> An editorial Saturday on Justice Sandra Day O'Connor said the Supreme Court in its last session had 13 5-4 decisions and that

O'Connor had been in the majority on all of them. The number of 5-4 decisions during the court's 2004-2005 session exceeded 13 (the number is up to 24, counting 5-3 decisions with Chief Justice William H. Rehnquist not voting, and other vagaries). O'Connor sided with the minority in a number of these 5-4 splits.[2]

The handover of power from the Coalition Provisional Authority to the interim Iraqi government in late June 2004 garnered a good deal of coverage in the mainstream media. A factual inaccuracy in some of that reporting garnered a good deal of attention in the blogosphere. As in the preceding example, it is worth noting that the factual inaccuracy is far from trivial, in that the story frame in some of the mainstream press accounts relies in large measure on that crucial detail.

On June 29 *The Washington Post* ran a story about the handover and the departure of the Coalition Provisional Authority administrator, L. Paul Bremer. The lede of the story (Chandrasekaran, 2004) indicates its pessimistic frame for the event:

> L. Paul Bremer arrived here almost 14 months ago with a seemingly limitless reserve of energy and a mission unparalleled in U.S. diplomatic history: to remake a nation by using near dictatorial powers. When he left Iraq on Monday after surrendering authority to an interim government, it was with a somber air of exhaustion. There was no farewell address to the Iraqi people, no celebratory airport sendoff. Instead of a festive handover ceremony on Wednesday, the date set for the transfer, an improvised event occupied five minutes on a Monday morning.

Later in the story, Chandrasekaran offered a summary comment of the Iraqi population's reaction: "To some Iraqis, it seemed as if Bremer had slighted them one final time by not making the handover into a grander gesture." The story ended by reiterating that Bremer had not made a farewell speech: "Without making any public comments, Bremer walked up the steps of an Air Force C-130 Hercules transport plane. As he reached the top step, he turned, waved and ducked into the military aircraft that would take him back to America."

A story in the *Los Angeles Times* (Rubin, 2004a) also reported that Bremer had not made a farewell speech to the Iraqis. This story described in detail Bremer's last visit to Hillah, touring the newly-founded Hillah University and its Memorial to Mass Grave Victims, and made this reference to a lack of a farewell speech to the Iraqi population in general:

> It was here, in the auditorium, before a few center employees and the clerics who accompanied him on his tour, that Bremer said farewell to Iraq. Twenty-four hours later, he would climb into a C-130 transport plane without a word of goodbye to the Iraqi people ... .

A number of bloggers observed a significant discrepancy between these accounts of Bremer's departure from Iraq and the personal accounts of Iraqi bloggers, regarding both the supposed omission of a farewell address to the Iraqi people and the Iraqi civilians' perceptions of Bremer. On *Iraq the Model*, Ali described watching a televised speech from Bremer with his coworkers at a hospital (Small Party and Great Hopes, 2004; minor errors in punctuation have been corrected in this excerpt):

> Then suddenly Mr. Bremer appeared on TV reading his last speech before he left Iraq. I approached the TV to listen carefully to the speech, as I expected it to be difficult in the midst of all that noise. To my surprise everyone stopped what they were doing and started watching as attentively as I was. The speech was impressive and you could hear the sound of a needle if one had dropped it at that time. The most sensational moment was the end of the speech when Mr. Bremer used a famous Arab emotional poem ... . Then he finished his speech by saying in Arabic, "A'ash Al-Iraq, A'ash Al-Iraq, A'ash Al-Iraq!" (Long live Iraq, Long live Iraq, Long live Iraq.)

Ali, a physician working in Baghdad, continued by describing his own reactions and those of two coworkers, which contrast strikingly with assertions about Iraqi reactions to the handover in *The Washington Post* reporting (syntax and punctuation as in the original blog post).

> I was deeply moved by this great man's words but I couldn't prevent myself from watching the effect of his words on my friends who some of them were anti-Americans and some were skeptic, although some of them have always shared my optimism.

I found that they were touched even more deeply than I was. I turned to one friend who was a committed She'at and who distrusted America all the way. He looked as if he was bewitched, and I asked him, "So, what do you think of this man? Do you still consider him an invader?" My friend smiled, still touched and said, "Absolutely not! He brought tears to my eyes. God bless him."

Another friend approached me. This one was not religious but he was one of the conspiracy theory believers. He put his hands on my shoulders and said smiling, "I must admit that I'm beginning to believe in what you've been telling us for months and I'm beginning to have faith in America. I never thought that they will hand us sovereignty in time. These people have shown that they keep their promises."

Iraq the Model contained another post about Bremer's departure, this one (From Um Mustaq, 2004) authored by Mohammed, a dentist in southwestern Iraq. The post first described Mohammed's conversation with a coworker who wanted to send a thank-you note to Bremer, then took the form of an open letter to Bremer from Mohammed. This passage contained a number of specific references to Bremer's farewell speech and, as had Ali's earlier post, described the relationship between Bremer and the Iraqi people in strikingly different terms than *The Washington Post* story (punctuation, capitalization, and syntax as in the original).

We miss you Sir and we know that it's been difficult for you too. Your speech has touched the hearts of all the Iraqis I have met just as your efforts have contributed in drawing the outlines of the bright future of Iraq, the new free democratic Iraq and we will never forget you. You worked hard as if you were a true son of Iraq and in fact you're one of Iraq's sons, that's how we look at you....

Sir, Iraq loved you just like you confirmed your love in your farewell speech. We were touched just as you were. You have taken a place in our hearts just as you said we've taken our places in your heart. We will be waiting for you to return with your grandchild Sophya (as you promised in your speech) and we'll share your will to teach her the history of Iraq and I'm sure she'll love Iraq as you do....

I was never surprised when none of the western media broadcasted your impressive speech because I doubt their interest in showing the world the nature of the relation between you and the people of Iraq. But I'd like to tell you this: Iraq loves you just as you love her.

Australian journalist Tim Blair quickly noted the contradiction between *The Washington Post* story and the Iraqi bloggers' personal accounts in a cleverly-titled post (Speechless, 2004) on his eponymous blog. He juxtaposed a lengthy passage from Ali's blog post describing the scene in the hospital with Chandrasekaran's paragraph flatly stating Bremer made no farewell address. Blair then made his criticism explicit, using irony to highlight the value of eyewitness accounts in the blogosphere.

> Ali says there was a speech; *The Washington Post* says there wasn't. Who to believe? A professional journalist, with access to every information stream on the planet and supported by a massive number of editors and researchers — or Ali, watching TV at a Baghdad hospital?
>
> My money's on Ali.

Several days later, Patrick Frey noted the same factual error (Yet Another Falsehood, 2004) repeated in a news analysis in the *Los Angeles Times* (Rubin, 2004b). In his post on *Patterico's Pontifications,* Frey quoted the second paragraph of the *Times* analysis.

> L. Paul Bremer III, the civilian administrator for Iraq, left without even giving a final speech to the country, almost as if he were afraid to look in the eye the people he had ruled for more than a year.

Frey linked Ali's post describing Bremer's televised farewell speech, and closed by turning the interpretive metaphor from the *Times* piece back on its author.

Why, it's almost as if the folks at the *L.A. Times* were afraid to look in the eye the facts that have been available on the Internet for days.

On *Countercolumn,* Jason Van Steenwyk posted the e-mail reply (*The LA Times* Reporter, 2004) he received from the author of the *Times* analysis (spelling, punctuation, and syntax as in the original).

> I am sorry you feel that my aim was to insult Amb. Bremer. I think if you look at my coverage of him through the year it has been quite consistently sympathetic. On the day he left and the day or two before that when I accompanied him on trips, he gave no farewell speech of the kind that one might give on the day or two before leaving. That was, I'm sure for security reasons. As you are probably aware, security had deteriorated badly or the the [sic] roughly three weeks before the transfer of sovereignty.

> Western reporters who follow Amb. Bremer would have been delighted to cover an event billed as a farewell to Iraq. However, I will gladly look at the material you have forwarded me and if indeed I should have included a qualification I will discuss doing so with my desk.

Van Steenwyk did not find that to be an adequate response to his e-mailed complaint about the analysis piece. He followed the text of the reporter's e-mail with a number of points in rebuttal, including these:

> [I]f she really feels that there were security reasons for Bremer remaining mum up until the transfer (and there obviously were) then why did she choose to omit that fact from the piece? Instead, she writes that Bremer seemed to have been afraid to speak to the Iraqi people....

> She should have gotten her facts straight no matter how the farewell speech was billed, or even if it wasn't billed at all. Her trying to blame Bremer's staff for her own screw-up is simply outrageous. Just because the event was not billed to Rubin as a "farewell speech" does not mean it did not happen.

Ryan, a Spokane journalist blogging on *The Dead Parrot Society*, was more sympathetic to the reporters from *The Washington Post* and the *Los Angeles Times.* He took something of an investigative reporting approach to the controversy in "The Mysterious Bremer Farewell Speech" (2004). Ryan began the post by recapitulating the complaints raised in a number of other blogs and noting the personal accounts of the Iraqi bloggers. He had found an article in a Lebanese paper which mentioned "a televised speech," and linked it. He had also found references to a farewell address by Bremer in reporting by ABC News and CNN, and linked their web pages. After carefully enumerating the bits of evidence he had been able to gather, he offered a theory explaining the discrepancy between the Iraqi bloggers' accounts of hearing a farewell address on television and *The Washington Post* and the *Los Angeles Times* reports that there had been none (emphasis in the original).

> I think I have a better guess: Bremer knew he'd be leaving quickly after the ceremony, so he taped a special farewell address in advance and left it for local media to broadcast. Print journalists, who would have been tagging along with him throughout that time, wouldn't have seen him give the speech, and obviously wouldn't have seen that broadcast either. They would have filed their stories, then, under the impression that there had been no farewell speech. (Whereas television news, like ABC, probably wouldn't have missed the broadcast.) If you'd have been with Bremer the whole time, and specifically seen him *not* give such an address, that's probably how you'd write the story too. Depending on how the deadline fell, it's easy to see how this error could reasonably get into print.

Ryan later updated the post with a quotation from a *Baltimore Sun* story which confirmed his theory.

> In a videotaped message he left for Iraqis, Bremer told them it was time for factions to come peacefully together to defeat those who would cause the country harm.

Ryan concluded his lengthy exploration of the controversy with his overall evaluation of the matter (emphasis in the original).

> So it was a pre-taped farewell address. Interesting. Now, this does not excuse the two papers from not correcting their initial reports

— and it doesn't excuse the cheap shot from the *Times* about seeming almost afraid to look the Iraqi people in the eye — but it sure does put the factual discrepancy from the Post and the *Times* in a more understandable context.

The following day, July 8, Patrick Frey posted a follow-up (*Los Angeles Times* Corrects False Statement, 2004) on *Patterico's Pontifications*. He quoted the *Times*'s just-issued correction to Rubin's analysis piece of July 4.

> A news analysis about the new Iraqi government in Sunday's Section A stated that outgoing administrator L. Paul Bremer III did not give a farewell speech to the country. His spokesman has since said that Bremer taped an address that was given to Iraqi broadcast media. The spokesman said the address was not publicized to the Western media.

Frey was nuanced in his reaction to the correction (emphasis, syntax, and capitalization as in the original).

> I'm pleased that the paper has acknowledged its error. However, it is not an excuse that the speech was "not publicized to the Western news media." Bremer's farewell address had been common knowledge among readers of internet blogs since at least June 30, when I wrote about Tim Blair's criticism of the *Washington Post* for making the *same exact error*. Yet the front-page *Los Angeles Times* news analysis appeared on *July 4 — 4 days later.*

On the following day, *The Washington Post* issued a correction (Corrections, 2004).

> An article June 29 on the departure from Iraq of U.S. administrator L. Paul Bremer stated that Bremer did not deliver a farewell address to the Iraqi people. Although he did not deliver prepared remarks to an audience on the day he left, a U.S.-funded television station in Iraq broadcast remarks he had taped two days earlier, his spokesman said.

Frey posted on this correction, also (*Washington Post* Issues

Correction, 2004), and included a lengthy e-mail he had received from the author of the original story. Chandrasekaran's e-mail concludes:

> The bottom line here is that I did not know anything about the taped remarks when I wrote that Bremer did not deliver a farewell address. Knowing what I now do, thanks in part to media watchdog bloggers, *The Post* has corrected the record. It's too bad, though, that the C[oalition] P[rovisional] A[uthority] did not do a better job in informing the Western and Arab press about the broadcast. Had we all known about it, I'm sure Bremer's comments would have received wider exposure inside Iraq and beyond.

Again, Frey did not find this explanation of the error completely satisfying.

> Although it's odd that Bremer's speeches were not better publicized by the Administration, this does not excuse the mainstream media's poor research on this issue. Still, it's nice to see "media watchdog bloggers" get some credit for correcting the record.

This example of fact-checking in the blogosphere is particularly interesting in several respects. The factual error was of substantial consequence to the interpretation of the event being reported. Personal accounts from people outside the journalism industry — in this case, the Iraqi bloggers — played a crucial role in the detection of the error in mainstream media reporting of the event. A number of other bloggers, one from outside the U.S., added pieces of evidence and interpretations of what was known about the erroneous reporting. E-mailed responses from mainstream journalists clarified the sequence of events which led to the error, and themselves became part of the archival materials relating to this controversy.[3]

A rather peculiar case of fact-checking concerns an op-ed about the integrity of election results, written by *The New York Times* columnist, Paul Krugman. The thesis of his August 19, 2005, column (Krugman, 2005a) was that the Republican party had in recent years won elections through various manipulations of the voting process. As an illustration of this alleged pattern of impropriety, Krugman flatly asserted that the two consortia of mainstream media outlets which reviewed Florida ballots, after the disputed 2000 presidential election was resolved by a Supreme Court decision, had found Al Gore to have won that state.

> Two different news media consortiums [sic] reviewed Florida's ballots; both found that a full manual recount would have given the election to Mr. Gore.

Later in the column, Krugman commented on the 2004 presidential election and made a factual assertion about a county in Ohio, a state which Bush had won. He offered an unusually higher voter-turnout figure for this county as evidence that there had been vote fraud on a statewide level.

> Miami County reported that voter turnout was an improbable 98.55 percent of registered voters.

As is customary in op-ed material, source citations in the column were vague. In context, it appears that the source for Krugman's assertion about the 2000 Florida ballot audit was a book called *Steal This Vote*, written by British journalist Andrew Gumbel. The source for the unusually high voter turnout figure in Miami County is less clear. A few paragraphs earlier, Krugman had mentioned two Democratic Party analyses of the 2004 election in Ohio, but the wording of the passage suggested the number came from some official source.

It is common practice in mainstream journalism that op-ed writers enjoy more latitude in their interpretative statements than straight news reporters. Nonetheless, some expectation of factual accuracy persists, regardless of what interpretation the op-ed writer may make out of the facts stated in the piece. A number of bloggers quickly challenged one or both of these assertions of fact in Krugman's column.

With the time zone difference between east and west coast and the online availability of newspaper copy before the print versions have been distributed, the first blog criticism of Krugman's column bears a date one day earlier than the column itself! James Bennett, a software engineer, posted his point-by-point rebuttal (Geez, Paul Krugman Lies a Lot, 2005), known in blog jargon as a fisking (Fisk, n.d.), on his *Chief Brief* blog. Most of the post consisted of objections to Krugman's interpretive statements, including the characterization of Gumbel's book as a "very judicious work"; of interest here is the way Bennett identified Krugman's thesis and called into question the factual support for it. The post began in the pugnacious style typical of fisking (punctuation and capitalization as in the original):

> The man [i.e., Krugman] is a guaranteed Fisking, it is really lazy work for a blogger. Now his latest attack is claiming BOTH of the last two presidential elections are fraudulent. Of course he only manages this through innuendo and half truths.

Bennett then quoted Krugman's assertion that the media consortia which conducted post-election ballot audits found Gore to have carried Florida, and raised his objection to that assertion (punctuation and capitalization as in the original).

> Of course what he is leaving out is that these "media consortiums" only said that this might have happened in certain scenarios, NONE of which were called for by the Gore campaign.

As evidence of this, Bennett quoted from *The New York Times* article about the consortium in which it had been involved (Fessenden & Broder, 2001), noting the irony that the *Times* was the newspaper which employed Krugman and ran his column. Bennett added emphasis to highlight how the *Times* story on its ballot audit contradicted Krugman's assertion.

> Contrary to what many partisans of former Vice President Al Gore have charged, the United States Supreme Court did not award an election to Mr. Bush that otherwise would have been won by Mr. Gore. <u>A close examination of the ballots found that Mr. Bush would have retained a slender margin over Mr. Gore if the Florida court's order to recount more than 43,000 ballots had not been reversed by the United States Supreme Court.</u>

> Even under the strategy that Mr. Gore pursued at the beginning of the Florida standoff [—] filing suit to force hand recounts in four

predominantly Democratic counties [—] Mr. Bush would have kept his lead, according to the ballot review conducted for a consortium of news organizations.

But the consortium, looking at a broader group of rejected ballots than those covered in the court decisions, 175,010 in all, found that Mr. Gore might have won if the courts had ordered a full statewide recount of all the rejected ballots. This also assumes that county canvassing boards would have reached the same conclusions about the disputed ballots that the consortium's independent observers did. The findings indicate that Mr. Gore might have eked out a victory if he had pursued in court a course like the one he publicly advocated when he called on the state to "count all the votes."

Several hours later a post appeared on *The Corner*, one of the blogs associated with the *National Review Online* site. John Podhoretz, a mainstream journalist himself, also questioned Krugman's assertion that both news media consortia had found Gore to have won Florida (Krugman Tries To Pull a Fast One, 2005). While Bennett had rebutted Krugman's statement with *The New York Times* article about its consortium's findings, Podhoretz quoted the lede of the *USA Today* article about the earlier consortium to which it had belonged (Cauchon, 2001).

George W. Bush would have won a hand count of Florida's disputed ballots if the standard advocated by Al Gore had been used, the first full study of the ballots reveals. Bush would have won by 1,665 votes — more than triple his official 537-vote margin — if every dimple, hanging chad and mark on the ballots had been counted as votes.

Podhoretz posted a second time later that day (More Krugmania, 2005), this time about *The New York Times* report on its consortium's findings (Fessenden & Broder, 2001).

Paul Krugman this morning said in *The New York Times* that two media consortiums [sic] retrospectively awarded the 2000 election to Al Gore. I pointed out earlier this morning that Consortium #1 said the opposite. So did Consortium #2 — in words that appeared in *The New York Times* itself ... .

Podhoretz quoted the first three paragraphs of the article, describing the consortium's major finding that Bush had prevailed in its ballot audit, then took note of the consortium's cautious statement about the recount scenario under which Gore might have carried the Florida vote.

> Only at this point in the piece does the consortium recount allow for the possibility of a Gore victory.

>> But the consortium, looking at a broader group of rejected ballots than those covered in the court decisions, 175,010 in all, found that Mr. Gore might have won if the courts had ordered a full statewide recount of all the rejected ballots. This also assumes that county canvassing boards would have reached the same conclusions about the disputed ballots that the consortium's independent observers did.

> But given the major variable in this example — that the county canvassing boards would have counted each rejected ballot the way the *Times* and its brethren organizations did — this scenario borders on the science-fictional.

Another blogger challenged the voter turnout figure Krugman had stated for Miami County (Ohio) in the 2004 election. On *Brainster's Blog,* commercial real estate analyst Patrick Curley offered evidence (Paul Krugman: Liar, or Just Sloppy?, 2005) that the figure applied to only one precinct in the county, a precinct which had a low total of number of votes. Ironically enough, the source Curley cited was an article alleging vote fraud in that state (underscore indicates an embedded link in the post; capitalization as in the original).

> [I]t looks like the myth of the 98.55 percent figure is now established for history. Here's an <u>article claiming fraud in Miami County</u> at a Web site called "Free Press", whose motto is "Speaking truth to power"; I think it's safe to assume that they are not part of the vast right-wing conspiracy.

> The Free Press article shows the percentage turnout at various precincts around Miami County. One precinct, CONCORD SOUTH WEST, is shown as having a 98.55 percent turnout; the

others range from 50% to 94%. CONCORD SOUTH WEST had a grand total of 679 voters; the entire county had over 52,000. It is pretty obvious that the county as a whole did not have anywhere near a 98.55% turnout.

Curley went on to point out how this factual misstatement in Krugman's column was highly relevant to the meaning of the passage in which it appeared.

> That one precinct certainly did have extraordinary turnout. But at the same time, that precinct delivered a net margin of 363 votes for Bush. It's completely <u>de minimus</u> in the overall context of his [statewide] margin of over 118,000 votes. So not only is Krugman probably lying when he claims a 98.55 percent turnout for the county, but he's misleading his readers into thinking that this might be significant in the overall picture.

The following day John Hinderaker, a lawyer, took up both these questions in a post on *Power Line* (Krugmania, 2005). He began with Krugman's assertion that the ballot audits commissioned by two consortia of news outlets found Gore to have won the 2000 Florida presidential vote.

> Yesterday's column, which darkly accused Republicans of stealing one election after another, was a classic of Krugmania. Krugman begins with the casual assertion that Al Gore "really" won the 2000 election:
>
> > Two different news media consortiums reviewed Florida's ballots; both found that a full manual recount would have given the election to Mr. Gore ... . But few Americans have heard these facts.
>
> Yes, well there's a reason for that ... .

Hinderaker linked the *USA Today* story on the findings of the first consortium, of which it was a member. He simply pointed out that the article (Cauchon, 2001) bore the headline, "Newspapers' Recount Shows Bush Prevailed." As James Bennett and John Podhoretz had done, Hinderaker quoted at some length from *The New York Times* article (Fessenden & Broder, 2001) describing the findings of the second newspaper consortium to examine the Florida ballots, the consortium of which the *Times* had been a member. Hinderaker included the first sentence of the article:

> A comprehensive review of the uncounted Florida ballots from last year's presidential election reveals that George W. Bush would have won even if the United States Supreme Court had allowed the statewide manual recount of the votes that the Florida Supreme Court had ordered to go forward.

Hinderaker then challenged the improbably high figure Krugman had mentioned for the 2004 turnout in Miami County (Ohio), as evidence of some sort of fraud in that state. Hinderaker located the countywide 98.55% figure in a document issued by the Democrat congressman, John Conyers. Krugman had stated the figure was reported by Miami County; Hinderaker linked the Web site of the Ohio Secretary of State, and pointed out that the official turnout for Miami County was listed as 72.2%, a figure typical of the entire state.

Thus far this was a straightforward issue of factual accuracy and source documentation. The controversy took a peculiar turn, however, when Krugman responded to his critics in the body text of another column a few days later, on August 22 (Krugman, 2005b). He first argued that his critics had misunderstood his assertion about the consortia's findings in the August 19 column, when they took him to say the consortia found that the intervention of the United States Supreme Court had altered the outcome of the election, and consequently offered concrete documentation to the contrary. In his follow-up column, Krugman explained he had been referring to some number of hypothetical manual recounts — hypothetical in the sense that they considered a variety of ballot-counting procedures different from any of those actually requested by the Bush or Gore campaign organizations, or considered in the election-related litigation (punctuation as in the original).

> About the evidence regarding a manual recount: in April 2001 a media consortium led by *The Miami Herald* assessed how various recounts of "undervotes," which did not register at all, would have affected the outcome. Two out of three hypothetical statewide

counts would have given the election to Mr. Gore.

Krugman's August 26 column (Krugman, 2005c) included a correction to the August 19 column, the one which started the controversy. The correction read:

> In my column last Friday, I cited an inaccurate number (given by the Conyers report) for turnout in Ohio's Miami County last year: 98.5 percent. I should have checked the official state site, which reports a reasonable 72.2 percent. Also, the public editor says, rightly, that I should acknowledge initially misstating the results of the 2000 Florida election study by a media consortium led by *The Miami Herald*. Unlike a more definitive study by a larger consortium that included *The New York Times*, an analysis that showed Al Gore winning all statewide manual recounts, the earlier study showed him winning two out of three.

While the correction to the 2004 voter turnout in Miami County was a straightforward acknowledgement of an error, the part of the correction referring to the findings of the media consortia about the 2000 Florida vote set off another round of criticism in the blogosphere, and followed a similar fact-checking trajectory. On her eponymous blog, political commentator Michelle Malkin observed (The Krugman Correction, 2005) that the correction appearing in the August 26 column repeated what Krugman had asserted in his August 22 column (emphasis in the blog original).

> The second correction addresses Krugman's characterization of the findings of a media consortium led by *The Miami Herald:*
>
> > [T]he public editor says, rightly, that I should acknowledge initially misstating the results of the 2000 Florida election study by a media consortium led by *The Miami Herald*. Unlike a more definitive study by a larger consortium that included *The New York Times*, an analysis that showed Al Gore winning all statewide manual recounts, <u>the earlier study showed him winning two out of three.</u>

> Well, OK. But take a look at what Krugman wrote in his earlier column:

About the evidence regarding a manual recount: in April 2001 a media consortium led by *The Miami Herald* assessed how various recounts of "undervotes," which did not register at all, would have affected the outcome. <u>Two out of three hypothetical statewide counts would have given the election to Mr. Gore.</u>

Confused? You're not the only one.

Patrick Frey, on *Patterico's Pontifications* (Paul Krugman Just Can't Get It Right, 2005), had expressed a similar puzzlement about the correction (emphasis in the blog original).

Okay, stop. Isn't Krugman saying the same exact thing he said in his *correction*? Paul Krugman initially said "Gore won two out of three" — and corrected that statement today to "Gore won two out of three." Call me crazy, but this appears to be the <u>same exact claim.</u>

I'm really starting to wonder whether Paul Krugman is looking at a different 2001 study of undervotes by a consortium including the *Miami Herald* than I am. Every time I look at my link to the *USA Today* article on the study, it says Bush won 3 out of 4 times.

As had been the case with the body text of the columns, Krugman had made an assertion of fact in the correction without specifying a source. Like Frey, financial analyst Donald Luskin had obtained an article describing *The Miami Herald* consortium's audit of undervote ballots (Cauchon, 2001). In a post on *The Conspiracy to Keep You Poor and Stupid*, Luskin likewise noted (Krugman Officially Corrects, 2005) that Krugman's statement in the correction was still inaccurate.

But the truth is that the study Krugman is talking about involved four methods for statewide recounts, and Bush won in three of them. Here's the way *USA Today* tells it (emphasis added):

USA Today, The Miami Herald and Knight Ridder newspapers hired the national accounting firm BDO Seidman to examine undervote ballots <u>in Florida's 67 counties</u>. The accountants provided a report on what they found on each of the ballots.

The newspapers then applied the accounting firm's findings to

<u>four standards</u> used in Florida and elsewhere to determine when an undervote ballot becomes a legal vote. <u>By three of the standards, Bush holds the lead. The fourth standard gives Gore a razor-thin win.</u>

Michelle Malkin (The Krugman Correction, 2005) speculated that although Krugman had specifically mentioned recounts of undervotes in the correction, he might have been referring to a later *USA Today* article (Cauchon & Drinkard, 2005) which described hypothetical recounts of both undervotes (i.e., ballots without a machine-readable vote for president) and overvotes (i.e., ballots with more than one vote for president). She noted, though, that no analysis described in this article — manual recount of four counties, statewide manual recount of undervotes, or statewide manual recount of undervotes plus overvotes — supported Krugman's factual assertion in the correction, either. The article included this summary of the hypothetical recounts:

> Who would have won if Al Gore had gotten the manual counts he requested in four counties? Answer: George W. Bush.

> Who would have won if the U.S. Supreme Court had not stopped the hand recount of undervotes, which are ballots that registered no machine-readable vote for president? Answer: Bush, under 3 of 4 standards.

> Who would have won if all disputed ballots — included those rejected by machines because they had more than one vote for president — had been recounted by hand? Answer: Bush, under the 2 most widely used standards; Gore, under the 2 least used.

This case of fact-checking by bloggers is particularly noteworthy for a number of reasons. Again, the factual errors are nontrivial in that the erroneous assertions were vital support for the thesis of the column. While criticism of this sort often is a collaboration among a number of bloggers and unfolds over time, there appears to have been parallel discovery occurring on the day Krugman's first column was published; that is, a number of bloggers independently identified the same passages as suspect, and performed similar fact-checking activities — in this case, searching archival documents — to reach the conclusion that these were factual misstatements. Oddly enough, the formal correction to an error became, itself, the subject of another round of fact-checking. It is also interesting to note that one of the bloggers involved in the criticism was, himself, a mainstream journalist. The issue of error correction in the mainstream press will be explored in more depth in a later chapter.[4]

Fidelity of Quotations

In the course of producing a news story, reporters routinely summarize statements made by public officials, or other people involved in newsworthy events. Typically these summary accounts will include brief direct quotations attributed to the those parties. This is common practice and makes good sense as a way of conveying the essence of the statement, given time and space constraints on both the journalists and the consumers of their products. In and of itself, there is no problem with the practice; the public relies on the journalist to reduce a relatively lengthy text into a concise summary passage in the news story, just as the public relies on the journalist to convey complex events with a judicious selection of representative descriptive details about them.

A question frequently raised by bloggers, however, is whether the journalist's summary fairly and accurately represents the words and thoughts of those actors, when condensed into a small amount of print space or a small duration of air time. This criticism can go well beyond the typical complaint that the remarks were taken out of their context; with the ready online availability of transcripts, bloggers often identify substantial discrepancies between the actual words of a party's statement and the capsule summary of his or her thoughts contained in the reporting. Nor is this type of criticism confined to mere nitpicking about wording; often the blogger points out that the meaning of the statement has been substantially altered in the reporting of it.

An example of this type of criticism concerns an Associated Press story describing a television interview of Israeli Prime Minister Ariel Sharon (Lavie, 2005). The story is headlined, "Sharon Rules Out Attacking Iran Over Nukes," and the lede is this:

Israel will not mount a unilateral attack aimed at destroying Iran's nuclear capability, Israeli Prime Minister Ariel Sharon said Wednesday in a CNN-TV interview. Sharon said he did not see "unilateral action" as an option.

This print account of Sharon's interview with Wolf Blitzer drew a critical commentary by Brendan Loy on *The Irish Trojan's Blog* (AP Puts Words in Ariel Sharon's Mouth, 2005). Loy noted that the lede of the AP story implies that "unilateral action" were Sharon's words, but the interview transcript indicated the phrase was Blitzer's, and that Sharon never used the word "unilateral" at any point in the interview.

In and of itself, this could be dismissed as a trivial complaint about the reporter's word choice in the summary article, since Blitzer might have asked Sharon directly about the possibility of Israel's unilateral military action against Iran and Sharon might simply have replied, "No;" in that case the ambiguity about the speaker of the word "unilateral" would not have substantially altered the meaning of Sharon's response. That is not what actually took place in the interview, however. Loy linked the interview transcript, and reproduced the exchange between Blitzer and Sharon in which the question occurred.

BLITZER: A lot of our viewers will remember in 1981, when Israel unilaterally bombed an Iraqi nuclear reactor at Osirak. Are you considering — let me rephrase the question, at what point would Israel take unilateral military action to try to prevent Iran from building a nuclear bomb?

SHARON: I remember, of course, that raid in Iraq and was always proud to [have been] a member of the inner Cabinet...I think that decision then has saved many lives. Just imagine what could have happened if Iraq would have had — Iraq under Saddam Hussein — would have had atomic weapons. I think that here the situation is different. And the problem is different and much wider. And I think that here it should be a coalition of democracies who believe in the danger, led by the United States, in order to put pressure upon Iran.

BLITZER: Have you ruled out a unilateral military strike against Iran?

SHARON: We don't think that's what we have to do. We're not going to solve the problems for nobody. And then the thing that —

I'd say the danger is so great that it should be an international effort. Altogether, I would like you to know that Israel is not leading the struggle. Of course we exchange intelligence. We exchange views, we discuss these issues, but it's not that we are planning any military attack on Iran.

It will be left to the reader to judge whether the AP reporter accurately summarized Sharon's statements, concerning the possibility of Israel taking unilateral military action against Iran. Brendan Loy was sharply critical of the AP headline and lede, however, arguing that Sharon equivocated rather than answered Blitzer's question directly, and that by no means had Sharon categorically ruled out the option of an Israeli strike against Iran, as the AP story flatly stated. In short, the blogger's complaint was that the AP story inaccurately conveyed, in summary form, Sharon's statements in the television interview, and he offered the full context as support for his criticism.[5]

Another interesting example of this genre of criticism concerns using a quotation out of its context in such way as to grossly distort its meaning; it occurred during the controversy over the Senate filibuster of judicial nominees, in 2005. An opinion piece printed in *The Washington Post* took the position that the fight between the political parties was a power struggle, rather than a principled disagreement about the propriety of using a filibuster to prevent floor votes on nominees (Neal, 2005a). As evidence, the columnist stated that Senator Orrin Hatch had supported the filibuster of judicial nominees a decade earlier when his party was in the minority in the Senate, even though in the contemporary situation Hatch was arguing that judicial nominees should be put to a vote on the floor as a matter of procedural integrity. The columnist used a short quotation from Hatch.

Eleven years ago, when Republicans were still in the minority, Sen. Orin [sic] Hatch (R-Utah) said the filibuster tool should be used because "the minority has to protect itself and those the minority represents."

This quotation caught the attention of radio commentator Hugh Hewitt, who critiqued it in a post on his blog (Introducing Washington Post Reporter, 2005). Hewitt argued that the meaning of the quotation had been grossly distorted by taking it out of context; he linked to a statement by Hatch to the Senate Judiciary Committee in 2003, objecting to a similar use of that quotation by a witness before the committee. In that statement Hatch noted that his words had been taken from a 1994 floor debate on a Federal appeals court nominee, but he had actually spoken in opposition to the filibuster of judicial nominees, rather than in support of it. Hatch repeated his 1994 comments for the record, including the passage in which the brief quotation had appeared. In context, it is apparent that Hatch was objecting to the Senate majority leader's tactic of filing a cloture resolution rather than negotiating floor time for debate preceding a vote on the nominee, and Hatch was by no means supporting the filibuster of a judicial nominee.

> Naturally, in the last week or so of a session, there is going to be the threat of some filibusters. It is one of the few tools that the minority has to protect itself and those the minority represents. But this is not a filibuster. I find it unseemly [for the majority leader] to have filed cloture on a judgeship nomination — where I have made it very clear that I would work to get a time agreement — and make it look like somebody is trying to filibuster a Federal court judgeship. I think it is wrong, and I think it is wrong to suggest in the media that this is a filibuster situation, because it is not. I personally do not want to filibuster Federal judges.

Hewitt's post was picked up by *Power Line* (Misreporting the Filibuster, 2005). Echoing Hewitt's suspicion that Neal, the author of *The Washington Post* article, might have relied on a partisan source for the Hatch quote, John Hinderaker added a stinging comment on journalistic practice:

> No self-respecting blogger would just reproduce a portion of sentence fed to it [sic] by one of the parties without at least doing some research to determine what Hatch really said: what was the full quote, and what was the context? But Neal's standards apparently are not so high.

As a parting shot, Hinderaker observed that Neal's column had misspelled Hatch's first name.

It is also interesting to note that *The Washington Post* ran a revised version of this story (Neal, 2005b) two days after the original version (Neal, 2005a). The paragraph to which the bloggers had objected had been substantially rewritten, and although it still contained the quotation it no longer implied that Hatch had actually supported a filibuster:

> Eleven years ago, when Republicans were still in the minority, Sen. Orin [sic] Hatch (R-Utah) described the filibuster as "one of the few tools that the minority has to protect itself and those the minority represents." And while Hatch didn't support a filibuster of any judicial nominee, he has voted to block at least one Democratic presidential appointment from receiving a straight up or down vote on the Seante [sic] floor.

A correction was appended to the end of the revised article (Neal, 2005b).

> An earlier version of this column erroneously reported that Sen. Orin [sic] Hatch said in 1994 that the filibuster tool "should" be used. Hatch described the filibuster as "one of the few tools that the minority has to protect itself and those the minority represents," but he did not say that it "should" be used to oppose a federal judge's nomination.

The misspelling of Hatch's first name persisted, however.[6]

Perhaps the most flagrant case to be exposed, so far, of a mainstream journalist distorting the meaning of a quotation involves the widely-syndicated, Pulitzer Prize-winning *New York Times* columnist, Maureen Dowd. In May 2003 Dowd wrote a column critical of the Bush administration's effectiveness in damaging Al Qaeda's operations in the Middle East (Dowd, 2003a). In its irreverent, caustic style the column is consistent with Dowd's other work; likewise, with regard to its hostility to the Bush administration. The column appeared two days after a terrorist attack in Riyadh, Saudi Arabia; its thesis was that Al Qaeda's ability to engage in terrorism was still potent, contrary to the administration's statements that the organization had been weakened.

As evidence of what she called "[t]he administration's lulling triumphalism" about the damage it had inflicted on Al Qaeda, Dowd briefly quoted President Bush.

> Busy chasing off Saddam, the president and vice president had told us that Al Qaeda was spent. "Al Qaeda is on the run," President Bush said last week. "That group of terrorists who attacked our country is slowly but surely being decimated ... . They're not a problem anymore."

Robert Cox, who wrote a blog called *The National Debate*, appears to have been the first to notice that Dowd had shortened the President's actual statement in a way that significantly altered its meaning. He has since described his role in this scandal in an article on *The National Debate* (The Evolution of the Maureen Dowd Ellipsis-Distortion Story, n.d.).

> I first learned of Dowd's column listening to [Don] Imus on the Radio. The column struck me as odd. I hopped online and read the column for myself. The line Dowd quoted was a standard part of Bush's recent speeches on his tax cut plan but she had truncated the line. I immediately knew Dowd had not just taken the quote out of context but had altered the quote to invert its meaning.

Cox found a transcript of the Bush speech on the White House Web site (President Visits Arkansas, 2003), and e-mailed *The New York Times* to complain about the quotation (Not Sure Who to Send This E-mail To, 2003) as it appeared in Dowd's column (punctuation and syntax as in the e-mail original; embedded links to the Dowd column and the White House transcript omitted for readability).

> As a reader, I am not clear on the difference between selectively editing a quote to materially alter a statement and simply making up a quote? Perhaps you can explain it to me.
>
> For example, in today's column Maureen Dowd writes:
>
> "Al Qaeda is on the run," President Bush said last week. "That group of terrorists who attacked our country is slowly but surely being decimated ... . They're not a problem anymore."

Here is the full quote from President Bush:

"Al Qaeda is on the run. That group of terrorists who attacked our country is slowly, but surely being decimated. Right now, about half of all the top al Qaeda operatives are either jailed or dead. In either case, they're not a problem anymore. (Applause.) And we'll stay on the hunt. To make sure America is a secure country, the al Qaeda terrorists have got to understand it doesn't matter how long it's going to take, they will be brought to justice."

Cox went on, in the e-mail, to precisely identify how the ellipsis Dowd used to shorten the quote significantly distorted the meaning of the President's statement about Al Qaeda.

President Bush used the word "they're" to refer to his preceding statement "top al Qaeda operatives are either jailed or dead." By selectively editing the quote, the word "they're" has been made to appear to refer to Al Qaeda as an organization and not to the operatives who are "jailed or dead." This ommission [sic] materially alters the statement the President made in Arkansas this week.

Cox had copied this e-mail to an established media watchdog organization, the Media Research Center. While *The New York Times* made no response to Cox, the Media Research Center posted a brief article about the truncated quotation on its *Times Watch* Web site, crediting Cox with having noticed the problem (Maureen Dowd's Dishonest Deletion, 2003).

Columnist Maureen Dowd dishonestly quotes President Bush to make him look wrong about the dangers posed by Al Qaeda terrorists, notes a sharp-eyed reader ... .

It's clear Bush is only talking about the top Al Qaeda operatives that "are either jailed or dead" as being "not a problem anymore" — not the Al Qaeda organization itself. Dowd dishonestly deleted that sentence and the first three words of the next one to make Bush "say" Al Qaeda was no longer a threat. Bush's additional assertion "it doesn't matter how long it's going to take, they will be brought to justice" makes it clear Bush considers the war on Al Qaeda an ongoing one.

Andrew Sullivan, former editor of *The New Republic*, also commented on the quotation in a post on his blog, *The Daily Dish* (Dowd's Distortion, 2003). An established journalist himself, Sullivan had some harsh words for Dowd and *The New York Times*.

> It's perfectly clear that the president is referring, sardonically, only to those members of al Qaeda who are "either jailed or dead," not to the group as a whole. Everything we know about this president tells us that he has always warned of the permanent danger of groups like al Qaeda, has always talked of a long war, and would never say the words that Dowd puts in his mouth. So this is a willful fabrication. Will they run a correction? Don't count on it.

A week later, Brendan Nyhan posted a detailed article about this issue on the *Spinsanity* Web site (Dowd Spawns Bush Media Myth, 2003). Nyhan reviewed the disparity between the president's actual statement and Dowd's truncated quotation of it, then traced the spread of Dowd's misquotation among many other mainstream media outlets, including MSNBC, CNN, *The Sacramento Bee, The Roanoke Times,* and Fox News. He then called, as had Sullivan, for a forthright correction.

> Critics have every right to object to Bush's statement if they believe it mischaracterizes the threat from Al Qaeda. But they also have a responsibility to accurately represent what the President actually said, rather than repeating Dowd's distorted quotation. *The New York Times* — and the other outlets that have disseminated the myth — should let their readers know the full context of Bush's statement. The rapid spread of this myth is yet another sad commentary on the state of American political journalism.

In an update the following day, Nyhan offered additional evidence that Dowd had distorted the meaning of the President's statement: he quoted from six other presidential speeches referring to dead or captured Al Qaeda operatives in similar terms (underscore indicates links to transcripts; syntax as in the original).

In addition, Bush has repeatedly used the "not a problem" formulation and the similar "no longer a problem" phrase over the past year to refer to Al Qaeda terrorists who have been captured or detained rather than the group as a whole:

I bet you we've hauled in a couple of thousand of these killers. They're detained, they're no longer a problem. And like number weren't as lucky, thanks to the United States military. (October 8, 2002)

A couple of thousand of them have been hauled in and they're no longer a problem. Like number met a different fate, and I can assure you they're not a problem. (October 31, 2002)

We're on an international manhunt, one at a time. A couple of thousand have been hauled in; a couple of thousand met their fate a different way. They're not a problem. (November 2, 2002)

We're working with friends and allies around the world. And we're hauling them in, one by one. Some have met their fate by sudden justice; some are now answering questions at Guantanamo Bay. In either case, they're no longer a problem to the United States of America and our friends. (January 3, 2003)

All told, more than 3,000 suspected terrorists have been arrested in many countries. Many others have met a different fate. Let's put it this way — they are no longer a problem to the United States and our friends and allies. (January 28, 2003)

So far, more than 3,000 suspected terrorists have been arrested in many countries. Just about that number met a different kind of fate. They're not a problem anymore. (February 13, 2003)

Two weeks after her column which drew this criticism, Dowd repeated the same passage from the President's address in Little Rock. Her interpretation of the statement remained the same (Dowd, 2003b), but she provided the full wording of the quotation this time.

After the war, the triumphal administration bragged about its Iraqi, Taliban and Qaeda scalps, painting our enemies as being in retreat.

"Al Qaeda is on the run," the president said in Little Rock, Ark.

"That group of terrorists who attacked our country is slowly, but surely, being decimated. Right now, about half of all the top Al Qaeda operatives are either jailed or dead. In either case, they're not a problem anymore."

While Dowd revisited the quotation and reproduced it without alteration this time, she did not specifically acknowledge her earlier, edited version of the president's statement. This did not satisfy her critics, who felt that a forthright correction of the distorted quotation was required, given the large amount of media exposure the faulty quotation had received.

Robert Cox (Dowd's Dots, 2003) summarized *The New York Times*'s response to its blog critics in this way (syntax as in the blog original):

> What the *Times* did do was to print Maureen Dowd's column of May 28th which included the full version of the controversial quote without explanation and then announce with, to borrow from Ms. Dowd, "lulling triumphalism", that *The Times* considered the matter closed. See if you can follow *The Times*['s] logic: (1) they implicitly acknowledge that there was a problem with the truncated quotation; (2) they acknowledge that some action was in order; (3) they take an action that is completely transparent to the reader so that the false impression created by the previous column remains intact.

After he had broken the story of the distorted quotation in Dowd's May 14 column, Cox had tracked its spread to other outlets. He went on, in this post, to explain why he felt the distorted quotation in the May 14 column had been a journalistic transgression with serious consequences.

> As noted above, *The New York Times* matters and does so in a way that no other news outlet in this country matters. Over the past weeks I have reached out to various media outlets where their reporters, columnists, editorial writers or on-air personalities appeared to have relied on Maureen Dowd's manufactured quotation for remarks they made. All confirmed that they had relied on Dowd and most admitted that they had not bothered to fact-check the quote. Their reason? It came from *The New York*

Times. For the record, as one of a handful of people who bothered to fact-check the quotation, it took less than thirty seconds to copy the quotation from the *Times* Web site, paste it into Google and find the original text of the speech ... .

Cox was not the only blogger dissatisfied with the *Times's* response to the controversy. On *Belgravia Dispatch*, corporate lawyer Gregory Djerejian made his feelings plain in the title of his post, "Maureen Won't Come Clean So" (2003). He first noted Dowd's failure to acknowledge the problem in her column of May 14 (syntax and emphasis as in the blog original).

> So how does Maureen Dowd of the NYT handle the greatly misleading treatment of a Dubya quote per her May 14th column (insinuating that Dubya had declared the war on terror won)? She (two weeks later) prints the President's comments in full — *without in any way acknowledging the misleading nature of her earlier treatment of the relevant quote and then (rather amazingly) further compounding her erroneous analysis of Bush's comments.*

Djerejian recapitulated the passages in Dowd's May 14 and May 28 columns, and observed that while Dowd had provided the entire wording of Bush's statement in its second appearance in the May 28 column, she had persisted in interpreting it to mean that al Qaeda had been completely defeated. Djerejian thus had two distinct criticisms of Dowd and the *Times*: there had been no explicit correction of the distorted quotation in the May 14 column, and Dowd had — in Djerejian's view — continued to misinterpret the statement (syntax and punctuation as in the blog original).

> But rather than issue a correction — Dowd attempts to sidle out of her misleading column of May 14th by now quoting the President correctly — but still suggesting that the President represented that al-Qaeda was decimated (or vanquished, licked, beaten, trounced, "on the run" etc.) — a gross misrepresentation.

> Not only is she just too stubborn to admit error...but she's also seemingly arrogant enough to continue to misrepresent the President's remarks.

So let's be perfectly clear. A leading columnist in the leading newspaper in the land continues to insinuate that the President has declared victory in the war on terror — the dominant theme of his entire Presidency — when in fact he hasn't. She repeats this error twice in two weeks.

In the aftermath of this journalistic scandal, Dowd's name entered the lexicon of blogosphere jargon (Dowdification, n.d.). To dowdify, in blog-speak, is to selectively edit a quote in a way that distorts its meaning. Moreover, Andrew Sullivan's prediction that *The New York Times* would refuse to issue a correction to the distorted quotation proved to be correct. Dowd's May 14 column with the problematic quotation, retrieved two years later from LexisNexis, bears no correction or editor's note. Neither does the May 28 column which repeated the quotation without alteration. Rowbacks — in this case, the repetition of the intact quotation in a subsequent column without a forthright acknowledgement of the problem with its earlier version — will be discussed in greater detail in a later chapter.[7]

Authenticity of Documents

News stories sometimes center around some sort of document; either the document itself is newsworthy, or the document is evidence for an interpretive statement central to a story. Logically, the authenticity of such a document is crucial to such stories. While examples of this type of media criticism are less plentiful, there have been occasions on which bloggers questioned whether such documents, reported in the mainstream media, were, in fact, genuine.

Perhaps the most elaborate such controversy began with a CBS News story broadcast as a "60 Minutes" segment, reporting the discovery of memoranda about President George W. Bush's service in the National Guard. As the title of the CBS segment suggests (New Questions on Bush Guard Duty, 2004), the story cast an unfavorable light on Bush's military service during the Vietnam War era. CBS claimed to have obtained memoranda written by Bush's commanding officer, memos which indicated unsatisfactory performance and hinted at pressure to evaluate more favorably than Bush's performance merited. While the story did not disclose how CBS News had obtained the memoranda, it vouched for their authenticity (ellipsis in the original).

> But "60 Minutes" has obtained a number of documents we are told were taken from Col. Killian's personal file. Among them, a never-before-seen memorandum from May 1972, where Killian writes that Lt. Bush called him to talk about "how he can get out of coming to drill from now through November."

> Lt. Bush tells his commander "he is working on a campaign in Alabama…and may not have time to take his physical." Killian adds that he thinks Lt. Bush has gone over his head, and is "talking to someone upstairs."

> Col. Killian died in 1984. "60 Minutes" consulted a handwriting analyst and document expert who believes the material is authentic.

The story described two other memos, likewise casting doubts about Bush's military service.

> In a memo from Aug. 18, 1973, Col. Killian says Col. Buck Staudt, the man in charge of the Texas Air National Guard, is putting on pressure to "sugar coat" the evaluation of Lt. Bush … .

> On Aug. 1, 1972, Lt. Bush was suspended from flying status, due to failure to accomplish his annual medical examination. That document was released years ago. But another document has not been seen until now. It's a memo that Col. Jerry Killian put in his own file that same day. It says "on this date, I ordered that 1st Lt. Bush be suspended not just for failing to take a physical….[ellipsis in the original] but for failing to perform to U.S. Air Force/Texas Air National Guard standards."

On the following day the *Boston Globe* ran a scathing story (Robinson & Latour, 2004) based on the memos described in the "60 Minutes" segment. The *Globe* story described the documents in this way:

> CBS, on its Evening News and in an in-depth report on "60 Minutes", said it obtained the documents from Killian's "personal

files." Anchorman Dan Rather reported that the White House did not dispute the authenticity of the documents and said the network had used document authorities to verify their authenticity.

The New York Times also ran a story about the memos, likewise accepting CBS News's assertions about their authenticity at face value (Seelye & Blumenthal, 2004).

> President Bush's Vietnam-era service in the National Guard came under renewed scrutiny on Wednesday as newfound documents emerged from his squadron commander's file that suggested favorable treatment ... . The documents, obtained by the "60 Minutes" program at CBS News from the personal files of the late Lt. Col. Jerry B. Killian, Mr. Bush's squadron commander in Texas, suggest that Lieutenant Bush did not meet his performance standards and received favorable treatment.

CBS News had made images of the memos available on its Web site, linked from the page of the segment's transcript. On the conservative discussion site *Free Republic* someone had posted the text of *The New York Times* story about the memos, and visitors to the site had begun to comment on it (Documents Suggest Special Treatment, 2004). *Free Republic* is not a blog, as such. The format of the site consists of posts on separate pages, which can either be original writing or documents from media outlets, each followed by its own comment thread. Often the comments threads on *Free Republic* grow very long; in all fairness, some comments are essentially venting about the topic, while others do contain substantive thoughts about it or links to additional sources of information about it. Comment #11 on this thread contained the URL for the "60 Minutes" transcript, on which there were links to images of the purported memos. Comment #47 on this thread contained an observation about the appearance of the memos on the CBS Web site.

> [E]very single one of these memos to file is in a proportionally spaced font, probably Palatino or Times New Roman. In 1972 people used typewriters for this sort of thing, and typewriters used monospaced fonts. The use of proportionally spaced fonts did not come into common use for office memos until the introduction of

laser printers, word processing software, and personal computers. They were not widespread until the mid to late 90's. Before then, you needed typesetting equipment, and that wasn't used for personal memos to file. Even the Wang systems that were dominant in the mid 80's used monospaced fonts.

I am saying these documents are forgeries, run through a copier for 15 generations to make them look old. This should be pursued aggressively.

This comment was the beginning of what became a full-fledged journalistic scandal, ultimately resulting in widespread negative publicity for CBS News, an internal investigation by CBS, the resignations of three news executives, the firing of the segment producer, and the retirement of the network anchor (CBS Ousts 4, 2005). In the end, this *Free Republic* reader's suspicion that the documents were forgeries proved correct; under scrutiny by bloggers and, in time, other mainstream media outlets, CBS News was unable to support its assertion that the documents had been authenticated and went through a grinding series of defenses of the story about the purported National Guard memoranda, culminating in an announcement that it would conduct an inquiry into the production and broadcast of it. After some months, CBS released the report of its internal inquiry into the "60 Minutes" segment, which found that "CBS News had produced a story that was neither fair nor accurate and did not meet the organization's internal standards" (CBS Ousts 4, 2005). The web page containing the transcript of the segment at issue (New Questions on Bush Guard Duty, 2004) now bears a terse annotation acknowledging the malpractice of those involved with segment, yet still avoiding an explicit correction of the factual misstatement that the purported memos were genuine documents:

(CBS) Editor's Note: A report issued by an independent panel on Jan. 10, 2005 concluded that CBS News failed to follow basic journalistic principles in the preparation and reporting of this Sept. 8, 2004 broadcast.

A full exploration of this scandal could be the subject of an entire book in itself; here, we will note only highlights of bloggers' criticism of the documents' authenticity and of CBS News's journalistic practices in bringing the segment to broadcast.

Readers of *Power Line* alerted the bloggers to that comment on *Free Republic.* Scott Johnson linked the "60 Minutes" and *Boston Globe* stories (The Sixty-First Minute, 2004), and quoted the comment about the typeface from *Free Republic.* The post was updated thirteen times with material contributed by readers before Johnson closed it, indicating they would continue the story with separate follow-up posts for the sake of readability! The *Power Line* readers disagreed among themselves about some details of the available typefaces of the time; one said that in fact IBM did make a typewriter which used a proportionally spaced font, while another who had worked for IBM at the time pointed out that only the top-of-the line machine had that capability. Over the course of these updates, other questions arose about the authenticity of the purported National Guard memos, apart from the proportional spacing of the typeface. One reader pointed out the superscript characters in the memos (punctuation slightly altered, for clarity).

> The "Memo To File" of August 18, 1973 also used specialized typesetting characters not used on typewriters. These include the superscript "th" in 187th, and consistent right single quote used instead of a typewriter's generic apostrophe.

Other readers noted that the wording of certain passages in the memos did not accord with what they had seen in their own military service.

> I am amused by the way "147 th Ftr.Intrcp Gp." appears in the August 1, 1972 document. It may have been written that way in non-forged documents, but as someone who worked for ComCruDesLant, I know the military liked to bunch things together.

Another reader raised a question relating to recordkeeping, based on his own military specialty (emphasis in the blog original).

> I served in the Air Force for 21 years — 1968 to 1989 — the first 7 as a Personnel Specialist and the remainder as a PSM (Personnel Systems Manager). I also spent 2 years as an inspector at Hq SAC,

Offutt AFB, NE in Omaha, inspecting Personnel Offices at all 26 SAC bases. As a PSM I had to know every job in Personnel, including the proper filing of documents in individual military records. Memos were NOT used for orders, as the one ordering 1LT Bush to take a physical. This would have been done as a letter, of which a copy should have been sent to the CBPO (Consolidated Base Personnel Office) to be filed in 1LT Bush's military record. Memos DID NOT get filed in personnel records.

Another reader made an additional observation about the typeface, apart from the proportional spacing (capitalization and punctuation as in the original].

The type in the document is KERNED. Kerning is the typ[e]setter's art of spacing various letters in such a manner that they are "grouped" for better readability. Word processors do this automatically. NO TYPEWRITER CAN PHYSICALLY DO THIS.

To explain: the letter "O" is curved on the outside. A letter such as "T" has indented space under its cross bar. On a typewriter if one types an "O" next to a "T" then both letters remain separated by their physical space. When you type the same letters on a computer next to each other the[y] are automatically "kerned" or "grouped" so that their individual spaces actually overlap...Two good kerning examples in the alleged memo are the word "my" in the second line where "m" and "y" are neatly kerned and also the word "not" in the fourth line where the "o" and "t" overlap empty space. A typewriter doesn't "know" what particular letter is next to another and can't make those types of aesthetic adjustments.

The reader continued with an observation about the line breaks in the purported 1970s' memos (capitalization as in the original).

The sentences have a wide variance in their AMOUNT of kerning and proportional spacing. Notice how the first line of the first paragraph seems squished together and [a] little hard to read but the last line of the first paragraph has wider[,] more open spacing. Even the characters themselves are squished in the first line (as a computer does automatically) and more spread out on the last line where there is more room.

There's no way a typewriter could "set" the type in this memo and even a good typesetter using a Linotype machine of the era would have to spend hours getting this effect.

On *Little Green Footballs*, desktop publishing expert Charles Johnson thought of an interesting way to test whether the memos had actually been produced on a word processor rather than a typewriter. In "Bush Guard Documents: Forged" (2004), he described how he had retyped the text of one of the memos using the current version of Microsoft Word and compared its appearance to the purported 1973 memo (emphasis in the original).

> I opened Microsoft Word, set the font to Microsoft's Times New Roman, tabbed over to the default tap stop to enter the date "18 August 1973," then typed the rest of the document purportedly from the personal records of the late Lieutenant Colonel Jerry B. Killian. And my Microsoft Word version, typed in 2004, is an *exact match* for the documents trumpeted by CBS News as "authentic."

Johnson posted an image of the purported memo from the CBS News Web site, and followed it with an image of his recreation of the text using Microsoft Word. He then concluded (emphasis in the original):

> The spacing is not just similar — it is identical in every respect. Notice that the date lines up perfectly, all the line breaks are in the same places, all letters line up with the same letters above and below, and the kerning is exactly the same. And I did not change a single thing from Word's defaults; margins, type size, tab stops, etc. are all using the default settings.

Several days later, Johnson posted an animation which overlaid the CBS News memo with his recreation (The Smoking Memo, 2004). The animation alternated between the CBS News image and that of his word processor recreation of the text; as Johnson asserted, there was no appreciable difference between the two.

Power Line continued to post comments from its readers. Two are particularly noteworthy in that they raised detailed questions about wording of the purported memos, which was discrepant with military usage of the time. "An Officer Weighs In" (2004) contained these observations (syntax and capitalization as in the original, minor punctuation errors corrected):

> But MOST GLARING is the omission of an "SSCI" code, the Standard Subject Classification Indicator code which is found on every piece of US military correspondence. The SSCI must appear in the upper right hand corner and include a subject code, the originator's initials, the clerk-typist's code and the date. Every official military document must include an SSCI — this officer (who most likely never typed an official document in his career) forgot to include it and probably could not even remember the correct subject abbreviation code.
>
> ALSO ON US MILITARY CORRESPONDENCE THE SUBJECT LINE IS ALWAYS CAPITALIZED — no self-respecting military clerk typed this forgery nor would they type the date "14 May,1972" instead of the correct military style of "14 MAY 1972."
>
> Other errors:
> "Lt Colonel" should be "LC" or "LTCOL" or more correctly "Lieutenant Colonel (branch of service)."
>
> "Commander" should read "COMMANDING."

"Another Officer Speaks" (2004) contains similar observations about the content of the memos from another veteran. His comments began with a description of his extensive administrative experience in the Air National Guard, beginning in the time period of the purported memoranda. The *Power Line* reader then detailed more formatting discrepancies in the memos.

> 1. The format used in this letter, dated 04 May 1972, which was allegedly prepared/published 16 months prior to Lieutenant Bush's request for discharge, is completely wrong, as the letter is formatted in a manner that was not used by the Air Force until the very late 1980s/early 1990s.
>
> 2. The terminology "MEMORANDUM FOR" was never used in the 1970s.

3. The abbreviations in this letter are incorrectly formatted, in that a period is used after military rank (1st Lt.). According to the Air Force style manual, periods are not used in military rank abbreviations.

4. The abbreviation for Fighter Interceptor Squadron (FIS) includes periods after each capital letter. Again, periods are not used.

5. In paragraph 1, the phrase "not later than" is spelled out, followed by (NLT). NLT was, and is, a widely recognized abbreviation for "not later than" throughout all military services, so the inclusion of "not later than" was not a generally accepted practice and completely unnecessary in a letter from one military member to another.

6. Lt Col Killian's signature element is incorrect for letters prepared in the 1970s. This letter uses a three-line signature element, which was normally not used. Three-line signature elements were almost the exclusive domain of colonels and generals in organizations well above the squadron level.

7. Finally, the signature element is placed far to the right, instead of being left justified. The placement of the signature element to the right was not used or directed by Air force standards until almost 20 years after the date of this letter.

On the following day, Hinderaker posted about Dan Rather's appearance on CNN (apparently CNN Wolf Blitzer Reports, 2004; see also Blitzer, 2004), in which the CBS network anchor vouched for the authenticity of the purported memoranda. Hinderaker described Rather's statement in this way (Rather Puts Neck on Chopping Block, 2004):

> A half hour ago, Dan Rather went on CNN and said he knows the Jerry Killian documents to be authentic, and knows that they are not forgeries. Therefore, he said, there will be no retraction, no correction, and — apparently — no investigation.

Hinderaker thought this suggested Rather himself had been intimately involved in the CBS story.

What does this mean? Last night, it was reported that senior executives at CBS News were promising an investigation. Today, Dan Rather is personally vouching for the documents' authenticity. This can only mean that Rather himself is the source of the documents. This makes sense; if a staffer on the "60 Minutes" payroll had come up with the purported records, the story never would have run without the documents being authenticated. Who has the power to drive this story onto the air without an investigation that would include, for example, contacting Killian's widow, or his son? Dan Rather does.

This controversy over the purported National Guard memos had already generated comments in all corners of the blogosphere, and the capsule summary here may seem to suggest that the viewpoints were uniformly suspicious of the memos' authenticity. The blogosphere in fact is characterized by a great heterogeneity in opinion; along that line it is useful to note a rebuttal to the *Power Line* and *Little Green Footballs* bloggers which appeared on *The Daily Kos*. A blogger using the pseudonym Hunter addressed the issue of proportional fonts at great length in a post titled "TANG Typewriter Follies" (2004). Hunter felt that Charles Johnson's recreation of the memo using a word processor did not establish that the memo was a contemporary forgery (syntax, punctuation, and emphasis as in the original).

> You see, a "typeface" doesn't just consist of the shape of the letters. It also is a set of rules about the size of the letters in different point sizes, the width of those letters, and the spacing between them. These are all designed in as part of the font, by the designer. Since Microsoft Word was designed to include popular and very-long-used typefaces, it is hardly a surprise that those typefaces, in Microsoft Word, would look similar to, er, themselves, on a typewriter or other publishing device. That's the *point* of typefaces; to have a uniform look across all publishing devices. To look the same.

Hunter also addressed at length the issue of whether the National Guard office could have had, in the 1970s, equipment capable of producing proportionally-spaced documents (syntax, punctuation, and emphasis as in the original).

The IBM Executive electric typewriter was manufactured in four models, A, B, C, and D, starting in 1947, and featured proportional spacing ... . It was an extremely popular model, and was marketed to government agencies ... .

The IBM Executive is probably the most likely candidate for this particular memo. There is some confusion about this, so to clear up: The IBM Selectric, while very popular, did <u>not</u> have proportional spacing. The <u>Selectric Composer</u>, introduced in 1966, did, and in fact could easily have produced these memos, but it was a very expensive machine, and not likely to be used for light typing duties. The proportional-spacing Executive, on the other hand, had been produced in various configurations since the 1940's, and was quite popular ... .

Did they have a font that looked like Times New Roman? Unclear; they apparently were manufactured in a range of configurations, and with different available typefaces. Not that these were not "typeball" machines, like the Selectrics; they had a normal row of keys. But it is worth noting that IBM had what we will call a "close" relationship with Times New Roman.

Hunter's comments drew a reply on *Power Line* (The Daily Kos Strikes Out, 2004). John Hinderaker noted that while Hunter had found that typewriters capable of proportional spacing existed at the time the memos were supposedly generated, he had not considered the actual likelihood that Killian's office had such equipment.

Kos' entire effort is devoted to showing that there was a typewriter in existence in the early 1970s that was capable of producing proportional spacing, superscript and Times New Roman font. There is no evidence, of course that Jerry Killian used such an exotic machine, and certainly no other authentic documents generated by the Texas Air National Guard used such a machine.

Hinderaker went on to observe that Hunter's rebuttal had not touched on the matter of kerning at all (syntax, punctuation, and emphasis as in the original).

But these are minor points. Kos never addresses the smoking-gun issue of kerning. We discussed this extensively yesterday, but briefly, "kerning" is the ability of letters in word-processed documents to intrude on one another's space. If you type the word "my" in Word or any other word processing program, the tail of the "y" will curl slightly under the "m". This cannot be done on any typewriter, because a typewriter cannot know what the adjacent letter is. A letter on a typewriter must have its own space.

Hinderaker also summarized his readers' comments on the discrepancies in formatting, syntax, and content of the memos (syntax and punctuation as in the original).

Kos also never addresses any of the substantive issues: the absurdity, on its face, of writing a memo whose subject heading is "CYA;" the memos' inconsistency with various military usages of the early 1970s; and, most of all, the anachronism in the August 18, 1973 memo, where Killian allegedly writes: "Staudt has obviously pressured Hodges more about Bush." Brigadier General "Buck" Staudt retired in 1972.

Two days after its initial reporting on the purported National Guard memos, the *Boston Globe* ran a follow-up story (Latour & Rezendes, 2004) asserting that document experts had judged the typeface in the memos to be consistent with the available technology of the time. The headline was unequivocal: "Authenticity Backed on Bush Documents." The lede of the story followed suit.

After CBS News on Wednesday trumpeted newly discovered documents that referred to a 1973 effort to "sugar coat" President Bush's service record in the Texas Air National Guard, the network almost immediately faced charges that the documents were forgeries, with typography that was not available on typewriters used at that time. But specialists interviewed by the *Globe* and some other news organizations say the specialized characters used in the documents, and the type format, were common to electric typewriters in wide use in the early 1970s, when Bush was a first lieutenant.

The story then went on to cite the opinion of one document expert the reporters had contacted.

> Philip D. Bouffard, a forensic document examiner in Ohio who has analyzed typewritten samples for 30 years, had expressed suspicions about the documents ... . But Bouffard told the *Globe* yesterday that after further study, he now believes the documents could have been prepared on an IBM Selectric Composer typewriter available at the time.

Later, the story elaborated on the supposed change in Bouffard's expert opinion.

> Bouffard, the Ohio document specialist, said that he had dismissed the Bush documents in an interview with *The New York Times* because the letters and formatting of the Bush memos did not match any of the 4,000 samples in his database. But Bouffard yesterday said that he had not considered one of the machines whose type is not logged in his database: the IBM Selectric Composer. Once he compared the Bush memos to Selectric Composer samples obtained from Interpol, the international police agency, Bouffard said his view shifted.

The *Globe* article caught the attention of Bill Ardolino, a marketing manager who writes *INDC Journal*. Ardolino contacted Bouffard directly, and reported that Bouffard said he had been misquoted in the *Globe* article (Dr. Bouffard Speaks, 2004).

> [H]e's angry that the *Globe* has misrepresented him ... and he wants me to correct the record. He did not change his mind, and he and his colleagues are becoming more certain that these documents are forgeries.

Ardolino went on to quote from his conversation with Bouffard.

> "I did not change my mind at all! I would appreciate it if you could do whatever it takes to clear this up, through your internet site, or whatever.
>
> "All I'd done is say, 'Hey I want to look into it.'
>
> "What I said to them was, I got new information about possible Selectric fonts and (Air Force) documents that indicated a Selectric machine could have been available, and I needed to do more

analysis and consider it.

"But the more information we get and the more my colleagues look at this, we're more convinced that there are significant differences between the type of the (IBM) Composer that was available and the questionable document."

As a sidenote to this capsule summary of the controversy, the *Globe* story now bears an appended correction, added four days after its publication.

CORRECTION: Because of an editing error, the headline on a Page One story Saturday on whether documents released by CBS News about President Bush's Texas Air National Guard service are genuine ("Authenticity backed on Bush documents") did not accurately reflect the content of the story. The story quoted one analyst saying that the documents could have been produced on typewriters available in the early 1970s, but the analyst did not vouch for the authenticity of the documents. A second analyst quoted in the story said he doubts the documents are authentic.

An extremely detailed expert analysis of the typeface-related issues appeared on a computer scientist's company Web site on the same day; this analysis quickly drew a good deal of attention in the blogosphere, and three days later was featured in a *Washington Post* story about the questions surrounding the memos (Dobbs & Kurtz, 2004). One of the pioneers in word processing and desktop publishing, Joseph Newcomer, declared the purported memos to clearly be forgeries (The Bush "Guard Memos," 2004). His essay on the memos is quite lengthy and technical; this summary can only include highlights and the reader is encourage to view it.

Newcomer began his essay by making explicit his interest in the controversy, and his personal attitudes toward the parties involved in it (syntax as in the original).

First off, before I start getting a lot of the wrong kind of mail: I am not a fan of George Bush. But I am even less a fan of attempts to commit fraud, and particularly by a complete and utter failure of those we entrust to ensure that if [sic] the news is at least accurate. I know it is asking far too much to expect the news to be unbiased.

But the people involved should not actually lie to us, or promulgate lies created by hoaxers, through their own incompetence.

Newcomer then stated the conclusion he had reached, regarding the purported National Guard memoranda (syntax as in the original).

[I]t takes approximately 30 seconds for anyone who is knowledgeable in the history of electronic document production to recognize this whole collection is certainly a forgery, and approximately five minutes to prove to anyone technically competent that the documents are a forgery ... . At time I a[m] writing this, CBS is stonewalling. They were hoaxed, pure and simple. CBS failed to exercise anything even approximately like due diligence.

Newcomer disagreed with the earlier arguments that the purported memos had been kerned, but nonetheless reached the same conclusion that the purported memos were contemporary forgeries. He distinguished between true kerning and a simulation of it routinely performed by word processor fonts (emphasis and syntax as in the original; minor punctuation error corrected).

Some have argued that the documents are forgeries because the characters are "kerned." Kerning is an operation which tucks characters together to compact space. However, Microsoft Word by default does not kern text. The text of the memo is not kerned ... . However, Times New Roman uses a characteristic of Microsoft TrueType fonts called the ABC dimensions, where the C dimension is the offset from the right edge of the bounding box of the character to the next character. If this offset is negative, the character with the negative C offset will overlap the character which follows...This gives the illusion of kerning, or what I sometimes call "pseudo-kerning" ... . ALL technologies I am aware of in 1972 that would have been available for office work (not, say, the sort of production book typesetters that major publishers might have had) could only advance an integral number of units, and could not "tuck in" the characters like Microsoft's Times New Roman font under Microsoft Word does, by using a negative partial-character offset ... .

Not even Word supports kerning without selecting a special option (and if selected, the resulting document does not look like the memo). But somehow, magically, the font used by some hypothesized piece of equipment in 1972 works the same was [sic] as a font that uses a set of ABC width parameters that did not exist until TrueType fonts existed. Microsoft delivered the first version of TrueType for Windows in April of 1992, and the original TrueType font format was developed by Apple and delivered in May, 1991.

Newcomer gave detailed examples of the pseudo-kerning found in the purported memos, with tables of the ABC dimensions of a few characters to illustrate differences in their C dimensions. He also noted the problem with quotation marks, as they appeared in the purported memos.

Many have commented on the anomalies of the curly quotes, another piece of Word automation which would not have been found in documents of the era. I know that our fonts [a reference to Newcomer's early work in the development of electronic publishing] did not have left and right quote marks because of limitations of the character sets, which could only have 95 or 96 printable characters. Most of our contemporaneous printers used 7-bit ASCII fonts, which had no option for specifying curly quotes, nor did our software automatically generate them, as Word does.

Newcomer tried the same test Charles Johnson had devised, and reached the same conclusion.

Based on the fact that I was able, in less than five minutes, to replicate one of the experiments reported on the Internet, that is, to type in the text of the 01-August-1972 memo into Microsoft Word and get a document so close that you can hold my document in front of the "authentic" document and see virtually no errors, I can assert without any doubt (as have many others) that this document is a modern forgery. Any other position is indefensible.

Newcomer then reviewed the evidence concerning the typeface in the purported memos, and reiterated his conclusion that the memos were forgeries (syntax as in the original).

Attempts to recreate the memos using Microsoft Word and Times New Roman produce images so close that even taking into account the fact that the image we were able to download from the CBS site has been copied, scanned, downloaded, and reprinted, the errors between the "authentic" document and a file created by anyone using Microsoft [W]ord are virtually indistinguishable.

The font existed in 1972; there were technologies in 1972 that could, with elaborate effort, reproduce these memos, and these technologies and the skills to use them were used by someone who, by testimony of his own family, never typed anything, in an office that for all its other documents appears to have used ordinary monospaced typewriters, and therefore this unlikely juxtaposition of technologies and location coincided just long enough to produce these four memos on 04-May-1972, 18-May-1972, 01-August-1972, and 18-August-1973. ...

All I can say is that the technology that produced this document [i.e., the purported memos] was not possible in 1972 in the sort of equipment that would have been available outside publishing houses, and which required substantial training and expertise to use, and it replicates exactly the technologies of Microsoft Word and Microsoft TrueType Fonts.

It is therefore my expert opinion that these documents are modern forgeries.

One of the corroborating witnesses mentioned in the "60 Minutes" segment (New Questions on Bush Guard Duty, 2004) was Robert Strong, whom CBS News had described as "a friend and colleague of Col. Killian." Strong had been quoted, in the "60 Minutes" story, as having said

"They [the memos] are compatible with the way business was done at the time. They are compatible with the man that I remember Jerry Killian being...II don't see anything in the documents that is discordant with what were the times, what was the situation and what were the people involved."

John Hinderaker picked up this thread of the controversy in a *Power Line* post titled "The Real Robert Strong" (2004). He observed that the quote from Strong was, in itself, a very weak sort of evidence for the authenticity of the documents, in that Strong was only saying he had not noticed any particular discrepancies between their content and his personal recollections of the time. The post is of particular interest here because Hinderaker went on to describe a *Power Line* reader's face-to-face conversations with Strong, concerning the "60 Minutes" segment. In essence, this post is investigative reporting by a blogger, made possible by interaction between the blogger and a reader (capitalization as in the original).

> Robert Strong is a professor of English who lives in a rural area west of Austin, Texas. One of his neighbors happens to be a *Power Line* reader. Last Wednesday afternoon, shortly before CBS broke the fake document story, our reader encountered Strong on the road that passes by their homes. Strong noted that the sign leading to their road had been knocked down, and asked our correspondent not to put it back up for a while because "I have things going on in my life...reporters are trying to talk to me." [ellipsis in the blog original]

> Our correspondent asked, About what? Strong answered, About Bush's National Guard service. Strong said that in his opinion, President Bush hadn't properly completed his service. Strong told our correspondent that "some new documents have turned up..."

> Strong said that he had served with President Bush in the Texas Air National Guard, which was news to our correspondent, who had never heard Strong mention such National Guard service.

> In a follow-up conversation, Robert Strong told our correspondent that he worked with Jerry Killian in the Air National Guard from 1968 to the early 1970s. He said that he believed that the CBS documents were genuine, but admitted that he "cannot vouch for the documents' authenticity." Further, Strong said that he doesn't think it matters whether the documents are genuine [or] not.

> At the same time, notwithstanding his claim to have served in the Texas Air National Guard, Strong admitted that he had never served with or even met Lt. Bush. He admitted further that Jerry Killian had never discussed Lt. Bush with him. Strong acknowledged that he had "no personal knowledge about Bush's

service."

Hinderaker felt this new contextual information, supplied by a *Power Line* reader, vitiated what corroboration CBS News had claimed Strong provided for the authenticity of the memos.

> Bottom line: Robert Strong is an inoffensive English professor who dislikes, but has never met, President Bush; he has no idea whether the CBS documents are authentic; he never discussed Lt. Bush with Jerry Killian; and he has "no personal knowledge" about President Bush's National Guard service.

Scott Johnson, another *Power Line* blogger, took note of a shift in CBS News's continued defense of the purported memos over the next couple days, from its claim the memos had been definitively authenticated by document experts to what it claimed was the factual consistency of their content with military records. In a post titled "CBS Keeps Digging" (2004), Johnson quoted from a new CBS report on the controversy.

> In addition to talking to handwriting and document analysts, CBS News said Monday it relied on an analysis of the contents of the documents themselves to determine their authenticity. The new papers are in line with what is known about the president's service assignments and dates, CBS said.

This prompted a rather sarcastic rejoinder from Johnson, himself a lawyer.

> CBS is inverting the OJ defense: If the document fits, you must acquit! Unlike OJ's glove defense, however, CBS's is a non sequitur.

> Moreover, the August 18 "CYA" memo refers to pressure from "Staudt," the brigadier general who had retired the year before. I guess the new papers are "in line with what is known about the president's service assignments and dates," except when they're not, and that's good enough for CBS.

A sidenote seems appropriate here. This author could not obtain, in the summer of 2005, the text of the CBS News story from which Johnson quoted on September 13. At the time of this writing the embedded link in the *Power Line* post brought up the September 22 story on the panel chosen to investigate the "60 Minutes" segment. This would appear to be a rowback on CBS News's part.

By this point the controversy had crossed over from the blogosphere into the mainstream media, and other outlets had begun their own investigations into the authenticity of the purported National Guard memoranda. While CBS News doggedly maintained that the memos were authentic, other mainstream media outlets reported evidence to the contrary. A *Power Line* post on the morning of September 14 (Naked, 2004) quoted extensively from a *Washington Post* story which largely refuted CBS News's claims about its authentication of the memos (Dobbs & Kurtz, 2004). It is interesting to note how many of the points mentioned in *The Washington Post* story had already been raised in the blogosphere.

> A detailed comparison by *The Washington Post* of memos obtained by CBS News with authenticated documents on Bush's National Guard service reveals dozens of inconsistencies, ranging from conflicting military terminology to different word-processing techniques. The analysis shows that half a dozen Killian memos released earlier by the military were written with a standard typewriter using different formatting techniques from those characteristic of computer-generated documents. CBS's Killian memos bear numerous signs that are more consistent with modern-day word-processing programs, particularly Microsoft Word.

The Washington Post story cited Joseph Newcomer's detailed analysis of the memos' font, noted many of the formatting discrepancies the *Power Line* readers had earlier pointed out, and included a statement they had independently obtained from CBS News's lead document expert, Marcel Matley. That statement was quite different from CBS News's assertion that Matley vouched for the authenticity of the memos.

> "I knew I could not prove them authentic just from my expertise," he said. "I can't say either way from my expertise, the narrow,

narrow little field of my expertise."

Another *Power Line* post later on the same day (Last Nail in the Coffin, 2004) quoted from a *Dallas Morning News* story (Slover, 2004), in which Jerry Killian's secretary declared the memos to be fake, and resolved the speculation about the typewriter the office used.

> "These are not real," she [Marian Carr Knox] told *The Dallas Morning News* after examining copies of the disputed memos for the first time. "They're not what I typed, and I would have typed them for him." ...

> She said the typeface on the documents did not match either of the two typewriters that she used during her time with the Guard. She identified those machines as a mechanical Olympia typewriter and the IBM Selectric that replaced it in the early 1970s.

A few days later, Hinderaker returned to the allegation, featured in both the "60 Minutes" segment (New Questions on Bush Guard Duty, 2004) and the first *Boston Globe* story (Robinson & Latour, 2004), that Killian had been pressured by his commanding officer, Gen. "Buck" Staudt, to sugar-coat Lt. Bush's performance evaluation. Early in the development of the controversy, bloggers had questioned the veracity of the allegation since Staudt had retired over a year prior to the date of the purported memo containing the reference to him pressuring Killian. ABC News later broadcast an interview with Staudt, and Hinderaker observed (Catch-22, 2004) that this interview destroyed what little evidence might have been remaining to support the authenticity of the memos.

> Yesterday, we noted that General Staudt had given an interview to ABC in which he denied that he had pressured anyone about Lt. Bush, and put to rest the claim that he had somehow come out of retirement to do it. In addition, Staudt drove a stake through the heart of the claim that Bush received preferential treatment in getting into the Guard. Staudt said that he was the person who accepted Bush as a pilot, that he did so solely because he thought Bush would make a fine pilot, and that he received no communications from anyone in relation to Bush's application ....

Staudt's testimony would seem to definitively put the lie to CBS's faked memos, but that's not how CBS sees it.

On the following day *The Washington Post* ran a story (Kurtz, Dobbs, & Grimaldi, 2004) describing the sequence of events by which the "60 Minutes" segment was produced and broadcast. It cast an unflattering light on CBS News regarding both the creation of the segment and its subsequent defense of it.

> An examination of the process that led to the broadcast, based on interviews with the participants and more than 20 independent analysts, shows that CBS rushed the story onto the air while ignoring the advice of its own outside experts, and used as corroborating witnesses people who had no firsthand knowledge of the document.

John Hinderaker noted the story (*The Post* Recaps Rathergate, 2004) and quoted some passages from it. Of particular interest here is Hinderaker's comment on the relationship between blogs and mainstream media outlets in the evolution of the scandal (punctuation as in the blog original).

> My only quarrel with the *Post*'s recap is that it downplays the importance of the [I]nternet to the story, focusing on the belated response of the mainstream media. For example, the *Post* writes that "major news organizations" began questioning the story on Friday, September 10. In recounting the events that occurred between Friday and Monday, the Post says:
>
> A new problem surfaced when reporters found that the man cited in a 1973 memo as pushing to "sugarcoat" Bush's record, Col. Walter B. "Buck" Staudt, had been honorably discharged a year and a half earlier.
>
> In fact, we reported this critical fact by the middle of the day on Thursday, based on a tip from a reader, and millions of people knew about the Staudt retirement issue before the mainstream press finally tumbled to it. "Reporters" didn't "find" this issue, they read it on *Power Line* and other blogs.

While questions still lingered about the source of the memos and the way they had come into the segment producer's possession, CBS News finally ceased defending the authenticity of the memos and announced an inquiry into the production of the segment on September 20 (CBS Statement on Bush Memos, 2004).

> ...CBS News President Andrew Heyward issued the following statement:
>
> ..."Based on what we now know, CBS News cannot prove that the documents are authentic, which is the only acceptable journalistic standard to justify using them in the report. We should not have used them. That was a mistake, which we deeply regret."
>
> ...CBS News and CBS management are commissioning an independent review of the process by which the report was prepared and broadcast to help determine what actions need to be taken. The names of the people conducting the review will be announced shortly, and their findings will be made public.

Nearly four months would go by before the promised internal review was released (CBS Ousts 4, 2005).

Perhaps the "60 Minutes" memo scandal, which came to be known as Rathergate because of the network anchor's central role in it, is the most familiar case so far of media criticism by bloggers. Many aspects of this controversy are of particular interest here. The controversy began with a critical observation about a mainstream outlet's story on a discussion board; that idea gained wider distribution when it was quoted on a blog with a large readership. Other critical observations accumulated, as readers of that blog e-mailed with additional questions about the documentary evidence reported in the story. Bloggers did their own investigation into the evidence, and reported expert opinion apart from that claimed by the mainstream outlet. Bloggers also critically examined the logical bases for assertions made by the mainstream outlet. Ideas which originated in the blogosphere were, after a short time, picked up by other mainstream media outlets. In the end, the bloggers' doubts about the authenticity of the documents proved to be correct, and the mainstream outlet which had created the faulty report was forced to acknowledge this. Apart from the issue of the accuracy of mainstream reporting, this case also illustrates the symbiotic relationship of the blogosphere and the mainstream media. A later chapter will explore this point in more depth.[8]

Perhaps because their suspicions about the authenticity of the National Guard memorandum had proven correct, some bloggers had similar doubts about what became known as the "talking points memo." In the end, the document proved to be genuine but the mainstream press's reporting about its authorship and distribution proved to be substantively inaccurate. This case again provides an illustration of blogs' ability to detect factual misstatements in mainstream reporting, and to make additional relevant information available. It is particularly interesting in that it illustrates both the fallibility of blog critics and also their willingness to acknowledge and correct their errors.

The controversy originated with a broadcast news report in March 2005 that Senate Republicans had circulated among themselves a memo of talking points about the Teri Schiavo controversy. The wording of the report raised doubts in Mick Wright's mind about its factual accuracy, and he described those doubts in a post on his relatively small blog, *Fishkite* (New Doc, 2005). Wright first linked the web page on the ABC News site (DeLay Says, 2005) and quoted a passage from it.

> ABC News obtained talking points circulated among Senate Republicans explaining why they should vote to intervene in the Schiavo case. Among them, that it is an important moral issue and the "pro-life base will be excited," and that it is a "great political issue — this is a tough issue for Democrats."

The wording of those purported talking points struck Wright as peculiar, as did the attribution of them.

> The base will be excited.
> This is a great political issue.
>
> How are those talking points?

And if they are talking points, why couldn't ABC News just interview any given Senate Republican, rather than "obtaining" them? Or they could have embarras[s]ed one of them by seeing if he read directly from the page.

Two days later, John Hinderaker, one of the *Power Line* bloggers, expressed similar doubts about a *Washington Post* story (Allen & Roig-Franzia, 2005) reporting on the Schiavo controversy. His post (Is This the Biggest Hoax, 2005) began by quoting two passages from the story which described the memo.

> In a memo distributed only to Republican senators, the Schiavo case was characterized as "a great political issue" that could pay dividends with Christian conservatives, whose support is essential in midterm elections such as those coming up in 2006.

> An unsigned one-page memo, distributed to Republican senators, said the debate over Schiavo would appeal to the party's base, or core, supporters.

Hinderaker had his doubts about the provenance of the memo, as described in *The Washington Post* story.

> But I have to wonder: is the memo genuine, or is it a Democratic dirty trick? I haven't seen a complete copy of the memo, and to my knowledge, none is available online ... . It is described as "unsigned." What does this mean? Most Senate and House memos are written on letterhead that show[s] whose office they came from. Is this memo on such letterhead? Apparently not. As best I can tell, it is anonymous. Is it simply a one-page memo on blank white paper that purports to come from a Republican? If so, is there any reason to assume that it is genuine?

The wording of the purported talking points raised further doubt in Hinderaker's mind, as it had in Wright's.

> Based on the fragments from the memo that were reported by the *Post*, I question its authenticity. It does not sound like something written by a conservative; it sounds like a liberal fantasy of how conservatives talk. What conservative would write that the case of

a woman condemned to death by starvation is "a great political issue"? Maybe such a person exists, but I doubt it. And who would send an anonymous missive to all 55 Republican Senators, commenting on tactics and strategies? That seems very odd. Who would send a memo to Senators like Lincoln Chaffee, Arlen Specter and Olympia Snowe, to the effect that "the pro-life base will be excited"? That requires an extraordinary level of political obtuseness.

I haven't even seen the memo yet, so I am reluctant to proclaim it a Democratic fraud. But, for the reasons stated, my suspicions are aroused.

He later updated the post with a link to a page containing only the text of the memo. Hinderaker did not feel that the text alone was adequate proof of its purported origin, and wanted to see an image of the memo. He also mentioned that he had queried *The Washington Post* reporter about his source for the story.

ABC reports the alleged complete text of the memo here. This means little or nothing, however; what we need is the memo in PDF. I've sent an e-mail to Mike Allen of *The Washington Post* asking for a copy of the memo, and asking him to explain what he did to verify its authenticity.

Both *Power Line* and *Fishkite* followed the story the next day. Hinderaker posted an e-mail he had received from a reader (Show Us the Memo, 2005), describing the customary procedure for circulating memos in Congress (punctuation and capitalization as in the original).

I worked on the Hill for some time and now work for the State Department. The S[tandard] O[perating] P[rocedure] for moving memos around is that you have a cover sheet that has a "distribution" list on it. Also on the cover sheet is a "Drafter" space where you enter the person's name who drafted the Memo. You cannot just walk around distributing memos to people on the hill. There is a strict protocol on how staffers/intern deliver memos to another congressman's office.

This appears to be an anomaly. I can['] t say that it is fake. But it most certainly does not mesh with the SOP of moving memos around.

Later in the day (So: Where Did It Come From?, 2005) Hinderaker pressed the question of the provenance of the memo. He had obtained an image of the memo; he linked the page, and commented on its appearance.

> The memo is not only "unsigned," as it was described by *The Washington Post*; it is not on House or Senate letterhead, nor is there any indication of source or authenticity.

Hinderaker quoted *The Washington Post* reporter as saying, in an online question-and-answer session (Allen, 2005a), "Because of the conditions under which it was provided to us, we frustratingly cannot tell our readers all that we know about its provenance." This was an insufficient response, to Hinderaker (emphasis in the original).

> Allen thinks he's frustrated that he can't tell us what he knows about the memo's origins? Sorry, but the days are long gone when a reporter can respond to questions about the authenticity of a document by saying that it came from an unimpeachable source.

Hinderaker repeated his questions about the specific content of the talking points, his dissatisfaction with the reporter's account of how he obtained the memo, and ended with a speculation about the authorship of the memo.

> So, to sum up: The memo itself contains no clue as to its origins. That in itself is suspicious; the memo's contents are hardly appropriate for an anonymous communication. The fact that the memo appeared in Senators' offices (or for that matter, at ABC News) proves nothing, as anyone, including a Democratic dirty trickster, could have distributed it. Mike Allen of *The Washington Post* says he knows something he can't tell us, but his only argument for why the memo is authentic — some Senators had it — is silly. Further, the content of the memo is highly suspicious. Why would anyone mix political strategy points — the one the Democrats want to talk about — with talking points for Senatorial argument?...

Does this prove the memo is a fraud? Not at all. It is possible that somewhere in the House or Senate there is a Republican staffer dumb enough to have produced and circulated it. The question, though, is: what is the evidence that the memo is genuine? At this point, there is none. And, with all due respect to Mike Allen, "trust me" is no longer adequate proof.

Mick Wright posted a detailed time line of developments in what had become a controversy about the memo (Senate "Talking Points" Update, 2005). He made note of a couple more curious things about the content of the memo. The text of the memo which had been released by ABC News contained a misspelling of Schiavo's first name and several other misspelled words, and also referred to the pending Senate bill by the wrong number.

The following day brought more posts on *Power Line*. Scott Johnson, also a lawyer, commented that "If it was a Republican staffer who prepared the memo, he or she should be fired for more than one reason" (Show Us the Source, 2005). John Hinderaker wrote a lengthy post (A Fishy Story, 2005) which noted that *The New York Times* had couched its description of the memo (Kirkpatrick & Stolberg, 2005) in more cautious language than had *The Washington Post*. He quoted from that article, adding emphasis.

> As tensions festered among Republicans, Democratic aides passed out an unsigned one-page memorandum that they said had been distributed to Senate Republicans.

Hinderaker carefully weighed the factual assertion in that passage.

> So the memo has been traced to a group of Democratic staffers. What evidence is there that its origins go back any farther? None, that we're aware of.

Hinderaker then went on to offer what he saw as three possible explanations for what few facts had been established, at that point, about the memo.

> The memo has three possible origins. The first possibility is that it was created by a low-level Republican staffer. This seems possible,

but highly unlikely. Only a very dim-witted staffer would 1) copy word for word from the Traditional Values site, 2) get the Senate bill number wrong, 3) make a number of silly errors, including misspelling Mrs. Schiavo's name as "Teri," and 4) mix comments about political advantage into a "talking points" memo. Moreover, the *Post* and ABC have tried to create the impression that the memo is an official, high-level Republican strategy document. It clearly is not that.

The second possibility is that the memo was created by a lobbying group, presumably the Traditional Values Coalition, since most of the content of the memo comes word for word from their Web site. But the controversial political observations — "the pro-life base will be excited," etc. — are inappropriate for an organization like the Coalition. They sound as if they are written from the internal perspective of the Republican party ("this is a tough issue for Democrats").

The third possibility is that the memo is a Democratic dirty trick. At the moment, that looks most likely. It is easy to picture how the document could have been constructed. A Democratic staffer wants to put in some language that will sound authentic for a Republican memo. What does he do? He steals four paragraphs from the Coalition's Web site. Then he adds the explosive political observations which are the whole point of the exercise — weirdly out of place in a "talking points" memo, but good politics for the Democrats.

Hinderaker closed by repeating his call that the reporters who broke the story disclose their sources, and again questioning their frame for the story.

The onus is certainly on Mike Allen of the *Post* and ABC News, if they actually have evidence that the memo is genuine, to tell us what that evidence is. In any event, however, the suggestion that this is some kind of high-level Republican strategy memo is ludicrous.

On her eponymous blog, Michelle Malkin documented how the idea that the memo was an official party document had spread throughout the mainstream press (What Exactly Did the *Post* Say,

2005) and come to be taken as established fact. She quoted from stories in the *Seattle Times*, the *Oakland Tribune, Contra Costa Times,* and *Yahoo! News*, all containing the phrase, "one-page memo, distributed to Republican senators by party leaders," and all bylined either to *The Washington Post* or to Allen and Roig-Franzia. She also noted the "distributed to Republican senators by party leaders" passage appearing in two Reuters articles about the memo. One of Malkin's readers had observed the phrase in the *St. Louis Post-Dispatch.*

It took two full weeks for the uncertainty about the memo to be cleared up, in both the mainstream press and the blogosphere. On April 6, Hinderaker posted "Mystery Solved?" (2005). In it, he said that he had received an e-mail from *The Washington Post* reporter, Mike Allen, with an AP story (apparently Yancey, 2005) attached. Hinderaker quoted at length from the AP story, which detailed how the talking points memo had been authored, without authorization, by an aide to Republican Senator Mel Martinez and accidentally been given to Democrat Senator Tom Harkin. It also reported that the aide had been terminated. Hinderaker accepted this account as reliable, but noted that it directly contradicted the initial *Washington Post* reporting about the authorship, party approval, and distribution of the memo. He quoted passages from the story and added emphasis.

> But the story that Allen wrote with a *Post* colleague on March 19 is not consistent with the current version of the facts. On March 19, Allen wrote:
>
> > Republican officials declared, in a memo that was supposed to be seen only by senators, that they believe the Schiavo case "is a great political" issue that could pay dividends...
> >
> > A one-page memo, distributed to Republican senators by party leaders, said the debate over Schiavo would appeal to the party's base, or core, supporters.
>
> In fact, if the current AP account is correct, the amazingly inept "talking points memo," which got the number of the Senate bill wrong, misspelled Terri Schiavo's name, and contained a number of other typographical errors, did not come from "Republican officials" or "party leaders," but rather from an anonymous,

unknown staffer ... . Also the reporting by ABC and the *Post* suggested that the memo was widely or universally distributed among Republican senators, while a survey reported by the *Washington Times* indicated that none of the 55 Republican senators had seen it. So, if the current AP story is correct, it confirms that ABC and the *Post* misreported the story — in the *Post*'s case, in an article that was picked up by dozens of other newspapers off the paper's wire service.

An update to this post noted Allen's new reporting of this development in the story (Allen, 2005b), now consistent with the AP story, but Hinderaker emphasized that Allen still had not accounted for his earlier attribution of the memo to Republican party leaders.

> Otherwise, his [Allen's new] story doesn't add much that is new, and doesn't attempt to explain the discrepancies between his original reporting and the most recent version. In particular, Allen offers no explanation as to why the anonymous memo was attributed to "Republican officials" or "Republican party leaders," or why it was said to have been distributed "to Republican senators," when the current story provides no support for those statements.

Two days later, Hinderaker did a lengthy recapitulation of the weeks-long controversy (Real Memo, Fake Story, 2005). He acknowledged that his, and other bloggers', earlier speculation that the memo was a forgery and part of a "dirty trick" had been incorrect, but noted that essential points in the mainstream press's reporting of the memo had proven false.

> While the creation of the "talking points memo" didn't turn out to be a Democratic dirty trick, the media's treatment of the memo was misleading at best. An ineptly produced memo, written by an unknown aide, which represented no one's opinions but the aide's and, as far as we now know, was distributed to almost no one, was widely trumpeted as the handiwork of the Republican party's leaders and an expression of the party's political strategy. Only when bloggers questioned the story did reporters from *The Washington Post* and ABC back off and admit that they had no reason to believe that the memo was the product of the party's leadership or had any official status. How the memo came to be

misreported in the first place is a story that has yet to be told.

The talking points memo is a complex case of fact-checking in the blogosphere, and it is worthwhile to review the points both the bloggers and the mainstream journalists got correct and incorrect as the controversy evolved. Early speculation by bloggers that the document might be a forgery by a Democrat dirty trickster proved inaccurate; when the facts about the authorship of the memo became known, they acknowledged the mistake. One blogger's speculation that the document might have been authored by a rogue Republican staffer proved to be correct; another's comment that such a staffer ought be terminated came to pass. At the height of the controversy one blogger offered a number of alternative explanations for what was known to that point; he was wrong in his choice of the most likely, but the actual sequence of events was one of the alternative explanations he offered.

The early reporting by ABC News and *The Washington Post* that the memo was an official document of the Republican senate leadership proved to be false, and assurances by *The Washington Post* reporter that not only was the document genuine but his description of its distribution was accurate also proved to be false. Reporting about the memo was not uniform across the mainstream news outlets; *The New York Times* was more cautious in its assertions about the distribution of the memo and the *Washington Times* reported, correctly, that the memo had not in fact been distributed to Republic senators. Under scrutiny by bloggers, *The Washington Post* reporter who broke the story subsequently backtracked on a number of his earlier assertions about the provenance of the memo at the center of the controversy.

It is also worth noting that both ABC News and *The Washington Post* appear to have done a rowback in their coverage of the story. (Rowback is the trade jargon for revising errors in previous reporting with follow-up stories, but failing to issue a formal correction to the inaccuracies in the previous reporting. Rowbacks will be discussed later in this book.) When this author, in July 2005, followed links to ABC stories embedded in *Power Line* posts during the week of March 20, he found the early stories simply to have been replaced on the ABC site with a story about Martinez's aide, dated April 7. In reviewing *The Washington Post* coverage of this controversy, this author noted that there had been no correction or editor's note appended either to the initial story attributing the memo to the Republican senate leadership or to the transcript of the online question-and-answer session in which the reporter affirmed that authorship, despite the significant factual error contained in those documents.[9]

Interpretation of Statistics or Scientific Studies

It is no simple task for a journalist to write about technical topics in a way that is both accessible and interesting to a lay reader. Particularly in the social sciences, the findings of a scholarly study are usually stated in carefully-qualified and precise language; this sets up the translation problem facing a journalist reporting on the study. Scholars are trained in such arcana as probability, confidence intervals, and null hypotheses; moreover, they understand that the findings of scientific studies ought not be taken as definitive statements of truth but are best thought of as provisional, subject to further testing and possible disconfirmation. Neither the general news audience nor most journalists have that background in research methods, yet the reporter must try to convey such highly nuanced technical information in non-technical language to a non-specialist audience, which is prone to expect a higher degree of certainty in the findings than the scientific method can guarantee.

It is not surprising, then, to find news stories about scholarly studies are often subject to criticism in the blogosphere. Oftentimes the blogger is more skilled in the interpretation of social science literature than the reporter; similarly, blog posts often include comments from readers with special expertise, including statistical methods. Typically, the criticism does not dispute the accuracy of factual statements in the news story so much as the journalist's vernacular interpretation of the findings of the study. Sometimes the critique involves knowledge of sophisticated research techniques, but sometimes the bloggers simply identify shoddy reasoning or selective interpretation of study's findings in the news media accounts of the study. Again, the purpose in examining several examples here is not to imply that mainstream journalists are generally failing to meet reasonable performance expectations, but rather to illustrate how the blogosphere makes a constructive contribution to public discussion of technical reports relevant to public policy.

A concise example of this type of criticism can be found on the blog of financial writer Meagan McArdle, *Asymmetrical Information* (Department of Awful Statistics, 2005). A scathing passage in a *New York Times* editorial (Crumbs for Africa, 2005) had caught her eye, and she began the post by quoting it.

> The United States currently gives just 0.16 percent of its national income to help poor countries, despite signing a United Nations declaration three years ago in which rich countries agreed to increase their aid to 0.7 percent by 2015. Since then, Britain, France and Germany have all announced plans for how to get to 0.7 percent; America has not. The piddling amount Mr. Bush announced yesterday is not even 0.007 percent. What is 0.7 percent of the American economy? About $80 billion. That is about the amount the Senate just approved for additional military spending, mostly in Iraq. It's not remotely close to the $140 billion corporate tax cut last year.

Posting under the pseudonym Jane Galt, McArdle explained why the last sentence of that passage seemed peculiar to her.

> I follow tax policy pretty closely, and I hadn't noticed a corporate tax cut last year. And a $140 billion tax cut would be pretty large, given that, according to the IRS, the corporate income tax only generated $167 billion dollars last year. I felt like I would have noticed an 83% tax cut.

McArdle found and linked a source (Weisman, 2004) for the $140 billion figure mentioned in the *Times* editorial. She then explained why she considered the editorial to have made deceptive use of an economic statistic (emphasis in the original).

> It's the ten-year estimate for the cost of tax cuts in last year's change to the export subsidy, <u>before the various clawbacks in that bill are subtracted.</u> This is naughty in two ways. First, comparing

the ten year cost of a tax bill to the one year cost of aid is not the done thing in economics circles — any more than you can compare the amount you'll spend on food over the next decade to the amount you'll spend on your mortgage over the next year, and declare that you spend more on food than shelter. And second of all, it is not quite playing the straight bat to include all the costs of the bill, and accidentally leave out the revenue generation.[10]

Clearly, David Brooks meant his op-ed piece on a medical study to be humorous (Brooks, 2005), but it drew a good deal of blog criticism for its oversimplification of the study's findings about the relationship of body weight and longevity. The lede reads, "The release of a report in *The Journal of the American Medical Association* indicating that overweight people actually live longer than normal-weight people represents an important moment in the history of world civilization," and the piece continues by poking fun at fitness enthusiasts. On *Unfogged*, a blogger using the pseudonym Ogged posted an equally colorful rebuttal titled "Choke on that Cinnabon" (2005) but made the substantial point that Brooks misrepresented the study's findings when he suggested it indicated an individual's fitness- and diet-consciousness could actually decrease that person's life expectancy.

On *JustOneMinute*, retired investment executive Tom Maguire characterized Brooks's piece as "an almost perfect misreading of the latest report linking obesity, overweight, and early death" (Their Worst Nightmare, 2005). Of particular interest here is the way Maguire linked to an online copy of the study, pointed out that the researchers had carefully qualified their findings and acknowledged the data limitations of the study so as to preclude an interpretation such as Brooks's, and pulled from the study a passage reading, "Other factors associated with body weight, such as physical activity, body composition, visceral adiposity, physical fitness or dietary intake, might be responsible for some or all of the apparent associations of weight with mortality." Maguire summed up his critique by saying, "contra Brooks, the study surely did not conclude that exercise was futile, or harmful."

One might sensibly wonder if there is any point to these blog critiques of a mainstream media piece which was clearly intended as a humorous slice-of-life commentary. To the extent that Brooks's article might have inadvertently fostered a meme (which will be discussed later in this chapter) and left *New York Times* readers with the impression that a legitimate medical study had actually found being overweight to increase a person's longevity, the bloggers' criticism would seem nontrivial. It seems that such a meme actually did start to develop, given that Consumer's Union published an article a few months later (Is It Healthier, 2005) which refuted the slightly-overweight-is-better meme along much the same lines as the bloggers had, and mentioned Brooks's piece in its first paragraph.[11]

As noted above, bloggers sometimes have specialized expertise about the topic of a story. Critiques of news stories concerning economic policy issues frequently appear on *The Conspiracy to Keep You Poor* and *Stupid*, a blog written by financial analyst Donald Luskin. In a bluntly-worded critique (Shiller Shills for the Left, 2005), Luskin took issue with both a *Washington Post* story (Weisman, 2005b) about an economist's study of a Social Security reform proposal, and with the method of the study itself. Of interest here is the critique of the newspaper story's lede, which Luskin quoted:

> Nearly three-quarters of workers who opt for Social Security personal accounts under President Bush's "default" investment option are likely to earn less in benefits than those who stay with the traditional Social Security system, a prominent finance economist has concluded. A new paper by Yale University economist Robert J. Shiller found that under Bush's default "life-cycle accounts"...nearly a third of workers would bring in less in benefits than if they remained in the traditional system.

Luskin pointed out what seems an obvious contradiction: the references to three-quarters of the working population in the first sentence, and to one-third in the second sentence. Luskin also questioned the story's characterization of life cycle accounts as the "default investment option" in the reform proposal, saying that while the White House had made mention of life cycle accounts as a possibility, it had not yet committed to a particular investment design for personal accounts; he linked to policy documents and press briefings to support his point.

Luskin then linked the Shiller study which was the basis for the news story, and went on to critique the computer model used to simulate the performance of life cycle accounts. (Oddly enough, the paper was only available as a manuscript in PDF format on Shiller's personal Web site. At the time of *The Washington Post* story about it, March 2005, the study had not been published in a peer-reviewed scholarly journal, which is the customary venue for this type of academic work. As of this writing, in July 2005, it still had not.) Luskin objected to using money market funds as a significant proportion of the model portfolio, saying they tend to underperform bond returns over time; he also objected to using an average of 15 countries' market returns to project the return on the simulated accounts, instead of the actual historical returns of the United States market. Doing these things in the study, Luskin argued, would bias the data to considerably understate the probable returns of a personal portfolio based around a life cycle account.

As evidence of his personal expertise regarding life cycle accounts, Luskin linked his two patents on that investment device, and offered a concise explanation of the way they operate:

> In a nutshell, a life cycle account automatically moves an investor from higher risk holdings such as stocks into lower risk holdings such as bonds — much as a professional investment counselor might advise you to do as you get older.

In sum, Luskin's critique was twofold: the newspaper story did not accurately convey the findings of the study, and the findings of the study lacked validity because of a serious methodological flaw.[12]

With the popularity of news stories about poll results — and the direct involvement of mainstream news organizations in conducting political opinion polls — it is commonplace to find critique of those stories in the blogosphere. A good example is the *Power Line* post (More Bad Poll Data, 2005) about an ABC News/*Washington Post* poll (Morin & Balz, 2005). John Hinderaker noted something in the reporting of a poll question about judicial filibusters. He quoted the lede and third paragraph of the article in his blog post.

> As the Senate moves toward a major confrontation over judicial appointments, a strong majority of Americans oppose changing the rules to make it easier for Republican leaders to win confirmation of President Bush's court nominees, according to the latest *Washington Post*-ABC News poll.

> [B]y a 2 to 1 ratio, the public rejected easing Senate rules in a way that would make it harder for Democratic senators to prevent final action on Bush's nominees.

The newspaper story, as is customary, did not include the actual poll questions, but Hinderaker was able to obtain them from a link on *The Washington Post* Web site. The question about which the article was headlined read: "Would you support or oppose changing Senate rules to make it easier for the Republicans to confirm Bush's judicial nominees?" Hinderaker felt the wording of the poll question was leading, and contrasted it with another way to ask about the filibuster controversy.

> That is an absurd question, to which I would probably answer "No," too. The way the question is framed, it makes it sound like a one-way street, as though the Republicans wanted to change the rules to benefit only Republican nominees. If they asked a question like, "Do you think that if a majority of Senators support confirmation of a particular nominee, that nominee should be confirmed?" the percentages would probably reverse.

Hinderaker raised another methodological issue about the survey. As is customary in such news stories, the article reported the number of respondents to the poll, the dates on which the telephone poll was conducted, and the margin of error. Hinderaker checked the respondent demographics on the *Post* Web site, and noted that 35% of the respondents identified themselves as Democrats, and 28% as Republicans. He felt this indicated a problem in the sampling which was likely to bias the data, and commented, "Given that slightly more self-identified Republicans than Democrats voted in last November's election, this represents an egregious, seven-point over-sampling of Democrats."[13]

A study published in a British medical journal, reporting an estimate of what the authors called "excess" deaths from Operation Iraqi Freedom, sparked a very lively debate in the blogosphere some months afterward. Of particular interest in this example is the contribution of blog readers to a detailed and high-level discussion about the interpretation of statistical analyses.

What became known in the blogosphere as "the *Lancet* study" (Roberts, Lafta, Garfield, Khudhairi, & Burnham, 2004) was published online at the end of October 2004. The study used a cluster survey of Iraqi households to derive civilian mortality rates, before and after the invasion. Comparing those mortality rates, the authors concluded that "about 100,000 excess deaths, or more have happened since the 2003 invasion of Iraq." The study quickly drew a scathing critique on *Slate* magazine (Kaplan, 2004), raising a number of methodological questions about the study (including the representativeness of the clusters chosen for survey administration and the validity of the baseline mortality rate), but primarily concentrating on the unusually wide confidence interval surrounding the finding that 100,000 civilians had died because of the war: 8,000-194,000. Kaplan characterized the major finding of the study as "so loose as to be meaningless."

The second anniversary of the invasion, in March 2005, prompted renewed attention to the study in the mainstream media and the blogosphere. On *That Liberal Media*, Brian Crouch linked the Kaplan critique and commented, about the major finding of the *Lancet* study, "It's troubling to see how frequently this meaningless and distorted projection appears in the mainstream media" (Persistent, Pervasive and Pernicious, 2005). Crouch linked a number of favorable references to the study in the mainstream media, and termed the uncritical reliance on its finding "propaganda." Bloggers sometimes include a personal experience relevant to the topic of the post; Crouch also described a local meeting he had attended, at which the statistic from the study was cited and taken as established fact (punctuation and capitalization as in the original).

Two days ago I attended a Seattle community forum called "Veterans Reflect on the Iraq War," featuring Terry Thomas, a Marine lieutenant who had served in the initial push into Iraq, Josh

Rushing, from CENTCOM, and John Oliviera, a naval press officer. The veterans were diverse in their position on the war: Thomas described his moral clarity in favor of it growing from meeting families in the Marshes of the south who had each lost a family member to murders by the fedayeen, and seeing Hussein's torture facilities. Rushing was optimistic about the Middle East's reforms but thought more could have been done to avoid war and to engage the Arab media, and Oliviera felt the administration had lied and let the troops down.

Questions from the audience referred to the *Lancet*'s figure. "Even though they're voting, how can you justify killing 100,000?" or "Don't you feel angry that you were a part of killing 100,000 people for a lie, for oil?" The vets could have refuted the premise of those questions, if only the myth begun in October last year had been more effectively, dedicatedly debunked by journalists and the DoD. They seemed caught off-guard by this, even the anti-war vet didn't seem to believe it, but didn't know how to contend with the claim.

Brendan Nyhan had received an "action alert" e-mail from the media watchdog group Fairness and Accuracy in Reporting (Counting the Iraqi Dead, 2005), asking its list subscribers to contact the three major US broadcast networks and request that the *Lancet* finding be given more prominence in their news coverage. Nyhan took a dim view of FAIR's e-mail; he linked the text of it on his eponymous blog, and critiqued FAIR's critique (FAIR Hypes Shaky Estimate, 2005):

The political abuse of statistics continues. In an action alert sent to its e-mail list today, the liberals at Fairness and Accuracy in Reporting claim that Iraqi casualty estimates of 16,500-20,000 offered by the network newscasts, including NBC's Brian Williams, were too low.

Nyhan quoted a passage from the FAIR e-mail referencing the *Lancet* figure of 100,000 casualties, and echoed Kaplan's concern about the confidence interval surrounding that number.

Saying that "about 100,000 Iraqi civilians" have died vastly overstates the precision of the number that was found. As Fred Kaplan explained on *Slate*, the 95% confidence interval of the

Lancet study extended from 8,000-196,000 [sic] deaths. That means that the researchers are 95% sure that the true figure lies between those two vastly different numbers. While the Iraq Body Count estimates may indeed be too low, can you blame the networks [for] avoiding such a shaky estimate?

In an update the next day, Nyhan added a further point to his criticism of FAIR's action alert: "The study estimates the total number of 'excess deaths,' not civilian deaths. Thus FAIR's claim is doubly wrong."

On *InstaPundit*, law professor Glenn Reynolds initially made only a brief comment (That Liberal Media, 2005) seconding Brian Couch's criticism, and linking the Kaplan article. Reynolds updated his two-sentence post several times, as his readers sent him comments on the interpretation of the statistic reported in the *Lancet* study. Eventually the updates accumulated into a high-level discussion on the meaning of the finding and the study's validity. A graduate student took issue with Kaplan's understanding of the confidence interval (punctuation and emphasis as in the original).

> *Slate* has the statistical analysis of the piece wrong — though the confidence interval is 8000-194000, the median/mean in this case is actually far more likely to be true than either of the tails. These studies are conducted under the premise that the data fits a standard normal curve (imagine a mountain with low hills leading to a peak, then descending back to low hills.) 8000 and 194000 are the very end of the tails, and are thus FAR more unlikely to occur than the instances in the middle of the curve. What is most likely, and in this study statistically significant at the 95% level is that 101000 civilians have died as a result of violence attributable to the war.

A later update contained a management professor's reply to the graduate student (capitalization as in the original).

> Sorry to burst that grad student's bubble, but there are a few problems with his debunking of the debunking of the *Lancet* article.
>
> 1) the distribution of probable dead is not normal. It actually probably resembles a Poisson distribution.

2) the study distribution's 95% confidence range covers so much of the possible range as to be a nearly flat distribution (at least relatively speaking).

3) even if the statistics were acceptable, there are serious questions about the sample, as pointed out in the original debunking.

4) the author of the original study is known to have biases related to the research.

Another reader raised a question concerning the face validity of the study's finding (syntax as in the original).

> Are we honestly to believe that twice as many non-combatants have died as a result of the liberation of Iraq as were American combatants in 8 years of VietNam? In a war designed and fought to minimize civilian casualties with things like GPS guided bombs?

A doctoral student in economics contributed a detailed comment on the meaning of confidence intervals and null hypotheses (punctuation and capitalization as in the original).

> In non-Bayesian statistics, it is the interval that is random, not the population parameter of interest. The correct interpretation for, say, a 95% confidence interval around a given unknown parameter (in this case, the # of casualties) would be that the interval contains the true number about 95% of the time ... . Based on this information, [it is] technically incorrect to claim that 8000 or 194,000 would be "rare" events. Instead, the correct conclusion, as in the "debunking" article by Kaplan, is that we can be 95% confident that the true number of casualties lies between the bounds. It says nothing of the probability of any of these outcomes.

> Another way to think about this is in the form of a hypothesis test, in which the null hypothesis is that the true number of casualties (call it y) equals x. Based on the confidence interval, we would not reject the null hypothesis that y=x (against the alternative y <> x) based on our sample evidence, so long as x lied [sic] between the 8000 and 194000 bounds. In other words, our test produces exactly the same results for testing the hypothesis that the true number of

casualties is 8,000, 100,000 or 194,000...namely, do not reject.

Note that we do not "accept" the null hypothesis, either...[I]n statistics, one looks for evidence against the null, but there are many null hypotheses consistent with the data. A great quote on this that might provide some illumination to an illustrious law professor [presumably, a reference to Reynolds] comes from Jan Kmenta in his 1971 Elements of Econometrics book...

"just as a court pronounces a verdict as 'not guilty' rather than 'innocent', so the conclusion of a statistical test is 'do not reject' rather than 'accept.'"

Reynolds ended his post by linking to a lengthy defense of the *Lancet* study by another academician blogger, computer science lecturer Tim Lambert (Lancet Post Number 41, 2005).

On *The Age of Unreason*, a blogger using the pseudonym Andy S posted twice on the *Lancet* study, raising methodological questions appropriate to surveys. In the first (That Lancet Study!, 2005), he pointed out that survey respondents will not always give valid answers to questions (punctuation and capitalization as in the original).

...[A] bane of all sample surveys is the item called in the literature "Non Sampling error". One major source of non sampling error in surveys which collect responses from people is that people do not always tell the truth. Famously, surveys on how many cigarettes people smoke daily show far fewer cigarettes smoked than are known to be sold. Survey respondents typically understate the number of cigarettes they smoke daily, they are embarrassed to admit the truth, they may even be lying to themselves.

As I understand the *Lancet* survey, interviewers went to selected households and asked about family deaths in the period between the invasion of Iraq and the day of the interview. To say none (as most people probably did) is kind of boring so some respondents would be tempted to invent a dead relative. If the interviewee had an anti American agenda, as some surely did the temptation to lie would be even greater.

In his second post, Andy S questioned the cluster sampling (More on those Dead Iraqis, 2005).

Of Iraq's 18 provinces only 12 were actually visited. The sample design is a cluster sample survey (actually Cluster with sub Clusters). Now clusters assigned to the unsurveyed provinces were replaced in the sample by selecting clusters in adjacent provinces as proxies ... . The net effect of this is that of the five provinces in northern Iraq only Ninawa and Sulaymaniya were surveyed ... . In a similar manner Iraq's three southernmost provinces were left unsurveyed. Somehow or other the Northern Kurdish population and the Southern Shiite population were undersampled whilst the Sunni provinces were completely covered!

Judging the merit of the *Lancet* study will be left to the reader. Of interest here is the interactivity among the bloggers and their readers, the specialized expertise readers are often able to contribute to the discussion — expertise beyond what one could reasonably expect journalists to possess — and the collaborative nature of the blog criticism.[14]

Trustworthiness of Memes

The term meme is now a commonplace in the blogosphere, but did not originate in it, or even in the domain of computer-mediated communication in general. A scholar of animal behavior coined the term in 1976 as a way a way of applying the theory of genetic evolution to the realm of human cultural change (Dawkins, 1989, p. 189 ff.). He felt it would be fruitful to think about cultural transmission of ideas, practices, or artifacts by way of analogy to the reproduction and evolution of genetic code. This novel idea was enthusiastically received, and elaborated to quite a level of sophistication as a tool for cultural analysis (Blackmore, 2000; Blackmore, 1999).

Given that computer networking provides an excellent vehicle for the replication of ideas, it is unsurprising to see the concept adopted in the blogosphere. *Samizdata.net* maintains a helpful glossary of blogosphere terminology, and offers this entry for meme (Meme, n.d.):

noun. A meme is considered to be a discrete idea that replicates itself, with the connotation that memes replicate themselves and are propagated by people through social and technological networks, much like both real and computer viruses.

In itself, that definition would not explain why blog criticism of memes has become so prevalent. The point is worth exploring in greater detail.

While people often talk about memes as if they were simple statements of fact, there is an important distinction which needs to be noted. In the strict sense of the term, a factual statement can be verified or disproved with the use of observation or appropriate evidence; after it was tested in that way, we would expect a very high degree of intersubjective agreement on whether the factual statement was true or false. A trivial example would be the statement, "Dr. Cooper's eyes are blue." Direct observation of this author's eyes would show that to be a false statement. In short, a statement of fact can be tested by the application of evidence, after which there would be little or no controversy about its truth value. While the factually false idea that this author's eyes are blue might indeed propagate to a very limited extent for a very limited time, the defect in the meme — analogous to a defect in a gene — would work against its long-term survival.

In contemporary blogosphere usage, a meme is a more complex proposition in that it typically combines both facts and judgments about those facts into a single proposition. Because of that quality they are inherently more arguable, and — because of the tendency for people to take them as simple facts — more problematic. An example might be, "Dr. Cooper is a nice guy." That would be a summary judgment of this author's personality, based on some number of facts about this author's past behaviors and a particular understanding of what "nice guy" means. Once that meme had been created, replicated itself among some group of people, and come to be jointly understood as fact, it would become the context in which this author's subsequent behaviors would be interpreted. Once the meme had become established in the idea pool of that group of people, its further replication would be fostered, in that factual discrepancies — Cooper doing something mean, for instance — would tend to be discounted or ignored, at least until some tipping point at which the accumulated factual discrepancies were duly noted and the meme "died."

This simple illustration of a meme hints at some of the complexities which arise when memes are created in news reporting, and become used as building blocks of subsequent stories. Facts which might debunk a meme tend to be glossed by it, over time, and the meme alone comes to be taken as an established fact in itself. Bloggers often criticize memes in mainstream news coverage, either by disputing the factual basis for the meme or by identifying and questioning the judgments subsumed by the meme.

A good example of a blogger objecting to a meme in the mainstream media can be found in an April 2005 post on *InstaPundit*. This post is also a good illustration of how posts are frequently updated and developed over time, and how blog readers often contribute material to those updates, even when the blog does not offer a dedicated comments area for them to use. Blogs offer both archiving and interactivity capabilities that are new to the media mix.

While Glenn Reynolds did not label it a meme (Out-and-out Dishonesty, 2005), the passage he critiqued in a *New York Times* editorial (Losing Ground in Iraq, 2005) clearly contains one. Reynolds quoted this paragraph from the editorial, and added the emphasis.

> The only plausible reason for keeping American troops in Iraq is to protect the democratic transformation that President Bush <u>seized upon as a rationale for the invasion after his claims about weapons of mass destruction turned out to be fictitious.</u> If that transformation is now allowed to run off the rails, the new rationale could prove to be as hollow as the original one.

Reynolds commented, "this claim that democratic transformation was some sort of new rationalization is, not to put too fine a point on it, an out-and-out lie," and linked to an earlier post of his offering a large amount of evidence that the President had often mentioned democratization in speeches prior to the beginning of Operation Iraqi Freedom.

That *InstaPundit* post (More Historical Revisionism, 2005), from about two weeks earlier, was a critique of an opinion column in the *St. Louis Post-Dispatch* (Brown, 2005), which had included the sentence, "I don't recall any prewar speeches about delivering democracy to the

Middle East." In the original version, Reynolds linked to the 2003 State of the Union address and quoted several paragraphs containing references to United Support of democratization in both Iran and Iraq, as refutation of the columnist's remark.

The post continued to evolve over time with updates which included a considerable amount of material contributed by *InstaPundit* readers. One reader pointed out two prewar mentions of democratization in Iraq as a policy goal. The first in the update was Bush's 2002 speech to the U. N. General Assembly, which Reynolds linked to and quoted from, again adding emphasis:

> The United States has no quarrel with the Iraqi people; they've suffered too long in silent captivity. <u>Liberty for the Iraqi people is a great moral cause, and a great strategic goal.</u> The people of Iraq deserve it; the security of all nations requires it. Free societies do not intimidate through cruelty and conquest, and open societies do not threaten the world with mass murder. The United States supports political and economic liberty in a unified Iraq.

The second was from a NewsHour broadcast on PBS about a month before the start of Operation Iraqi Freedom. Reynolds linked to the show transcript, and quoted from it at length, including Margaret Warner's statement in a bridge between video clips of a Bush speech, "The President further asserted that a democratic Iraq could transform the entire region in a similar way."

An interesting sort of evidence supporting Reynolds's critique of this meme came from another reader. This person had found a number of passages in web documents created prior to the war, disagreeing with administration statements about democratization as one of the reasons for going to war. Reynolds linked three of these, and quoted from them. One came from the Web site *Counterpunch*, and read, "...he [Bush] proclaims that his war against the people of Iraq will bring about something called 'democracy' for the struggling peoples of the Middle East." To these quotes, Reynolds added the ironic comment, "So back then the claims were bogus — and now they're new!"

Another reader drew attention to the congressional resolution authorizing the war. Reynolds linked the document, and quoted a passage from the preamble.

> Whereas the Iraq Liberation Act (Public Law 105-338) expressed the sense of Congress that it should be the policy of the United States to support efforts to remove from power the current Iraqi regime and promote the emergence of a democratic government to replace that regime ... .

Again, it is not this book's purpose to argue for particular policies or to defend specific political actors. Of interest here is the nature of the critique, the way the blogger identified a meme which had developed in the mainstream media and offered documentary evidence as refutation of it. Also of interest here is the collaborative nature of the media criticism, the way readers contributed further material to it as the post evolved.[15]

Press coverage of the 7/7 London suicide bombings prompted blog criticism of memes concerning the root causes of terrorism. Stephen Green's post on *Vodkapundit* is notable for its economy of words in questioning a commonly-accepted explanation for terrorists' motives. In "Middle Class Blues" (2005), Green quoted the lede of a *Times of London* story (Winnett & Leppard, 2005) about British intelligence about terrorist activities there.

> Al-Qaeda is secretly recruiting affluent, middle-class Muslims in British universities and colleges to carry out terrorist attacks in this country, leaked Whitehall documents reveal. A network of "extremist recruiters" is circulating on campuses targeting people with "technical and professional qualifications", particularly engineering and IT degrees.

The title of the post hinted at the meme Green critiqued, and he added only a one-sentence comment of his own to make it explicit: "Remember, the root cause of terrorism is poverty."

A pseudonymous guest blogger on *Rantingprofs* contributed a longer post about that root cause meme, and touched on another as well. The post ("They Were Good Muslims", 2005) was titled with a quote pulled from a different *Times of London* story (Norfolk & Jenkins, 2005), this one describing the backgrounds of two young men

British investigators had identified as suicide bombers in the 7/7 attack. The post began by naming the two memes the blogger, who identified him/herself as Paleologos, felt were called into question by facts reported in the Times story.

> The profile of the alleged bombers coming out of London is the worst-case scenario. It is also more proof that the allegations that "third world poverty" and "Western foreign policy" cause terrorism have no basis.

Paleologos next quoted the lede of the *Times* story.

> If ever there were model immigrants, they were the Tanweers. The close-knit family, originally from Pakistan, had made a good life in Britain, running their fish and chip shop and living in a large detached house in the Beeston area of Leeds, with two Mercedes cars parked outside. They were good Muslims, respected in a local multi-ethnic community of whites, Africans, East Europeans, Pakistanis and Bengalis. But then Shehzad, one of their four children, went missing last week from the family home in Colwyn Road. Police believe that he was not only a victim of last Thursday's London bombings, but one of the perpetrators.

Paleologos then made his/her critique explicit by summarizing facts reported in the *Times* story that were inconsistent with the root cause memes, and suggesting an alternative explanation for the young men's participation in a terrorist act.

> A perfect storm of anti-expectations. Good family. Loving family. Stable family. Well-liked. No trouble with the law. No social disabilities. No prior terror connections. From a country untouched by Anglo-American "aggression." The only profiling tip: "an intense religious faith." We can only hope that for young men such as this, somebody will have to revise what being a "good Muslim" means.[16]

Another way bloggers criticize a meme is to provide visual images which call its trustworthiness into question. Val Prieto, a Cuban emigre living in the United States, took issue with the meme that the Castro regime provides its citizens good quality, free healthcare. Prieto began the fiery post on his *Babalu Blog* (Cuban Mythology, 2005) by noting the prevalence of the meme in the mainstream media (capitalization, punctuation, and emphasis as in the original).

> Every single time the island of Cuba and fidel castro's revolution are covered anywhere in the media one of the points always mentioned is Cuba's free healthcare. You can practically time it. If it's in print, you get the lead issue in the first and second paragraph[s], a mention of fidel castro or one of his cronies in the third paragraph and then the plug for the lauded free healthcare available to Cubans in the fourth. I dont think Ive ever read an article about castro or Cuba where the "healthcare" isnt mentioned ... . Of course, none of these *Free healthcare!* cheerleaders have ever been to a Cuban hospital. They've never been to a Cuban clinic. Hospitals serving the average Cuban, that is.

Prieto then posted three photographs he said had been taken in El Hospital Clinico Quirurgico de la Habana; he identified the source of the images as a Spanish-language periodical named *Gentiuno*, and linked the online article where he had obtained the images. The first image was a close-up of approximately two dozen dead cockroaches lying on a tile floor. The second image was a medium wide shot of a corridor with masonry walls, leading into a room; both floor and walls seem to be quite dirty, and there are no furnishings visible. The third image was a close-up of a wall and floor meeting; again, the surfaces appear filthy. Prieto then commented (capitalization and syntax as in the original):

> Quite unsanitary, no? Well, this is just a small reality of castro's lauded healthcare in Cuba. This is a hopsital [sic] in Havana, the nation's capital and the most populated city in the country ... . This is not a hospital that caters to foreigners, mind you. This is a hospital strictly for the Cuban people. Foreigners are treated quite differently and their facilities are state of the art and, at least, sanitary.

Prieto closed his post by again objecting to the meme (capitalization and punctuation as in the original).

I urge each and every one of you to check the remaining photographs out so that next time, when some fidel loving apologist mentions Cuba's free healthcare, you remember what they're really talking about: the myth of Cuba's vaunted healthcare system.

As is common, another blogger cited Prieto's post and added commentary of his own. In a post on *Captain's Quarters*, Edward Morrissey, a call center manager and part-time talk radio host, detailed how the meme played a role in debate about U.S. foreign policy (The Mythology of Cuban Medical Care, 2005).

For those who support or sympathize with Fidel Castro and his dictatorship of Cuba, no argument comes up more frequently than the supposedly marvelous health-care system that Castro has created for the Cubans. They routinely credit him with managing to deliver world-class facilities and treatment, equally for all Cubans, far surpassing even the United States in egalitarianism and effectiveness. For some people, that level of medical care outweighs Castro's oppression, which would be ludicrous even if they were right about the medical system they espouse. Unfortunately, that system is a myth, as Val Prieto points out ... .

He included the same picture of cockroaches, then several others from the *Gentiuno* article: a medium shot of a room with holes in the wall, a wide shot of a room in which a dropped ceiling seems to have collapsed, and close-ups of exposed electrical wiring from an open junction box and an open circuit breaker panel. Like Prieto, Morrissey closed with a stinging comment on the trustworthiness of the meme, and pointed again to the visual images as support of his critique.

When leftists tell you that Castro may have his faults but he provides for the Cuban people with his marvelous health system, try to remember these pictures. I wouldn't send a stray dog to a facility like this to get put to sleep, let alone receive treatment.[17]

CHAPTER 3

Framing

As many media scholars have noted, news coverage inherently does a lot more than simply provide an assortment of factual statements about an event, issue, or controversy (see Kuypers, 2002, pp. 4-11 for a concise review). Scholarly research into media effects on the audience and the characteristics of news products has a long history. One of the more interesting concepts to emerge in this tradition is framing, the organizing of facts around some central idea or issue (Gamson, 1989, p. 157). In colloquial language, the frame is the short answer to the question, "What's the story, here?"

Facts become comprehensible to us as they are linked into coherent interpretations of real life situations or real world actors. Put another way, making sense out of daily experience and observation necessarily involves fitting isolated factual data into some sort of pattern we understand and find meaningful. In a similar fashion, journalists weave their factual description of events into a coherent storyline, however nuanced or complex, in order to produce a competent news product. It is difficult to find a piece of journalism that offers no interpretation of the facts it contains; it is tempting to say that there could be no reporting without framing of the factual description, since the stories could not be written without suggesting a storyline. If framing is an intrinsic element of our sense-making of direct experience, it is unsurprising that journalists perforce do it in their mediation of remote experiences for our consumption.

There has been a lively debate, for some time, about whether the mainstream media favor particular viewpoints, interests, or ideologies in the frames of news reporting. While this is an interesting question (Cooper, 1994; Cooper, 2006; Kuypers, 2002), it is not crucial to take a position on the media bias issue here. Critique of the mainstream media's framing is a staple of blog criticism, and examples are plentiful. Just as framing seems to be an inherent feature in reporting, critique of framing seems to be a natural response of a reader to the reporting, a response that now finds an outlet in blogs. The critique may take the form of disputing the frame of a news story, reframing the facts into a distinctly different interpretation, or contextualizing a frame in a different way. Again these are not bright-line distinctions, but it is useful to consider examples of each.

Disputing the MSM Frame

Coverage of an Iraqi insurgent attack on an American military convoy in March 2005 offers an example of a blogger questioning the framing of mainstream news stories. *The New York Times* story about the event (Wong, 2005) drew a detailed critique from communication professor Cori Dauber on her blog, *Rantingprofs* (Bold, Aggressive Attack!, 2005). Dauber first noted that the headline itself of the story, "24 Insurgents Die in Attack Near Baghdad," struck her as unusually passive phrasing for the event, in that the insurgents "were killed in a military engagement they initiated when American forces shot back." She then quoted the first paragraph of the *Times* story, adding emphasis to wording which she thought indicated a misleading frame for the story.

> Iraqi insurgents <u>ambushed</u> an American military convoy <u>in daylight</u> outside Baghdad on Sunday, igniting a battle that left 24 of the attackers dead and 7 wounded, American military officials said. The <u>unusually bold assault</u> appeared to be <u>the largest by insurgents against an American target since the Jan. 30 elections</u>.

While it was factually accurate, Dauber felt the lede misframed the story in that it highlighted the potency of the insurgents in mounting the attack but glossed their defeat in the engagement.

> So, what's the news in the event that prompted a story? Not that the Americans routed the enemy, and badly. But that they were so bold as to launch a large assault, even larger than any other since the elections — and in daylight.

The fourth paragraph of Wong's story connected the ambush to the Iraqi election about 7 weeks earlier, stating that morale was deteriorating among the Iraqi civilian population as a result of insurgent attacks such as these. Dauber felt this, too, was misleading, and inappropriate in a straight news story.

> Of course, this little rant (in an article that, I note, is not labeled "News Analysis") ignores all the recent evidence that the momentum is building, and offers no evidence that the ordinary Iraqis have had it with the political process ... . The place ain't Shangri-la. But there are more and more people on the ground saying the situation isn't just getting better, but that it's getting better to the point that it genuinely looks as if the enemy is in real trouble ... . [I]t's all well and good for *Times* reporters to assert that the Iraqi street has lost hope, but those assertions don't stand up well against polling data when there aren't any reasons given to reject the polling data [that there is considerable support for democratization], but merely one article after another that avoids mentioning the fact that such polling data exists.

At the end of the post, Dauber offered what she thought would have been a more balanced way to frame this story of a firefight (emphasis in the original).

> Yes it was a bold, large, daylight attack. Fair point. The elections haven't ended the violence. Fair point *if* it's also noted that there is tremendous optimism right now. And if it's noted that the boldness of the attack is far less impressive given the fact that it was *crushed.*

On the next day, Dauber posted twice about the Associated Press coverage of the ambush (Another Frame, 2005; AP's Version of Events, 2005), and noted a stark difference in its framing compared to *The New York Times* story about the same event. The AP story (Carl, 2005) was headlined, "Iraq Sees Largest Militant Toll in Months," and the lede framed the event as a serious defeat for the insurgents, rather than evidence of their potency.

> U.S. soldiers, ambushed by dozens of Iraqi militants near the infamous "Triangle of Death," responded by killing 26 guerrillas

in the largest single insurgent death toll since last fall's battle for Fallujah, the U.S. military said Monday.

This prompted Dauber to observe that "the first paragraph almost completely inverts Wong's key paragraph." This frame continued into the daily roundup, the AP story bridging into the remainder of the article with, "It was one of several blows to the insurgency that were reported Monday." Dauber ended her "Another Frame" post with a wry and incisive comment typical of blog criticism: "Interesting comparison, don't you think?"

Rantingprofs contains a good deal of this genre of media criticism, and "Don't Be Afraid to Call It or Anything" (2005) offers another example. In this post, Dauber questioned the framing of an AP story about an engagement in Afghanistan (Graham, 2005). She began with a general observation about events in that area and coverage of them.

> Well, let's check out the news from Afghanistan, shall we? As promised, the Taliban are launching their spring offensive — and as promised, they're getting slapped down pretty hard (apparently without causing much damage). And also as promised [a reference to an earlier post of hers], that doesn't really seem to be the, um, emphasis of the press report here.

Dauber then made explicit her criticism of the AP story's frame.

> The headline reads, "U.S. Military: More Than 12 Insurgents Killed in Battle in Southeastern Afghanistan." Now, the phrasing, suggesting that this is only an unconfirmed claim from the military, is entirely appropriate, since this is, you know, only an unconfirmed claim from the military.

> But the thing of it is, the headline way underplays what it is the military is claiming. They're claiming they completely turned back two assaults and that that's evidence the offensive — and the "insurgency" as a whole — is in fact unraveling. But that macro claim doesn't appear until the 6th paragraph.[18]

Another good example of a blogger disputing the frame of a mainstream outlet's story can be found on *Bench Memos*, a group blog located on *National Review Online*. Ed Whelan noted something odd (*The Washington Post's* New Aversion, 2005) about the wording of a front page headline in *The Washington Post*. The *Post* story (Babington, 2005) described the defeat of a cloture vote on a controversial nominee for U.N. ambassador, and was headlined, "Democrats Extend Debate On Bolton." This prompted Whelan to wonder, "why the longer, less lively phrase 'extend debate' rather than the punchy 'filibuster'?"

Whelan provided evidence that the headline wording was unusual for a story covering this sort of political conflict.

> As it happens, a search of the *Post*'s archives reveals that the *Post* has used the term "filibuster" in headlines a total of 1,775 times. Until today, it had never used "extend debate" in a headline as synonym for "filibuster."

He ended the very brief post by speculating, "might the *Post* be providing rhetorical cover for Democrats?"[19]

The craft of writing a news story necessarily involves a choice of which facts to highlight and which to subordinate or omit entirely. Since the story frame is the central idea which organizes those facts given prominence in the story, disputing the story frame may well take the form of highlighting different facts. A post by radio producer Jon Henke on *QandO Blog* illustrates this type of critique.

Wryly titled "SS Reform is Dead; Long Live SS Reform" (2005), the post took issue with a *Washington Post* story reporting on a poll it had commissioned with ABC News (Weisman, 2005a). Henke quoted the lede of the story, which contained the frame that private retirement accounts were unpopular with the public.

> Three months after President Bush launched his drive to restructure Social Security by creating private investment accounts, public support for program remains weak, with only 35 percent of Americans now saying they approve of his handling of the issue, according to a new *Washington Post* — ABC News poll.

As John Hinderaker had done with his critique of another opinion poll story, described above, Henke found the survey questionnaire and polling data on *The Washington Post* Web site. He linked the document, and pointed out a questionnaire item the news story had not reported (emphasis in the original).

> But there's something very interesting buried deep in the polling data. Very interesting indeed. The public overwhelmingly disapproves of 1) the way Bush is handling Social Security (56%-35%), and 2) "Bush's proposals on Social Security" (55%-37%). But the public also overwhelmingly *supports* — by a margin of 56%-41% —*"a plan in which people who chose to could invest some of their Social Security contributions in the stock market."*

Henke linked a White House policy paper (Strengthening Social Security, 2005), and pointed out the section proposing voluntary personal retirement accounts. He then made his criticism of *The Washington Post* story's frame explicit (emphasis in original).

> And why does *The Washington Post* bury the fact that the public dislikes every part of Social Security reform except what has *actually been proposed* by President Bush? That seems important.[20]

Reframing a Set of Facts

Sometimes a blogger will provide an entirely different frame for facts contained in a mainstream outlet's story. Cori Dauber did this on *Rantingprofs,* in her critique (Well, What Would You Suggest?, 2005) of a *New York Times* story about a television show produced by the Iraqi police as part of their counter-insurgency efforts. The *Times* story described a program aired in Mosul which featured taped interviews with captured terrorists, "juxtaposing images of the masked killers with the cowed men they become once captured" (Hauser, 2005). Dauber objected to the frame of the *Times* story, which she quoted.

> The broadcast of such videos raises questions about whether they violate legal or treaty obligations about the way opposing fighters are interrogated and how their confessions are made public.

Dauber offered her own frame for a story about this show.

> After all the concerns that the Iraqi police aren't up to snuff, one group is coming up with an amazingly creative strategy ... . Sounds like pure genius to me.

She also noted that the *Times* story provided no specifics about how the television program might itself be questionable (emphasis in the original).

> Interesting, although the reporter never bothers to back that assertion up with so much as a list of which treaties or legal obligations are of concern. Apparently the simple assertion, sans argument, is presumed to be sufficient. Why, they're showing videos! Who cares if it might work! Surely there's some treaty out there *somewhere* this might violate!

Dauber later updated the post to amplify this point, and note the page position of the story (emphasis in the original).

> First, this is actually on the front page above the fold. Listen, if you're going to give a story this kind of placement, and therefore attention, you ought to be prepared to specify *which* treaties and laws the practices might violate and explain why ... . We expect actual arguments, not just assertions. We aren't supposed to be taking claims on faith because the *Times* said so, we're supposed to be believing things because the *Times* provides more information than any other paper.

Two months later Dauber posted about a *Washington Post* story (Murphy & Saffar, 2005) describing another Iraqi television show with a similar format. She linked her earlier critique of the *Times* story, and pointed out a distinct difference (Compare and Contrast, 2005) in the frame of *The Washington Post* coverage.

> While the role the program may be playing in helping the police is left mostly implicit, the concerns of human rights advocates is made clear — but is not the central focus of the story.[21]

An amusing example of reframing can be found on *Buzz*

Machine. Jeff Jarvis, director of the new-media program of the Graduate School of Journalism at the City University of New York, felt a *New York Times* story on a study of the prevalence of mental illness in the United States (Carey, 2005) was hyperbolic. Jarvis did not quote from the story, but he linked it. The *Times* story is headlined, "Most Will Be Mentally Ill at Some Point, Study Says," and the lede reads:

> More than half of Americans will develop a mental illness at some point in their lives, often beginning in childhood or adolescence, researchers have found in a survey that experts say will have wide-ranging implications for the practice of psychiatry.

Jarvis suggested, in his characteristic tongue-in-cheek style (The Person Next to You is Nuts, 2005), a much different frame.

> The *NY Times* reports today that more than half of us will be "mentally ill" sometime in our lives. Well, if more than half of us will, doesn't that make it normal? We're just screwed up, we humans.

Jarvis did a more substantial reframing in response to a *New York Times* story on the suicide bombers in the 7/7 London attack. "Angry Young Men" (2005) began by referencing an explanation for terrorist activity advanced by a *Times* columnist, and observing that what was known about the London bombers did not fit that explanation.

> When it turned out that the London bombings were carried out by four young Muslim men born in England, it seemed to give a lie to Tom Friedman's theory that Muslim terrorism sprouts from the anger of young men in Arab nations who have no hope of economic prosperity and freedom. Here were young men who may not have been born into Windsor Castle, but they were living in a land of freedom and opportunity. So how can they be portrayed as anything other than what they are: murderers? Well, today, the *Times* tries to continue portraying them as angry young men.

Jarvis then quoted a passage early in the story about the London suicide bombers (Fattah, 2005) containing the frame to which he objected.

> To the boys from Cross Flats Park, Mr. Tanweer, 22, who blew himself up on a subway train in London last week, was devout, thoughtful and generous. If they understood his actions, it was because they lived in Mr. Tanweer's world, too. They did not agree with what Mr. Tanweer had done, but made clear they shared the same sense of otherness, the same sense of siege, the same sense that their community, and Muslims in general, were in their view helpless before the whims of greater powers. Ultimately, they understood his anger.

Jarvis had a much different frame for the 7/7 terrorist attack.

> The problem with that analysis is that though it does not justify their actions — it tries to understand them — it gives a tacit logic, even a justification, to the horribly illogical, unjustifiable, uncivilized crime. What they did is a crime. That's all it is, nothing more. A crime.

As support for his reframing, Jarvis offered several examples of criminal acts and made a careful distinction between understanding criminal motives and condoning criminal behaviors.

> Do we justify vehicular manslaughter under the influence of alcohol because alcoholism is a disease? No, we treat the act as a crime and slap the killer in jail. Do we tolerate corporate fraud because the perpetrator was raised in a culture of competition, success, and greed? No, we treat the act as a crime and slap the thief in jail.

> Now it's fine to understand these acts insofar as it helps stop them ... . But that's not what's happening in the efforts to understand why these young men did this terrible thing in London ... . This is a sociological effort to understand them. And it begins with the presumption that we should accept their anger as real ... .

> Do we try to understand the BTK killer? Not really. Oh, we try to justify the sensationalistic coverage of the case in the media. But no one truly tries to understand him and justify what he did. No

one asks whether he was angry (or, as it turns out, horny). We know he is a deranged killer and that's how we treat him. We rejoice at catching him; we throw him in prison; some regret that we can't kill him; and we shake our heads at what a horrid person he is. We disdain him.

Well, these are crimes carried out by horrid criminals as well ... . Are they angry? Why even ask?

In an update Jarvis gave an even more pointed example to support his reframing.

Look at it this way: would you have tried to understand Edgar Ray Killen, the convicted Ku Klux Klan killer in the Mississippi Burning murders? Would you have explained his cultural shame at losing the Civil War and called him an insurgent or a militant or even a terrorist? Would you have blamed his grandparents for teaching him to have no respect for black people? Or would you simply condemn his hate and his act? The answer, of course, is C. So why should it be any different when condemning the crimes of these murderers?[22]

While its major topic was tacit support for terrorism in Europe, a very clear example of reframing can be found on *Rantingprofs* in a post by the pseudonymous guest blogger, Paleologos (The Fox Hunting Standard, 2005). The post began by contrasting the crowd numbers for three different public gatherings in England.

400,000 Britons marched in support of fox hunting in one day in 2002. 200,000 grooved for Live-8 in Hyde Park on July 2 ... . Yet, only about 2,000 massed against terror a few days ago. How would you headline these stories?

Paleologos next offered his/her sense of how the mainstream press tends to frame coverage of demonstrations such as these.

Press reports about the size and significance of crowds, demonstrations, or protests tend to vary according to how the media ideologically view the event. If they approve of the cause, a small number of people are described as important; if they don't, then the same number might be not reported at all or ridiculed as being paltry.

He/she then applied this idea to the recent terrorism protest in London, and reframed the event

> The anti-terror vigil in London was universally approved, and so it was treated as huge and important — but was it? Newspaper and television accounts say "thousands" were there; I read that as no more than 2,000... This is the kind of media analysis I hate to make but...the same stories could have been written as "Anti-Terror Vigil Draws Few."

The nomination of John G. Roberts to the Supreme Court in the summer of 2005 generated a good deal of media coverage. One of the early background stories on Roberts's judicial record (Yost, 2005) prompted a reframing by John Hinderaker on *Power Line* (Here Comes the Party Line, 2004). Hinderaker first noted the headline of the story, "Roberts Has Backed Administration Policies." He then quoted the lede:

> John G. Roberts has demonstrated strong backing for Bush administration policies, ruling against Geneva Conventions protections for detainees at Guantanamo Bay and in favor of keeping Vice President Dick Cheney's energy task force records secret. Roberts' record as a federal appeals court judge is short but clear, and he has a trail of solid conservative credentials dating back to the administration of President Bush's father.

Hinderaker bluntly stated the frame of the AP story, then offered his reframing of the same set of facts.

> There you have it: Bush nominates administration stooge to Supreme Court. Of course, some observers would say that the AP's headline could more accurately have read, "Administration's Policies Generally Upheld in the Courts."

As a lawyer, Hinderaker was familiar with the two decisions mentioned in the story's lede as evidence that Roberts was an administration supporter. Hinderaker noted that Roberts's opinions in those cases clearly fit in the mainstream of judicial opinion.

> Roberts was part of a D.C. Circuit Court panel that unanimously (and correctly) reversed a rogue district court ruling on Guantanamo Bay and the Geneva Convention. As for the records of Vice-President Cheney's energy task force, the Supreme Court agreed with Judge Roberts' position by a 7-2 vote.[23]

Contextualizing

In creating news products, journalists necessarily make choices about which facts will be included in the stories. Apart from their choices of facts about the immediate topic of the story, they make choices about additional facts to supply as context or background for it. This selectivity is unavoidable as part of the process by which news products are created, but it is fair to point out that the journalists' choice of facts to include or exclude, by way of context, tends to predispose a frame for the topic. Bloggers often critique the mainstream outlets' framing of an event or issue by supplying additional facts they feel are relevant to the story topic, but were not included in the story. For instance, they may quote prior statements by actors in the current events, they may refer to the opinions of different experts, or they may provide other documentary evidence.

A telegraphic example of this type of criticism can be found on *Power Line*, regarding the controversy over filibusters of judicial nominees in the spring of 2005. In a post titled "That was Then, This is Now" (2005), John Hinderaker pulled two quotations from the Congressional Record of March 2000. He added none of his own commentary, other than the title of the post, to past comments by Senators who, in 2005, were in support of the filibusters. Hinderaker quoted Senator Pat Leahy as saying, in 2000:

> The Chief Justice of the United States Supreme Court said:
>
> > The Senate is surely under no obligation to confirm any particular nominee, but after the necessary time for inquiry, it should vote him up or vote him down.

Which is exactly what I would like.

Hinderaker then quoted Senator Charles Schumer as saying:

> I also plead with my colleagues to move judges with alacrity —
> vote them up or down. But this delay makes a mockery of the
> Constitution, makes a mockery of the fact that we are here
> working, and makes a mockery of the lives of very sincere people
> who have put themselves forward to be judges and then they hang
> out there in limbo.

Hinderaker added no comments of his own to these quotations and did not identify any particular news story as the target of the post, but it seems fair to understand this post as an implied critique of stories framing the filibuster as a principled stand by Leahy and Schumer.

An example of contextualizing in which the critique of the mainstream outlet's frame is made explicit can be found on *Countercolumn*. Financial writer Jason Van Steenwyk gave this post the facetious title, "Amber Alert: Another Missing Headline" (2005); in it, he took issue with BBC reporting on a UN study of child malnutrition in Iraq (Children "Starving", 2005). The metaphor of a missing persons bulletin carries through the entire post. Van Steenwyk began the post by saying the proper headline for the story, "Iraq Child Malnutrition Rates Cut by Two Thirds," had been "abducted from the masthead of the British Broadcasting Service, and replaced with the misleading headline, 'Children Starving in New Iraq'." He quoted the lede of the BBC story:

> Increasing numbers of children in Iraq do not have enough food to
> eat and more than a quarter are chronically undernourished, a UN
> report says. Malnutrition rates in children under five have almost
> doubled since the US-led intervention — to nearly 8% by the end
> of last year, it says.

Van Steenwyk followed the quote by providing additional context he felt was relevant to the frame of the story, continuing the missing persons metaphor.

> In addition to the headline, several important and relevant facts

were also reported missing from the story. Among them was the 2000 report of a congressional Democrat and head of the Congressional Hunger Center.

He quoted Rep. Tony Hall as saying "he could verify reports estimating that more than 25 percent of Iraq's children are underweight and one-tenth are suffering from hunger and disease." The quotation was not linked in the blog post, but the passage appears in a CNN story (Congressman: Blame Iraq, 2000). Van Steenwyk continued the missing persons metaphor.

> Second among the reported missing facts was a prewar United Nations report, cited by PeaceAction.org and countless other sites, which found that 25 percent of Iraqi children were malnourished during the final years of Saddam Hussein.

As further evidence that child malnutrition had been prevalent in prewar Iraq, he linked the Peace Action press release (End Sanctions on Iraq, n.d.).

The comments thread of this post is of interest, also, for its lively discussion of Van Steenwyk's critique by contextualization. One reader pointed to the age qualifier in the BBC story (under five years); another questioned whether the terms "chronically undernourished" and "malnourished" had been conflated. One reader questioned the neutrality of the UN report upon which the BBC story was based, and linked to documents critical of the report's author; other readers provided links to additional documents relating to public health in Iraq during the Hussein regime. In sum, this post illustrates the informality common in blog criticism, the technique of criticizing the frame of a mainstream media story by providing additional context for a story, and the interactivity among the readers of the blog.

Another good example of critique by contextualization concerns a *New York Times* follow-up story about the Augusta National golf club, two years after a controversy over its exclusively-male membership policy (Hack, 2005). The *Times* follow-up described the current disinterest in what had been, in 2003, a national story, and included a brief recapitulation of that controversy. That prompted a lengthy and often bluntly-worded critique from Robert Cox — at the time of this writing, the president of the Media Bloggers Association — on *The National Debate* (*New York Times* Master's [sic] Coverage, 2005). Cox characterized the 2005 follow-up story as "highly sanitized," in that it made no mention of the *Times*'s own involvement in creating the 2003 controversy. Cox objected to what he saw as

> ... *The Times'* effort at revisionist history which omits any mention of *The Times*['s] role in manufacturing the controversy in the first place. For those who don't recall, Raines made the admittance of women to August[a] National a *Times* crusade, a campaign which sowed the seeds for his eventual departure from the paper.

As evidence, Cox linked to and quoted at length from an article in *American Journalism Review* (Smolkin, 2003), which described the saturation coverage former *New York Times* editor Howell Raines had devoted to the Augusta National story over a period of weeks, the front page and editorial page positioning of the coverage, the editorial decision to spike two sports columnists' defense of the Augusta National male-only membership policy, and the heavy criticism of the *Times*'s coverage in journalistic circles at that time.

Cox quoted and criticized several passages from the *Times'*s 2005 follow-up story, but one is of particular interest here regarding contextualization as a way to criticize a story frame. A passage early in the story contains the frame, and Cox quoted it, adding emphasis.

> Two years ago, the Masters tournament was ensnared in a debate over the absence of women in the Augusta National membership, a debate spearheaded by Martha Burk, the chairwoman of the National Council of Women's Organizations. But the 69th Masters is free of the controversy that prompted Johnson to pull advertisements from the tournament's television coverage for two years, beginning in 2003, to shield its sponsors from a campaign to force the addition of women to the private club. Johnson emerged unscathed, and the tournament appears as strong as ever.

Cox felt it was unacceptable for the *Times* to gloss its own role in the development of the controversy, and said so, bluntly.

> Ensnared is the right word but it was *The Times* doing the

"ensnaring." Martha Burk couldn't "spearhead" her way out of a paper bag. The entire controversy was patently a Raines-Sulzberger production. The *Times*'[s] Hack uses only the "third-person" trick to impugn the golf club without mentioning that the "questions" Augusta faced came primarily from *Times* editorials and in carefully selected quotes positioned in heavily slanted articles designed to pressure the club but published as "news" articles, often on the front page of the paper.[24]

CHAPTER 4

Agenda-Setting and Gatekeeping

As the term suggests, agenda-setting refers to the influence the news media have on the public's perception of the relative significance and urgency of events, issues, or situations. A good deal of media effects research has supported the thesis that press coverage tends to define an agenda of topics for public discussion and potential decision-making (a line of research beginning with McCombs & Shaw, 1972, and with intellectual ancestry tracing back to Cohen, 1963, p. 13). An essential step in the news cycle which shapes the public agenda is the editorial choice of which stories to create, in the first place; this has become known as gatekeeping (Lewin, 1947; White, 1950). In essence, this is a matter of news judgment; of all the events of the day or potential discussion topics, which should become news stories or opinion pieces and how much coverage should they receive, for how long a period of time? Those to which the mainstream media choose to devote column inches or airtime are the ones which will tend to be taken most seriously by the public and be seen as of most consequence.

As with other media effects identified through empirical research, it is a gross over-simplification to say that the press determines the public's sense of what matters deserve attention. Rather, the research on agenda-setting indicates that the press has an influence on the public agenda; heavy coverage tends to increase the salience of a story, minimal coverage tends to decrease the salience, and lack of coverage tends to inhibit consideration of the topic.

Criticism of the mainstream media's agenda-setting or gatekeeping is a staple in the blogosphere. Bloggers frequently question the news judgment of professional journalists, arguing, in effect, that the amount of coverage devoted to a story is disproportionately large to the actual significance of the topic. Conversely, bloggers often raise issues they feel are important but the press is giving short shrift to, or ignoring entirely. Moreover, they will often keep an issue alive, after the mainstream media have ceased covering it. Again, it will be useful to examine a few examples of these variants of agenda-setting and gatekeeping criticism.

Questioning the News Judgment

Bloggers are frequently critical of the mainstream press' decisions about what events to cover, and the relative prominence of those covered. Oftentimes the critique takes the form of simply noting what topics are featured on a given day, and questioning their actual importance to the general public compared to other possible topics.

For example, Cori Dauber commented on the "Today" show's choice of national stories to feature, on May 3, 2005, in a post on *Rantingprofs* (Yeah, That's a Winning Strategy, 2005), and suggested the choice indicated some degree of condescension toward the audience. She first listed the headline news stories: recovery of a pilot's body from a crashed F-18, the plea in the Lynndie England court-martial, a development in the BTK killer case, and an update on the Runaway Bride story. Dauber then described the extended news segments: an interview with the groom of the Runaway Bride, an interview with the groom's father, and an interview with the bride's pastor, followed by a segment on gas prices and a feature about a long-term coma victim regaining consciousness. Dauber found the story selection lacking in substance, and mentioned topics she felt would be of greater value to the public

> Wonderful, truly, but news? North Korean nukes? Iraq? Social Security, judicial filibusters? This looks an awful lot like the old "Today", not anything like some kind of new "Today" and as we know this strategy — assuming their audience to be a bunch of idiots with no interest in the world as it is — isn't exactly what we would call, uh, working.

Sometimes bloggers will note a story which gets less prominence than they would have expected, or think the story deserves, for whatever reason. A post by Will Collier on *Vodkapundit* provides an example of this kind of criticism. Collier had read a story in a local newspaper (Gerstein, 2005) and wondered why the national newspapers had not given it extensive play, since it contained the kinds of sensational elements which he felt would normally trigger heavy coverage (Oh, That Liberal Media, 2005).

> The first time I read this *New York Sun* story, I almost figured it was a put-on. I mean, it's got "punchline" written all over it: Ted Kennedy's brother-in-law pleads guilty to political corruption related to Hillary Clinton's campaign, it's revealed that he's been a secret informant to the FBI for years, and oh, by the way, he's also under investigation for trying to lure young girls into his car using a fake police light. But it's not a joke — it's a real story. And what a story! It's got corruption, Kennedys, secret informants, Clintons, even weird sexual allegations. You'd think it would be the lead headline from coast to coast. But funny thing — you can't find it much of anywhere.

Collier then described his search of the CNN, *New York Times*, and *Washington Post* Web sites for coverage, finding only a wire service story on the *Times*'s site. This prompted him to make a cutting remark on news judgment (punctuation and emphasis as in the original).

> Gee, I thought the *Times* was supposed to be the "newspaper of record," with the best reporters in the world — they couldn't even spare *one* of them to cover a story involving the Democratic Party's two most prominent elected officials, Ted Kennedy and Hillary Clinton?

As always, the merit of the critique is left to the judgment of the reader. In the comments thread, a number of Collier's readers felt he had made too much of the story's newsworthiness; one noted a *New York Times* story about the case run the day following Collier's post (Hernandez, 2005), but observed that the story was buried inside the B section of a Saturday edition. Of interest here is the way the blogger criticized the news judgment of the mainstream press, by pointing out elements of the story which he felt would warrant more prominence than it actually received, and questioning why this story did not follow the usual practice.

A similar critique of the mainstream press's news judgment concerns the capture of a sniper in Baghdad in July 2005. On *Jackson's Junction* (No Coverage of Soldier, 2005), a guest blogger posted about a story which had appeared in the *Army Times*. Pamela, a former newspaper executive, offered little commentary of her own, other than "From the *Army Times*, this you MUST SEE!" However, she linked the story (Soldier Survives Attack, 2005) and quoted the entire item (excerpted here from the blog original).

> During a routine patrol in Baghdad June 2, Army Pfc. Stephen Tschiderer, a medic, was shot in the chest by an enemy sniper, hiding in a van just 75 yards away. The incident was filmed by the insurgents. Tschiderer...was knocked to the ground from the impact, but he popped right back up, took cover and located the enemy's position. After tracking down the now-wounded sniper with a team from B Company, 4th Battalion, 1st Iraqi Army Brigade, Tschiderer secured the terrorist with a pair of handcuffs and gave medical aid to the terrorist who'd tried to kill him just minutes before.

On his more heavily-viewed site, *InstaPundit*, law professor Glenn Reynolds linked Pamela's post and raised an explicit question about news judgment (Given How Interesting, 2005).

> Given how interesting this story is, and the fact that there's video available, it's surprising that it didn't get more attention ... . Go figure.

Along a similar line, Cori Dauber wondered on *Rantingprofs* why a raid on a terrorist safe house near Iraq's border with Syria had gotten almost no play in the mainstream networks' broadcasts of that day (But Hey, 2005). She began the post by noting the day's heavy reporting on difficulties in negotiations over the Iraqi constitution, then wondered why only Fox had even mentioned a brief AP report (U.S. Military Says Airstrikes Destroyed Suspected Terror Base, 2005,

August 26) describing an airstrike on a gathering of Al Qaeda members. This struck her as particularly odd, as local Iraqi civilians had tipped off coalition forces on the use of the building as a meeting place for terrorists. She contrasted that to the mainstream media's routine coverage of casualties inflicted by Al-Qaida (syntax and emphasis as in the original).

> Why is it that when the enemy is active, has a good day, kills many, well, by God, that's *essential* news and must be covered. But when our forces are active, have a good day, kill many — because of the cooperation of average Iraqis no less — well, that can fall by the wayside. (And don't tell me it's a time issue, because this is information easily compressed to a sentence or two of wire copy.)

Dauber closed the post by making an observation about the long-term effect of such news judgments on public opinion about the situation in Iraq.

> Is it any wonder so many Americans think the war is going badly? Why on earth would they have any reason to think differently?[25]

A rather unusual example of bloggers questioning the mainstream media's news judgment concerned an announced network broadcast of a national address by the President in June 2005 (VandeHei, 2005). In the days preceding the speech, a few bloggers took the unconventional position that networks ought not broadcast it. On *Eschaton,* Duncan Black, who uses the pen name Atrios and describes himself as a "recovering economist," felt a press conference would be a more appropriate format (Don't Show It, 2005). The entire post was this:

> I don't think it matters much either way, but I agree with [fellow blogger] David Corn that it'd be pretty silly for the networks to show Bush's speech. I also agree with him that usually I'd be annoyed if they didn't. But, there's no actual event prompting this speech other than his declining poll numbers, and somehow that doesn't really seem like a good enough reason. Press conference, yes. Speech alone, no.

The comment to which Atrios alluded was on the eponymous blog of *Nation* magazine's Washington editor, David Corn. "No Reason for Networks" (2005) was a lengthy negative commentary on the Iraq war and the administration's public statements about it, but ended with the position that the upcoming Presidential address did not merit network coverage.

> I usually blast the broadcast networks when they do not air presidential addresses. But this time around I would find it tough to insist that they displace their usual assortment of sleazy reality shows and loaded-with-gross-details crime dramas for the latest White House word games.

On *AMERICAblog,* political consultant John Aravosis took the same position (The TV Networks Shouldn't Broadcast, 2005). The entire post was this (punctuation as in the blog original):

> I'd mentioned this last night. Atrios chimes in, as does David Corn. Bush's speech is nothing more than a PR stunt to raise his poll numbers. Nothing has happened to prompt the speech, there's no news on Iraq, no new policy he's unveiling, nothing. Why cover this speech?[26]

In the summer of 2005, the Pew Research Center released the report on its survey of public opinion in 17 predominantly-Muslim countries (Islamic Extremism, 2005). The major finding of this report was that support for Islamic extremism and terrorist activity had declined significantly over the past year in the Muslim world. *The Washington Post* ran a story summarizing the Pew Center's findings (Wright, 2005), which prompted Cori Dauber to pose a question about the mainstream outlets' news judgment. Her *Rantingprofs* post, "Don't Let Me Interrupt" (2005), first took note of the extensive coverage which negative poll results had garnered in the past (punctuation and emphasis as in the original).

> You know that at various times over the past three and a half years there have been doom and gloom polls telling us how hated we are throughout the Muslim world. And you know that every time one

of these polls comes out it's *huge* news.

Dauber linked *The Washington Post* story and the Pew Center's report. To emphasize her point that the survey included highly newsworthy information, she quoted a passage from the report.

> Large and growing majorities in Morocco (83%), Lebanon (83%), Jordan (80%) and Indonesia (77%) — as well as pluralities in Turkey (48%) and Pakistan (43%) — say democracy can work well and is not just for the West.

Dauber then made her question about the mainstream media's news judgment explicit, noting the minimal coverage of this survey.

> Since bad news polls are major news, how much attention will this poll, obviously timely given London [a reference to the 7/7 bombings], get? Keep one ear open as you listen to cable news today, will ya?

> The [N. Y.] Times, which has a story about the troubles of the Governor of California front page above the fold, puts the story on pg. A-8 below the fold ... . This does not come up in the "Today" show's golden twenty minutes ... .[27]

Those examples concerned the relative prominence of given stories, in the form of air time, column inches, or page position. A more fundamental question is the decision about what information to report at all. A good example of blog criticism of gatekeeping can be found on *Conspiracy to Keep You Poor and Stupid*. Donald Luskin thought it peculiar that a *New York Times* story covering one Senate resolution about Social Security failed to mention a competing resolution considered on the same day (The Senate Resolution You Didn't Hear About, 2005). Luskin quoted the *Times* (Stolberg, 2005) describing a resolution which failed to pass as a

> nonbinding measure declaring that Congress should reject any Social Security plan that would require "deep benefit cuts or a massive increase in debt." Five Republicans joined the Senate's 44 Democrats and one independent in voting for the resolution, a symbolic effort to demonstrate opposition to Mr. Bush's plan to

allow workers to invest part of their taxes in private retirement accounts. Although the measure failed with one vote short of a majority, Senator Charles E. Schumer, the New York Democrat who has been a leading opponent of the plan, later said it was a "significant vote."

Luskin felt there was a glaring omission, for a story reporting Senate consideration of the Social Security issue: the story described in some depth a resolution which did not gain majority support, but made no mention of another on the same day which did (emphasis in the original).

> But there's not one word in the *Times* story about another vote yesterday — a Republican-sponsored resolution declaring that *not* addressing Social Security's financing problems would trigger "massive debt, deep benefit cuts and tax increases." *That* resolution was carried by 56 to 43, garnering "aye" votes from every Republican except Snowe and George Voinovich of Ohio, and picking up Democrats Bill Nelson of Florida, Ben Nelson of Nebraska and Robert Byrd of West Virginia.

In a similar vein, Cori Dauber criticized the sparse early coverage of the Iraqi government (Where's the Follow-Up?, 2005). She first made a general observation about coverage of the situation in Iraq just before the formation of the new government, linking to a Google search of stories on Iraq as evidence of her point (punctuation and syntax as in the original).

> Over the last several days there have been multiple stories focusing on the "surge" in violence in Iraq, many suggesting that a contributing cause was the "political paralysis" in the country. Posing the theory that political paralysis is partially the cause for a surge in violence suggests that ending that political violence is of critical importance, and it also, in narrative terms, sets up a cliff-hanger of sorts. When will the Iraqis get a government? will it happen before the momentum of the elections completely be dissipated?

Dauber then made clear what she saw as a failure in news judgment by the mainstream press.

But you can't cover the first half of this story — the Iraqis don't have a government yet — without covering, with equal emphasis, the back half of the story — they got one. Yet during the 5 to 6 am hour, I didn't hear a single mention of the new Iraqi government.

Sometimes a compliment for one mainstream outlet implies an obvious criticism of others. This was the case with Dauber's post (The Beat Goes On, 2005) on a *Washington Post* story about the developing effectiveness of the new Iraqi army in handling urban combat situations. She noted with approval that *The Washington Post* was continuing to run front-page reporting on Iraq (Finer, 2005) even when hurricane damage to the Gulf coast had pushed this story off the agenda of broadcast news outlets.

Note that at *The Washington Post*, unlike the networks, the hurricanes haven't wiped Iraq away: not only is it still covered but it makes page one, and with a (relatively) upbeat report about [the] progress of Iraqi forces. U.S. commanders in the field here are smart to provide assessments that are never completely positive. That kind of talk lacks credibility.[28]

Setting an Alternative Agenda

Just as the mainstream press sets an agenda of topics for the public to consider, so does the blogosphere. The same media effects concepts apply: bloggers decide which topics to comment on (gatekeeping) and how much to say about them (agenda-setting). When the blogosphere substantially differs from the mainstream media, we can consider this as constituting an alternative agenda. It is apparent that the agenda constructed in the blogosphere is not necessarily congruent with that constructed by the mainstream news media; a good number of posts argue, in essence, that either the mainstream media have erred in their judgment of the relative importance of current events or are willfully ignoring events of consequence.

A concise illustration of an alternative agenda can be found on *TKS*, a blog on *National Review Online*. Jim Geraghty did a side-by-side comparison of the day's war coverage headlines in *The New York Times* and *The Washington Post* with the war coverage on two popular blogs, *Belmont Club* and *Captain's Quarters* (Have the *New York Times* and *Washington Post*, 2005). Geraghty made his thesis clear, at the beginning of the post.

> [T]here is a considerable amount of good news in the war on terror that you just cannot find in the mainstream media. If you do, you find it on the last few paragraphs of the jump page.

He then listed headlines from that day's edition of *The New York Times*, linking to the stories:

> Bush Says Russia Must Make Good on Democracy; President Calling for New Era of Western Unity After Iraq Strains
>
> Afghan Living Standards Among the Lowest, U.N. Finds
>
> Attacks By Militant Groups Rise in Mosul

He did the same for headlines from *The Washington Post*:

> Bush Seeks to Mend Transatlantic Rift
>
> Humvee Tragedy Forges Brotherhood of Soldiers; Iraqis Persevere to Recover Dead Americans
>
> For Some, A Loss in Iraq Turns Into Antiwar Activism
>
> Three Soldiers Killed in Baghdad

Geraghty then listed stories featured on *Belmont Club* and *Captain's Quarters* that day, including:

> EU to Open Baghdad Training Office; Officials Hail Unprecedented Unity over Iraq
>
> Bush, Chirac Call for Withdrawal of Syrian Troops From Lebanon
>
> Hillary Clinton Judges That the Insurgency in Iraq is Failing
>
> Taliban Giving Up in Afghanistan?

The contrast between the featured stories in the mainstream press and the featured stories on those blogs prompted Geraghty to comment on the comparative news agendas.

> If you get your news from the mainstream media, you simply do not see any good news in the war on terror. Progress goes unreported ... . That's not journalism. Sure, it involves being in these countries, collecting facts and quotes, and putting them together into an article. But it's basically shoehorning the facts to fit a prearranged template, that all of Bush's efforts are failing and that nothing is going right in Afghanistan or Iraq. News that is this selective and this shaded constitutes war-critic junk food — with no nutrition for the rest of us who want the whole picture, the good news and the bad.

In passing, the comments thread of the *Captain's Quarters* post which Geraghty referenced (Taliban Giving Up in Afghanistan?, 2005) contains two good illustrations of eyewitness accounts contributed by readers. One reader described his/her experience in Afghanistan, regarding economic development activity.

> I was in Kabul in late January (I work for a private enterprise oriented NGO) and from the evidence I saw during my time there, the Captain is spot on with his analysis. To put it bluntly, Kabul is booming. There is plenty of food in the markets (including oranges and other fruit from Pakistan), gasoline must be plentiful judging from the number of cars on the streets and everyone seems to be busy trying to rebuild the country. The infrastructure is in horrible shape, but the Afghans manage. Electricity is spotty and there are few municipal services, but there is peace. From what our expats tell me, the situation is similar in other cities such as Kandahar and Herat. My NGO is working to develop business associations and chambers of commerce and when we do trainings in how to do this, the number of people who want to attend far exceeds the capacity of the workshops.

Another reader offered a comment relating to the cultural dynamics of the reduction in terrorist activity.

From what I can see here — admittedly it is only 3 of the provinces of Afghanistan — things have calmed down a fair amount and the Taliban and the Hezb-e Islami Gulbuddin have been pushing out ten[t]ative inquiries about reconciliation. It is part of the culture here to accept the lower level folks back into the fold, and Karzai has made it perfectly clear that will be the case now.[29]

A remarkable example of a blogger setting an alternative agenda can be found in a long-running series of roundup posts on Arthur Chrenkoff's eponymous blog, *Chrenkoff*. These seem to have been a specialty of this blogger, a Polish emigre living in Australia, as he wrote an extensive series of lengthy posts on both Afghanistan and Iraq. There is so much material in these roundups that it would be impossible to adequately summarize even one of them; this passage should be taken as just a tiny sampler from the series, and the reader is encouraged to examine the roundups. The format is consistent across all of them: Chrenkoff collected what he called "good news" stories published in various mainstream outlets around the world, linked them, quoted representative passages from them, and bridged the excerpts with brief interpretive commentary of his own.

"Good News from Iraq, Part 23" (2005) opened with Chrenkoff's perception of a trend in the coverage, based on a miniature content analysis of his own roundup series.

> Is the situation in Iraq getting better? It's not really up to me to answer that question, but I can try to answer another one: is reporting from Iraq getting better? To find out, I decided to look back at the past installments of this series and do a little count. For the sake of simplicity I started with Part 6, which happened to be the first one to be also published by the *Opinion Journal*. When printed out, that July 19, 2004 edition of "Good news from Iraq" is 10 and a half pages long, and contains links to 71 "good news" stories. Since then, the length of each installment has fluctuated, but the overall trend has been up. So much so that the "Good news from Iraq" you're reading now is 23 and a half pages long and contains 178 links to "good news stories."

> The same trend i[s] evident in my "Good news from Afghanistan". The first installment published by the *Opinion Journal* (and second

overall in the series) of July 26, 2004, was 6 and a half pages long when printed out and contained 55 links. The latest one, number 10 of March 7, 2005, is 19 pages long and contains 124 links.

Either there is more and more good news coming out of both Iraq or Afghanistan, or the reporters are getting increasingly optimistic about the situation there, or both. Whatever's the answer, it's good news.

The remainder of the lengthy, link-rich roundup was organized in separate sections with the headings: Society, Economy, Reconstruction, Humanitarian Aid, Coalition Troops, and Security. An excerpt from the section on economy will illustrate the way Chrenkoff deftly wove together quotations from a variety of news stories and policy documents, embedding links in the hypertext which make it convenient for his readers to examine his source material for themselves. The embedded links are marked with an underscore, here; quotation marks are in the original blog post.

> "Dr. Hajim Alhuseini, the Iraqi minister of industry and minerals, announced the start of the implementation of a plan to transit the Iraqi economy to a free market economy." The authorities are expecting the economic revival to continue: "Dr. Fa'ik Ali Abed-Elrasoul, a deputy at the Iraqi ministry of planning said that the increase in investments may lead to general growth of about 17 percent in 2005, 15 percent in 2006 and 6 percent in 2007. The deputy expects that income per capita to raise form [sic] US$780 per year in 2004 to US$1156 in 2007." Another report reminds us about the improvement in the standard of living due to a significant increase in average salaries. Meanwhile, one estimate puts the figure of direct foreign investment in Iraq over the next few years at $44 billion, mainly in the fields of manufacturing, oil, and IT.

"Good News from Afghanistan, Part 14" (2005) followed a similar format. The section on society included this passage (again, links indicated here by underscore; quotations as in the blog original):

> Two new schools, each able to take in 1,500 pupils, have opened in Bagram district and Sinjit Dara of the central Parwan province.

The schools were a joint project of the local Provincial Reconstruction Team and UNESCO.

In higher education news, "the American University of Afghanistan's new female dormitory, which has been established with [the] assistance of the Afghan Wireless Communication System, AWCC, was opened [recently]...The foundation of the three-story building of new American University of Afghanistan was laid in the southwest of Kabul earlier this year. The initial academic programmes will include majors in information technology, business management and public administration."

Denmark has also been active in the area of education: "The Danish support to the Ministry of Education has already resulted in a new curriculum for 22 courses, better training of teachers, publication of 3.6 million schoolbooks and the construction of new schools." Overall, the Danish contribution is worth DKK 670 million ($108 million) and will extend at least until 2009. Meanwhile, the Afghan-Turkish School in Kabul has organised the first science fair in [the] country's recent history.

In one of the early Iraq roundups (Good News From Iraq, Part III, 2004), Chrenkoff made explicit his agenda-setting purpose in creating these posts: to increase the prominence of positive news from the Middle East.

The news from Mesopotamia hasn't been too bad lately, with the successful UN resolution, countdown to sovereignty, and the new Iraqi government generating a lot of good-will throughout the world. Still the prisoner abuse, terrorism, kidnappings, and casualties otherwise continue to crowd out and overwhelm any of the good news you'[ll] read below.[30]

Along a related line, Roger L. Simon wrote a long series of posts on his eponymous blog about the Oil-for-Food scandal at the United Nations in 2004 and 2005. Simon, a screenwriter and novelist, judged the scandal to be of great consequence and felt the mainstream news media did not devote nearly enough attention to it. Like Chrenkoff's good news roundups, the relationship of the blogger and the mainstream outlets is essentially symbiotic in this case; in most of the posts, Simon would link a story in the mainstream press and quote from it, then offer some comment of his own on the day's development in the story, raise additional critical questions about the scandal, connect the scandal to other news, or again criticize what he saw as insufficient attention to it in the mainstream media. He would often compliment the work of Claudia Rosett and Niles Lathem, nearly alone in their reporting of the scandal among mainstream journalists.

Distinct from the roundups as a form of alternative agenda-setting, this case illustrates a blogger pursuing a particular story with noticeably more vigor than the mainstream press. An interesting feature of Simon's posts is that he would sometimes share some personal comment about the scandal's importance to him. Another interesting feature — not entirely unexpected, given that Simon is a writer by trade — is the amusing word play often found in the titles of the posts.

This, too, is a form of alternative agenda-setting, in that Simon repeatedly asserted that the scandal was of far greater consequence than the amount and positioning of the mainstream coverage would suggest, and explained that his extensive posting about the scandal better reflected its true salience. It resembles the standard mainstream journalistic practice of a reporter following a story over its lifespan, becoming an expert on its details and ramifications, and generating a body of work pertaining to it; while many other bloggers did take note of the Oil-for-Food scandal, Simon followed it doggedly over a long period, and in time presented some investigative reporting of his own. This selection is only intended to give a sense of this series of posts as a form of alternative agenda-setting by a blogger; by no means are all the posts mentioned here.

In an early post, Simon reacted to the disclosure that the Oil-for-Food program's administrator, Benon Sevan, appeared to be one of the individuals who had made personal profit from it (Stonewalling on 46th Street, 2004). He quoted at length from a *Wall Street Journal* editorial about the developing scandal (Raphael, 2004), but of particular interest here are Simon's comments on what he saw as the humanitarian significance of the story and what he felt was the disproportionately low level of interest in it shown by mainstream journalists.

No matter that there's the little matter of the money — the grand larceny that seems to have occurred in Iraq and elsewhere under the auspices of the UN Oil-for-Food Program. Hey, what's a little corruption among friends? Enron did it. Several companies in the EU did it. We survive. Yeah, we do, except the management of those companies didn't harm people's lives (their physical ones anyway, at least directly), just their pocketbooks and their retirement. The UN corruption kept a homicidal dictator in office, operating human shredding machines. And given the extent of the accusations, how its tentacles reached our from the UN Secretariat across so many countries to so many individuals and groups, it's no wonder the United States wasn't getting much support from the UN for a firm stand against Saddam. That would have been like asking the Mafia to legalize heroin — it's simply not in its interest.

You would think the UN would want to "get out front" on this issue, even with a "limited hangout" in Nixonian parlance, but so far we have heard nothing much at all. You'd also think [the] Robert Woodwards of the world would be all over this, but to date they too have been remarkably silent on the list of names that came out of Iraq. They shouldn't be leaving it [to] amateurs to vet it, but they are so far. Why?

A number of Simon's posts elaborated on the point that the integrity of the UN was seriously threatened by this scandal. In a post two weeks later (Enron on the East River, 2004) he continued his comparison of media attention to corporate scandals with the attention to the Oil-for-Food scandal.

I hate to be so "hobby-horsical" in the words of the great Laurence Sterne about the continued non-investigation of the UN Oil-for-Food scandal, but it seems to me if we're fighting a War on Terror, which is really a War on Fascism in its various forms, we should be paying special attention to the lifeblood of that system, which is money. Greed and racism are its twin hearts.

And that if one of those hearts is pumping, or has been pumping, from the center of our most important international institution, we are in trouble. That must be dealt with — and fully. Yet few in our media seem to be paying attention, preferring to play gotcha games on the affairs of the day ... .

The N[ew] Y[ork] T[imes] et al were all over Halliburton like the proverbial you-know-what. But with all their powers of investigative journalism, as far as I know, the same papers haven't really approached the UN scandal, not in any serious way ... .

I have to assume it's a conscious/unconscious desire on the part of these media to protect a valued institution, but in ignoring this problem, they are actually participating in its demise.

In a number of posts Simon made reference to his own life experiences, by way of explaining the scandal's salience to him. An interesting example of this is found in a post titled "Kojo, Kofi & Kerry" (2004). He began the post by noting that a major theme of the John Kerry presidential campaign was America's working relationships with traditional allies; he wondered why the press had not asked Kerry for his reaction to the Oil-for-Food scandal, given the prominence of the UN in his campaign speeches. Simon then related this question to his own political identity.

Normally you would think a "liberal media" would be very interested in that. These are, traditionally as well, the liberal causes that I grew up on, that formed the common bond around the dinner table when I was a boy. But don't expect to see it. Most liberals in our media have actually forgotten their own ideology. They are no longer really liberals. They don't even rejoice in the democratization of Iraq, except by paying lip service to it.

The word play was evident in a post with a lengthy title imitating the patter of an old-time newspaper vendor: "'Oil-for-Food!' Get Yer Hot 'Oil-for-Food'...READ ALL ABOUDIT!" (2004). Simon complimented the *New York Post* for running a fairly brief story on the scandal (Lathem, 2004), but indicated his dissatisfaction that the 9/11 hearings had overshadowed it (punctuation as in the original; passage is not edited here).

While the Congress is playing the blame game with their 9/11 hearings...telling us all what we already knew (that no one did much about terrorism before 9/11 — duh!)...the real investigation is beginning on 44th Street with potential information that can tell us a hundred times more about the terror game...no make that a thousand times more...than the partisan sniping going on on (where else?) Capitol Hill.

In the post titled "Trouble at the UN — Opposing Papers on Same Side" (2004), Simon took note of two mainstream outlets with distinctly different editorial viewpoints validating his feelings about salience of the scandal.

> *The New York Times* and *The Wall Street Journal* have a rare confluence of opinion this morning. Both are running editorials urging reform at the United Nations.

Simon linked both editorials (Iraq Needs a Credible U.N., 2004; Saddam's U.N. Financiers, 2004), and quoted from both. He went on to speculate on the blogosphere's impact, and to compliment a reporter for *The Wall Street Journal*, who was essentially alone in the mainstream press with her coverage of the story (spelling error corrected).

> Does the blogosphere deserve credit for this simultaneous concern from the left and the right? It's hard to tell, but certainly the WSJ's Claudia Rosett merits special plaudits for driving this story. And I imagine with both sides opining in their editorials on this matter our politicians are listening. Will they act? We shall see. One thing I do know — bloggers will be watching, as will, no doubt, Ms. Rosett.

Simon repeated his criticism of the mainstream media's news agenda in "A Tale of Two Hearings" (2004). In this post he contrasted the "flood-the-zone" coverage of the 9/11 Commission's hearings with the sparse coverage of the Oil-for-Food scandal, which had by that point developed some colorful knick names in the blogosphere (punctuation, capitalization, and emphasis as in the original).

> First we have had to sit through one of the most meaningless hearings in modern American government history — the 9/11 Commission — which reached its apotheosis of self-serving puffery with the Jamie Gorelick I-refuse-to-recuse-letter ... .

The commission has informed us of absolutely nothing, unless you have been inhabiting the Crab Nebula for the last three years. All I got out of it is the following: 1. Neither the Clinton nor the Bush administration did nearly enough to stop terrorism before 9/11. 2. The CIA and the FBI likewise did not communicate nearly enough before that date (to which Ms. Gorelick contributed in her small way) and 3. Various bureaucrats make nasty claims about other peoples' culpability. The other people disagree.

I could have told you all that for ten cents.

Meanwhile, something of true significance — the internal investigation of the "UNSCUM" Scandal aka the UN Iraq Oil-for-Food Program — is in jeopardy. (Why is this one more important? Simple. It is about the allegation of *actual crimes* on a grand scale committed under the name of our most important international organization. It's not about alleged blunders and screw ups that are subject to more interpretations than the Babylonian Talmud.)

Simon had some harsh words for *The New York Times* as coverage of the scandal began to increase in other mainstream outlets. He began "UNSCAM Should Not Be Ideological" (2004) by complimenting a WashingtonPost.Com roundup about the scandal (Morley, 2004). He then made a very pointed contrast with the *Times's* coverage of developments (capitalization as in the original).

The one-time "newspaper of record" (even they now abjure this title) has dealt with the issue like a two-year old learning to swim, dipping their toe in the water and then running away. According to their Web site, over the last two days, while Congressional Hearings have been going on concerning the subject, they have only run one article on the scandal — and that one not of their own authorship, but from the AP about Kofi Annan's "response" to corruption charges.

He continued his comparison of the relative consequence of the 9/11 Commission and the Oil-for-Food scandal in "Blame Canada!" (2004). He began the post by linking and quoting from a story in a Canadian newspaper (apparently Ibbitson, 2004). The post's title was a play on a song from the television cartoon, "South Park," as Simon complimented the Canadian Prime Minister's criticism of the UN. Simon then reiterated his position that the Oil-for-Food scandal was of much greater consequence than the 9/11 Commission hearings (emphasis in the original).

> Meanwhile, we have been living through a kind of Tale of Two Scandals (or rather "Commissions") — the first being the September 11 investigation and the second being the House Investigation of the UN Oil-for-Food Program. The differences are huge but they come down to this: September 11 is about who screwed up *accidentally*. Oil-for-Food is about who screwed the Iraqi people and the world *deliberately*. One is about politics and one is about unconscionable global crime.

Some of Simon's posts were essentially alerts to his readers that a mainstream outlet had reported some new development in the scandal. "Important Oil-for-Food Update" (2004) is an example. Simon linked an Associated Press story (Butler, 2004) and quoted from it, including this passage.

> Interviews with dozens of former and current Iraqi officials by congressional investigators have produced new evidence that Saddam Hussein micro-managed business deals under the U.N. oil-for-food program to maximize political influence with important foreign governments like Russia and neighboring Arab states.

Simon added a brief interpretive comment, relating to the news agenda:

> This is positive news on two fronts. 1. The Congressional Committee seems to be on the case. (It's hard to trust the UN to investigate itself.) 2. It's nice to see another mainstream organ like the Associated Press reporting on this mammoth scandal. Good for them.

A similar post about the mainstream press's coverage of the scandal is "Important Oil-for-Food Breakthrough" (2004). Simon linked and quoted from the lede of an editorial in the *Chicago Tribune*

(The UN's Coalition of the Bribed, 2004).

> One after another, with the cadence of choreographed mortar fire, disclosures about the phenomenally corrupt United Nations program known as Oil-for-Food — it ranks as one of the greatest financial crimes of all time — are exploding into the news.

> With each troubling disclosure, last year's refusal of the UN Security Council to enforce its 17 resolutions against Iraq after the Persian Gulf war becomes more transparent.

Simon added only a terse comment of his own, indicating again his dissatisfaction with the lack of attention paid to the scandal by the mainstream press:

> Congrats to the *Chicago Tribune* for joining the few major M[ain]S[tream]M[edia] outlets to acknowledge the importance of this scandal.

Another post in the same vein was "Annan Family Values" (2004). Simon began by quoting from a Reuters story on that day.

> Annan's son, Kojo, received payments from the Geneva-based Cotecna firm until last February after the United Nations said he severed ties with the company in February 1999. Part of the payments involved an agreement not to compete with Cotecna in West Africa after he left the firm.

> "Naturally I was very disappointed and surprised," Annan told reporters, saying the discrepancy had not been brought to his attention.

Simon repeated his frustration with what he saw as the mainstream press' insufficient attention, and again affirmed the importance of the United Nations as an international organization (emphasis in the original).

> Where is the MSM in this? If Annan were an American politician, they'd be all over him like the cheapest suit on the planet. This is their UN too, in case they don't get it.

As a sidenote to this post, this author was able to retrieve the 650-word story in its entirety from the archivist at Reuters (Leopold, 2004), and verified that Simon had quoted it accurately. Consistent with Simon's complaint that the mainstream press showed little interest in the scandal, a LexisNexis search for this Reuters story in mainstream outlets yielded only a brief excerpt from it by an electronic clipping service (Annan "Disappointed and Surprised", 2004).

In the spring of 2005 Simon continued his commentary on the desultory mainstream reporting of the scandal, but also began generating some investigative reporting of his own. It appears from these posts that Simon had been in contact with one of the witnesses in the U.N.'s internal investigation of the scandal, headed by Paul Volcker. As had his running commentary on the scandal, the original reporting became extensive over time, and it is only possible to offer a sampling here.

"Special Report #1 — Oil-for-Food Investigation" (2005) was posted on the eve of a preliminary report by Volcker's group. At the beginning of this post the writing style is noticeably different from his personal commentary in the earlier posts, and more in keeping with the wording conventions of straight news reporting; most obvious is the use of the third person to refer to himself (capitalization as in the original).

> This blog has new information from sources close to the investigation of the United Nations Oil-for-Food Scandal by Paul Volcker's Independent Inquiry Committee. After some delay, the committee is releasing its preliminary results at noon Tuesday. This report may reveal, among other things, startling information tending to indicate Secretary General Kofi Annan had more knowledge of, or was closer to, his son Kojo's activities with Cotecna — the company whose role in the scandal seems so pervasive — than previously thought.

Simon then suggested what he would soon make explicit: his source was close to one of the witnesses who had provided testimony to Volcker's group.

> The committee has been interviewing Pierre Mouselli, a

businessman in Paris who was Kojo's business partner ... . Mouselli, who has been a cooperative witness and is not under investigation himself, has told the committee numerous interesting things, which deserved to be followed up.

"Special Report #2 — The Case of the 'Main Mentor' " (2005), posted a few days later, is written in his more customary, personal style. Simon disclosed that his source was Pierre Mouselli's lawyer, and he provided something of a "behind-the-scenes" description of the investigation.

> What follows is information that comes from only one source — Mouselli's attorney Adrian Gonzales-Maltes. So bear that in mind when you evaluate it, though I have no reason so far to disbelieve Mr. Gonzales-Maltes. Indeed, several things he has told me have already been validated by the report itself ... .

> The committee took the better part of a year to locate Pierre Mouselli, although Kojo's former business partner was not in hiding and well-known in Lagos where his brother is known as the Nigerian Donald Trump. He apparently readily agreed to talk with them, once they provided him with a lawyer.

Two days later, "Special Report #3 — Corruption in the Palace of Justice" (2005) foreshadowed an upcoming resignation by two of the principal investigators (punctuation as in the original).

> This blog has had a special look inside at how this investigation has been working.

> Most of the heavy-lifting, the interviewing of witnesses, has been conducted by three attorneys — Michael Cornacchia, Robert Parton and Miranda Duncan ... . Cornacchia is the lead investigator, though Parton is apparently the one doing the more serious questioning. Parton is not a happy camper, however, and seems to have threatened to resign a few weeks ago because the committee was not pursuing leads they thought went outside their purview. To have had an investigator quit at that point would have created a mini-scandal of its own and a compromise was worked out to keep him. This could account for some of the equivocal language in the report ... .

Gonzalez-Maltes has also provided the committee with a wealth of new details about Kojo's and Mouselli's business dealings (company names, documents, etc.), which open up many possible avenues for investigation.

"Special Investigation #4 — The Big Shame" (2004) made explicit Simon's disappointment with a *London Times* story (Winnett, 2005) about the Volcker group's preliminary report. An especially interesting feature of this particular post is the way Simon wove together his criticism of the mainstream outlet's reporting — and of the Volcker group's pursuit of leads in the inquiry — with the investigative reporting he had been doing on his own (parentheses in the original; bracketed material added by this author).

> Notably missing from today's *London Times* story on the interim report is any mention of the September/October 2002 contacts between Kojo's former business partner Pierre Mouselli and the Iraqis. According to Mouselli, Saddam's people (then on the brink of being invaded) suddenly invited the businessman to lunch at their embassy in Abuja, Nigeria. They told him they were extremely interested in locating Kojo Annan for (unspecified) reasons. They said Kojo owed them for (unspecified) favors previously done him and they needed then to speak with [the] Secretary General's son as soon as possible. They offered Mouselli a visa to Iraq to discuss this with them further.
>
> If anything in Mouselli's testimony is incendiary material, this is it. Its implications point in many directions. But I have no idea if this testimony was followed up by the committee or by the *London Times*. It should have been because there is evidence, including the October 24 visa shown here [a photograph of the visa appeared at this line], that Mouselli, despite whatever "instabilities" he may have had, is not just making things up. The offer from the Iraqi ambassador in Abuja came just days before Mouselli moved back from Nigeria to France. Though never used, this visa was picked up there by Mouselli from Nawaf Jassim, the "Conseiller, Iraqi Section" in Paris. Mouselli has given Jassim's business card to the committee. Was Mr. Jassim contacted by the committee for corroboration or other insights? I don't know, but given their lax investigation I would bet against it.

A post one week later (Uncovering the Coverup — More Mouselli On the Way, 2005) was primarily a criticism of what Simon viewed as the Volcker group's laxity in following up leads. It is of interest here because he provided photographs of Mouselli with Kojo Annan and with an Iraqi ambassador, as corroboration of the meeting described in the previous post.

> But why hasn't the committee itself followed up on Mouselli's several leads, most amazingly his encounter with the second Iraqi ambassador in 2002 who told him the Iraqis were looking for Kojo and that the Secretary General's son had done them a favor? It wouldn't take a Sam Spade or Sherlock Holmes to figure out that was worth pursuing. But as far as I know they haven't. The committee is moving on to the next phase of the investigation — operations — without having completed the first one.
>
> Meanwhile, here are some photos the committee might have found interesting:
>
> 1. Kojo with Mouselli at the French embassy in Lagos.
> 2. Mouselli with the Iraqi ambassador Taha Sukar.
>
> There's evidently more in Mouselli's scrapbook.

Simon continued his investigative reporting with "Trouble in (Volcker) Paradise?" (2005). Consistent with his earlier posts suggesting that the Volcker inquiry was not as diligent in following leads as it ought be, this one reported a rumor that two investigators might resign in protest. It is interesting to note that the writing style echoes that of tabloid investigative journalism, including the use of the third person to refer to the writer (punctuation and emphasis in the original; the post is not edited here).

> This blog has heard as yet unconfirmed ... repeat *unconfirmed* ... rumors of resignations of two key members of the legal staff conducting the investigations into the UN Oil-for-Food scandal on behalf of the Volcker Committee. What does this mean if true? It can't be anything good for public confidence in Mr. Volcker's committee.

A post on the following day (Your Foreign Relations Committee at Work!, 2005) contained an update that, in fact, the resignations had occurred (capitalization, punctuation, and emphasis as in the original).

> IMPORTANT UPDATE: <u>Investigators Robert Parton (senior investigative counsel) and Miranda Duncan (deputy counsel) have resigned because information was not being followed up by the Volcker Committee!!!</u> These are two of the top three field investigators for the committee. Only Michael Cornacchia remains.

A second update linked and quoted from an Associated Press story on the resignations (apparently Butler & Wadhams, 2005). Simon had doubts about the veracity of the official explanation of the resignations (capitalization and emphasis as in the original)

> MORE: Following several hours after this blog, the AP now has the story. The CYA has already begun:
>
> > A spokeswoman at Volcker's committee, who would speak only on condition of anonymity, said the resignations came after the investigators had completed the work they signed on to do.
>
> I wouldn't say that any other way but <u>anonymously</u> myself.

Later the same day, Simon added detail to his skeptical comment on that anonymous statement (Pinocchios of the Volcker Committee, 2005; emphasis in the original.)

> Why am I so sure this is nonsense? Because I have known *personally* about Parton's disaffection from the committee for <u>over a month</u> — that is long before the committee made its interim report and therefore long *before* Parton, Duncan or anyone else had "completed their work." Indeed, I had learned some time ago that somewhere around or about March 11 Parton had already *tried to resign*, but then was presumably persuaded to stay on or talked out of it by other members of the committee. What promises were to him at that about the "thoroughness" of the investigation I do not know, but I strongly suspect they were trashed within weeks or even days after having been made.

Confirmation of Simon's suspicions about the resignations came a few days later. His post titled "UPDATE: Oil-for-Resignations" (2005) began by noting two mainstream press accounts which contained statements attributed to Parton.

> Key UN Oil-for-Food investigator Robert Parton, whose resignation several days ago was first reported on this blog, is going public with his accusations toward the Volcker Committee in two news reports this evening ... .

He quoted this passage from an Associated Press story (Butler, 2005).

> The investigator, Robert Parton, confirmed a report by The Associated Press earlier this week that he had resigned along with another investigator to protest recent findings by the committee that cleared U.N. Secretary-General Kofi Annan of meddling in the $64 billion program. Parton's statement comes after a member of the committee discounted reports that the two investigators had left the Independent Inquiry Committee because they believe the report was too soft on the secretary-general.
>
> "Contrary to recent published reports, I resigned my position as Senior Investigative Counsel for the IIC not because my work was complete but on principle," Parton said.

Simon followed this with a quotation from a similar *London Telegraph* story (Laurence & Samuel, 2005).

> Last night, in the most explicit criticism so far directed at the report, Robert Parton, one of the senior investigators, told a lawyer involved with the Volcker inquiry that he thought the committee was "engaging in a de facto cover-up, acting with good intentions but steered by ideology."

There are many more posts in Simon's commentary about and reporting on the Oil-for-Food scandal than can be included here. The series is an elaborate example of an individual blogger following a story in much the same way as a mainstream journalist would; other outlets' material were often the starting point for his own contributions to it, and new information he had obtained or new interpretations he had to offer were woven into the publicly-available information. A particularly interesting feature of the series is the way the writing style at times tacked between the impersonal, third-person usage customary in the mainstream press and the highly personal, first-person usage familiar in the blogosphere, as if Simon were wrestling with the genre conventions of both. It appears that this series turned out to be a precursor of the blog-based news portal Simon later founded with Charles Johnson, of *Little Green Footballs*. Their portal, *Pajamas Media*, is described later.[31]

The preceding examples illustrate how bloggers often define a different priority order for existing stories in the mainstream media; put another way, their media criticism consists of assessing the salience of various current events or issues differently from the mainstream press. Another variety of alternative agenda-setting seen in the blogosphere consists of extending the lifespan of stories previously covered by the mainstream press, but then demoted in importance or abandoned entirely. These posts often consist just of mentioning the story, and wondering what has transpired since the initial coverage. Longer posts of this type may contain some amount of additional context, or recapitulate the earlier reporting on the subject.

A concise illustration of a blogger mentioning a story abandoned by the mainstream news media can be found on *InstaPundit*. Some time after the story had faded from the public eye, Glenn Reynolds brought up the case of Sandy Berger (Several Readers, 2005), the former National Security Adviser who had pled guilty to charges of mishandling classified documents. In its entirety, the post is this; the underscore indicates a link to a brief story in the online magazine *NewsMax*.

> Several readers have written to ask whether Sandy Berger was sentenced as scheduled on July 8. The answer is no, because the sentencing has been <u>postponed until September</u>, but this news account, which is all I could find, isn't very informative as to why.[33]

A more elaborate example of this kind of alternative agenda-setting concerns the follow-up to what can fairly be considered a journalistic scandal. In some quarters of the blogosphere, the controversy over CBS News basing a "60 Minutes" segment on forged memoranda about President Bush's service in the National Guard had become known as "Rathergate," because of the network anchor's involvement in the segment and ensuing controversy over the authenticity of the documents. In September 2004, CBS News announced an inquiry into the production of reporting it finally had acknowledged to be erroneous; after that the story died out in the mainstream press. In mid-November 2004, Glenn Reynolds wondered what had become of the inquiry (Rathergate Update, 2004).

> Rathergate update: or non-update, as the case may be. It has now been two months since CBS President Andrew Heyward promised that the investigation would be over and public in "weeks, not months." It's been months, now. Just another statement from CBS that turned out to be false?

As evidence that the report on the scandal was long overdue, Reynolds linked to a *Washington Post* story from September containing the quote from Heyward (Kurtz, 2004a).

Two days later, Reynolds noted early broadcast news reports of the network anchor's upcoming retirement (Fox News and ABC Radio, 2004).

> Fox News and ABC Radio are reporting that Dan Rather will be stepping down in March.

> Update: But we're still waiting for the Rathergate investigation.

The announcement of Rather's retirement (Kurtz, 2004b) prompted other bloggers to also note the delay in making the inquiry public; Reynolds linked some. Jim Geraghty recapitulated some information about the scandal, and mentioned the report which had not been released (First Thoughts, 2004).

> I guess I should be excited. CBS will say that Rather's departure has nothing to do with the infamous memo story that was based on

the unreliable word of Bill Burkett and a photocopied document that looked like it was printed out last Tuesday. They will say it has nothing to do with his stubborn refusal to retract the story when the facts were clear, when the skepticism of CBS'[s] own document experts was revealed, when the obsessive agenda of Mary Mapes [producer of the "60 Minutes" story] was revealed.... But I have my doubts.

And now I really want to see the results of that CBS internal investigation.

Andrew Sullivan thought it curious, given Rather's involvement in the scandal, that despite retiring as network anchor he would continue working for "60 Minutes". He, too, noted the delay in the CBS inquiry in a post on *The Daily Dish* (CBS'[s] Spin Control, 2004; emphasis in the original).

Why on earth is Rather staying on *full-time* at *Sixty Minutes,* the show whose reputation he besmirched by rashness and partisanship?...A simple question: How can you rehire a man for *Sixty Minutes* when you haven't even published your own investigation into the journalistic meltdown that he presided over? Shouldn't you wait until you know what actually happened before you declare that someone will stay on full-time? And how long does such an investigation take, for Pete's sake?

On *Captain's Quarters,* Ed Morrissey likewise noted the delay in CBS's response to the scandal (Rather Resigned, 2004).

Two years ago, this announcement [Rather's retirement] would have been a blockbuster. By this point, the reaction will mostly focus on why CBS waited so long to make the announcement.

By way of a postscript to this controversy, the internal inquiry conducted by CBS was finally made public almost two months after the announcement of Rather's retirement (Kurtz & Milbank, 2005). In January 2005 *The Washington Post* reported "the release of the outside panel's report that sharply criticized [Rather] yesterday."[33]

Perhaps the most explicit illustration of bloggers setting an alternative news agenda can be found in the blog-based online news portals. These pages are not blogs, *per se*, but instead are derived from blogs in one way or another. *Power Line News*, as the name suggests, is the news portal spun off the group blog, *Power Line*. The web page is a roundup of hyperlinks to selected mainstream media stories of the day from a variety of news outlets, to selected mainstream media video clips, and to the recent posts on a selection of blogs. The hyperlinks are formatted as the headlines of the selected stories, clips, and posts; at a glance, the reader sees the *Power Line* bloggers' alternative agenda for the day in the form of the stories, clips, and posts they choose to link.

Memeorandum is similar in that it consists entirely of a hyperlink roundup. A very interesting feature is that the page visually clusters links to mainstream media stories with links to blog posts related to them, reflecting the symbiotic relationship between the blogosphere and the established media outlets. Another interesting feature — to this author's knowledge, a feature unique to this site, as a news portal — is that the selection of mainstream media stories and blog posts is automated, and made by an algorithm devised by the site's creator, Gabe Rivera. He described the selection of stories and posts in this way (Q: Who's Included?, 2005):

> I'll start with the most common question: how are sources selected for inclusion?
>
> To answer that, I'll begin with my philosophy: I want writers to be selected by their peers. That is, I want the writers in each topic area to select which of their peers show up on the site. Not deliberately, but implicitly, by whom they link to and in what context they link. The source-picking algorithm is based on this philosophy and works roughly as follows: I feed it a number of sites representative of the topic area I want coverage [of]. It then scans text and follows links to discover a much larger corps of writers within that area.
>
> The decisions for including sources are continually reevaluated, in such a way that new sources can be included in real time ... . [S]ometimes the author of the most insightful analysis piece at 2pm was a relative unknown at 1pm. Real-time inclusion is possible on *memeorandum* provided that author receives prompt

enough recognition by peers ... .

In other words, the alternative agenda-setting evident on *memeorandum* operates at the collective level of the symbiosis of the mainstream media and the blogosphere: the algorithm searches for both mainstream media products and blog content related to them. Further, it is in essence a peer-review process centered on issue salience rather than a particular perspective: both critical and laudatory comments are included in the documents chosen, through a text-processing algorithm, for the site. Put in the vernacular, *memeorandum*'s alternative agenda is the "buzz" in online world.

Pajamas Media, founded by Roger L. Simon and Charles Johnson, differs from those portals in that it is a consortium of bloggers from around the world. Content written by bloggers is featured on its home page, much as the Web sites of mainstream media outlets feature their staff's content. The alternative agenda-setting on this site is evident in its choice of top blog posts of the day, just as a traditional broadsheet newspaper places its headline stories above the fold. A tease for each post appears on the *Pajamas Media* home page with full text linked on the individual bloggers' pages, much in the way a newspaper supplies the beginning of a story on the front page and continues with a jump to an inside page.

With regard to the format and appearance of the page, and to the editorial decision-making behind its agenda-setting, *Pajamas Media* is perhaps the most traditional. The innovation here, however, is that the featured content on the site is generated by bloggers, including first-hand reports of newsworthy events, background stories on remote locations and situations, and commentary on issues or events. Another aspect of the site worth noting is that the contributing bloggers represent an extraordinary variety of perspectives — far broader than most mainstream outlets' roster — as a perusal of its blogroll will show.[34]

CHAPTER 5

Journalistic Practices

The preceding chapters described genres of criticism which, in general terms, concerned the content of news products. There is also a good deal of media criticism appearing in blogs, centering on the craft of journalism in itself. This genre of criticism raises questions about the working methods and professional standards of mainstream journalists, rather than the specific content of news stories. We can distinguish three varieties of critique within this genre: newsgathering, writing and editing, and error correction.

Newsgathering

Critique of newsgathering concerns the way mainstream journalists obtain the information they put into their stories. Bloggers may object to mainstream journalists' use of anonymous sources; they may object to mainstream outlets' reliance on local stringers instead of having their own staff directly observe situations or events; on occasion bloggers have questioned the mainstream media's use of video footage or still pictures which may have been shot by terrorist groups or possible sympathizers. Bloggers may criticize the mainstream press's attention to sensational events at the expense of follow-ups or background stories on matters of enduring importance. Bloggers may wonder about the personal relationships between journalists and parties interested in issues they cover, and the potential for those personal relationships to influence the reporting about the issues. Along a similar line, bloggers may take note of journalists' reliance on advocacy groups for statistics or other factual information relating to some issue.

A good deal of criticism of newsgathering practices can be found on *Rantingprofs*, in particular. This is unsurprising since the blogger, Cori Dauber, is a communication professor whose scholarly interests include the news media. Her specialized expertise enables her to single out particular steps in the newsgathering, story creation, and dissemination process, and to often connect what she sees as deficiencies in this process to consequent media effects on public opinion.

The terrorist murder of an American activist in Iraq was the subject of considerable mainstream media attention in April 2005. Marla Ruzicka had formed friendships with many journalists in both Afghanistan and Iraq, and Dauber posted twice about Ruzicka's relationship with mainstream journalists working in those areas, and the implications of the relationship for news coverage. The first noted that stories about Ruzicka's death had provided little detail about her activities in Afghanistan and Iraq and her interactions with members of the press corps there. The opening line of this post was a continuation of its title, "Let Us Not Speak Ill of the Dead" (2005; emphasis in the original).

> But let us speak accurately.
>
> Both NBC and CNN produce hagiographic pieces about a young "humanitarian," or young "aid worker" killed today in a suicide bombing. What, precisely, she did of a practical nature in either Afghanistan or Iraq is left somewhat vague, besides *caring* an enormous amount, and *organizing* ... .
>
> Well, more power to her, I suppose, and rest in peace. But I think it would have been a better and more complete story if either of these networks had reported more fully on just who this young woman was — and why it was that both of them knew of this young woman, and themselves cared about her so much.

Dauber then quoted a lengthy passage from an article which had appeared in *Columbia Journalism Review* three years earlier (Massing, 2002). The author had spent a few weeks in Afghanistan to prepare a political analysis piece for *Nation* magazine; the *Columbia Journalism Review* article gave his detailed personal account of mainstream newsgathering operations in Afghanistan at the time, and happened to include a substantial description of both Ruzicka's activism and her personal interactions with journalists. The passage Dauber quoted (excerpted here), concerned the tendency towards uniformity in the mainstream press accounts of the events.

> These experiences, in turn, point to a second shortcoming in the press's approach to Afghanistan — its pack mentality. The "hacks" in Kabul, as they call themselves, tend to hang out with one another, eat together, party together ... . Many of these parties were organized by Marla, a bubbly, blond-haired woman who had come to Kabul for Global Exchange, the antiglobalization group based in San Francisco. Marla's mission was to organize Afghans who had lost family members to the U.S. bombing. She was hoping both to document the number of victims and to get survivors to demand compensation from the United States.

> I never did figure out if Marla's hostessing was specifically designed to snare the media's attention, but stories about civilian casualties began appearing regularly. And, on one level, they were welcome ... . Now the press was finally getting around to investigating the matter.

> Well-researched accounts, though, put the civilian death toll at about 1,000. While all such deaths are regrettable, that number seems low when measured against the positive effects of the bombing — the overthrow of the Taliban, the smashing of al Qaeda, the restoration of basic freedoms to the Afghan people. In fact, Marla told me that many of the families she had contacted were so pleased with the results of the bombing that they were reluctant to come forward to demand compensation. This reality, however, made its way into very few of the stories that appeared in the U.S. press. The coverage of the issue swung from complete silence to lockstep condemnation — a demonstration of how synchronized the reporting out of Kabul tends to be.

Two days later Dauber commented on a *Washington Post* correspondent's reminiscence about Ruzicka's popularity among the western journalists working in Iraq (Constable, 2005). In a post titled "What's Coming Out Now" (2005), she took note of the close personal relationships between the journalists and Ruzicka. Dauber felt this sort of relationship between journalists and activists was context that ought be provided to readers of the news stories, as the relationship at least had the potential to color the reporting.

> I want to be very careful here, because I don't want to make light of Marla Ruzicka's death, and I absolutely do not want to belittle the feelings of people who have clearly lost someone very dear to them. But when you read the note the *Post* published from one of their top foreign correspondents in Ruzicka's honor, there's something disturbing about it ... .

> [W]hat gets inadvertently revealed here, in a very sincere effort to honor someone respected and cared for, is that the n[on]-g[overnmental] o[rganization] and journalistic communities often mingle and become close. But the NGO [capitalization added] community is one with a point of view and an agenda to push.

Dauber observed that such personal relationships are perfectly understandable, since western reporters working in non-western areas — especially in dangerous environments — would naturally find the company of another westerner attractive. Nonetheless, she saw the potential influence of an activist on the coverage as context which ought be provided to the news audience.

> But it seems as if there ought to be some way for reporters to alert readers that sources they use are friends, issues they write about were brought to their attention by people they were partying with. Does that kind of relationship in some way change a reporter's ability to evaluate evidence? ...

> Should readers be "read in" to those relationships? Aren't the questions at least worth asking?[35]

During the incursion into Iraq in March and April 2003, the mainstream press made extensive use of reporters "embedded" with combat units. This was the term used to describe reporters who, in effect, became non-combatant members of military units. Embedded reporters traveled with their unit, and were allowed complete access to their unit's operations and to their unit's personnel; there was no military review of their copy, but unit commanders could require, with justification, short delays in publication for security reasons (see Cooper, 2003 for a summary of the embedding ground rules). The practice of allowing journalists to embed with combat units was a significant departure from the earlier press pool arrangements, and the new policy was for the most part received favorably by the mainstream press as it allowed first-hand observations of the war (Cooper, 2003). One study noted a considerable difference in the framing of stories from embedded reporters, compared to stories describing the same day's events by journalists based away from the combat theater (Cooper & Kuypers, 2004).

While the Department of Defense continued to make embed slots available after the fall of the Hussein regime, press interest in the slots dropped off. Coverage of the reconstruction and the insurgency in Iraq has largely taken the form of what some have termed "hotel journalism" (Grant, 2005), with journalists drawing on local stringers as much or more than their own direct observations of conditions and events in that area.

Cori Dauber has often posted favorably about embedding as a newsgathering practice; her *Rantingprofs* post titled, "There are Benefits to Embedding" (2005) is a good example. *The Washington Post* had published a story describing an attack on a convoy, written by a reporter riding in one of its vehicles (Tyson, 2005). Dauber linked the story, and offered this appraisal of it (punctuation as in the original):

> Today the *Post* runs a story that comes out of a reporter embedding for only a short period of time, and while it ends up being a "bad news story" (the short [H]umvee ride is attacked) it's superbly done. Another reminder, by the way, that good reporting is not a function of "good news vs. bad news."

Of particular interest here is Dauber's critical comment on hotel journalism as a substitute for embedding (emphasis and punctuation as in the original).

> As I've written repeatedly, I remain mystified by the argument that, although reporters feel they can't leave their hotels in many instances, but must rely on barely trained or untrained Iraqi stringers to do the actual reporting, embedding is not an alternative

because it would provide access to only one side of the story. Sitting in the hotel provides access to *no* sides of the story — embedding would at least balance what the stringers are getting.

That post contained an overall criticism of the mainstream press' routine failure to have their staff directly observe events and conditions in Iraq, and their heavy reliance on information supplied by organizational outsiders; the critique was developed by contrasting an example of high-quality embedded reporting with the practice of hotel journalism. A later post on *Rantingprofs* contains a related thought. In this case, Dauber offered a compliment to *The New York Times* for keeping its own reporter in Afghanistan (Give the *Times* Its Due, 2005) when other outlets had withdrawn from the area. She linked to a detailed story describing a woman campaigning for a parliamentary seat in Afghanistan (Gall, 2005), and noted the dearth of coverage of that important and complex election caused by the lack of staffing.

> I have spent my fair share of time complaining about *The New York Times* ... . But the fact remains that there are virtually no American outlets remaining in Afghanistan, which means almost no one even attempting to cover what's going on with their election campaign. So, bottom line, is there any other paper where you could read about the leading candidate for the women's position for representative for the nomadic peoples of Afghanistan?

In a bluntly-worded earlier post (Meanwhile, Back at the Hotel, 2005), Dauber had noted that while the mainstream press relied heavily on stringers for its Iraq coverage, it tended to ignore information supplied by military authorities. She included a link to a roundup post of favorable news (The Jaws of Victory, 2005) on another blog, the *Mudville Gazette*, which did include such reports. Dauber was careful to acknowledge that mainstream journalists ought not accept those accounts uncritically or to rely on them as their sole source of information about events in Iraq, but nonetheless questioned why that source of information about dangerous areas was underutilized (emphasis as in original; minor error in syntax corrected).

What do "hotel journalists" do from their hotels to get their information? Okay, sort of a rhetorical question. Because they don't seem too interested in the official press releases provided by CENTCOM.

On the one hand, it would be a mistake for the press to turn into nothing more than mouthpieces for the official *version* of events. On the other hand, if that official version involves the fact that those events, you know, took place to begin with, shouldn't the press be including that, telling us that those things are happening?[36]

The mainstream press coverage of the Iraq war has sometimes included video footage of hostages taken by terrorist organizations. On occasion the footage has been highly graphic in showing violent behavior, even including the execution of a hostage; strongly emotional content, at the least, has been routine. The broadcasting of a video of an Australian citizen taken hostage in Iraq prompted a *Rantingprofs* post about the practice of airing such motion images without providing information about how the footage had been acquired by the news outlet (A New Video, 2005). Dauber commented that such footage had the potential, as persuasive rhetoric, to deflect attention away from the captors.

So, given how powerful this new video is, as this man begs (in English) for our President, for the Australian Prime Minister, even for the Governor of California, to do something, anything, to assuage his kidnappers, placing the burden — and therefore the blame — not on the murderous thugs who are holding him, but on the civilized people who the kidnappers want to argue are now actually in control of his fate, let's go back to the questions Dorrance Smith wants to ask.

Her reference was to an op-ed which had appeared in *The Wall Street Journal* (Smith, 2005) questioning the arrangement between al-Jazeera and the American news outlets through which the American outlets obtained footage of hostages and terrorist attacks. Smith had taken the position that American outlets had an ethical obligation to report on the connection between al-Jazeera and terrorist groups, if those outlets chose to air footage provided by al-Jazeera. Dauber raised a number of questions about the clip of the Australian hostage (capitalization and punctuation as in the original).

> So, what is the provenance of this tape that all the networks are playing?
>
> Did it come from al Jazeera?
>
> Where did al Jazeera get it, if so?
>
> Did al Jazeera pay for it?
>
> Do the networks know the conditions of the relationship between al Jazeera and the groups that supply it with footage?

Dauber concluded the post by returning to her earlier observation that the footage appeared to have considerable persuasive power by virtue of its highly emotional content. She raised an additional question about the extensive play the clip was receiving: the tension between the newsworthiness of the footage and its potential to aid the terrorist groups through repeated broadcast (capitalization as in the original).

> What is gained from showing this footage? does the news value of this footage trump the harm of showing propaganda footage? if so, does that value remain the same every single re-showing on cable? is there a value to repeated showings? should the cable news networks continue to show this footage over and over and over? doesn't the news value wear off, while the propaganda value grows stronger and stronger, so that the balance begins to shift over time?

Along a similar line, Dauber noted an occasion on which an American broadcast network aired video footage from al-Jazeera purportedly showing a successful attack on Marine forces (Shame on NBC, 2005). Her objection to this broadcast was that military authorities had unequivocally stated that the footage, at a minimum, was being fraudulently represented. She began the post by describing the circumstances (syntax and emphasis as in the original).

> As I noted last night, NBC reports that al-Jazeera is showing video from a terrorist group that is claimed to be footage of the attack

that recently killed 10 Marines. While NBC notes that the military has told them that it can't be footage of that attack, since in the footage it's clearly daylight, while the attack in question took place at night, they go ahead and *show the video anyway.*

Dauber linked and quoted the Marine Corps's carefully-worded official statement (Disinformation Alert, n.d.) about the footage.

> A video posted to a terrorist Web site and aired by some media organizations purporting to show the improvised explosive device attack that killed 10 U.S. Marines on Dec. 1 is disinformation. The circumstances of the IED attack near Fallujah do not match those shown on the video. While we are unable to discern whether the video shown is authentic, the statement that the video shows the Dec. 1 IED attack near Fallujah is false.

Dauber then made her criticism of NBC explicit.

> Way to go, NBC. You aren't only disseminating terrorist propaganda, you're participating in a terrorist disinformation campaign. Let's not pull punches here: to air the video for the American public (even with hedges and caveats and qualifiers) is to participate in the disinformation campaign, period.[37]

The issue of the relationship between news outlets and terrorists had arisen before, in connection with a dramatic still photograph which eventually won a Pulitzer Prize for the Associated Press. The image which became known as the "Haifa Street photo" was included with an AP story describing the street execution of three Iraqi Independent Electoral Commission staff in Baghdad in late December 2004. Its lede clearly indicates the story's frame (Lekic, 2004), that the situation in Iraq was not favorable for the upcoming January election.

> A brazen daylight attack in the heart of Baghdad with rebels executing election workers in cold blood served as a chilling reminder Sunday of the deteriorating security situation in the Iraqi capital with just more than a month before crucial parliamentary elections. A series of pictures taken by an AP photographer show three pistol-wielding gunmen, who had earlier stopped a car carrying the election officials and dragged them into the middle of

Haifa Street in the midst of morning traffic.

The provenance of the photographs quickly became the subject of controversy in the blogosphere. On *Belmont Club*, Australian software developer Richard Fernandez posed the question how the AP photographer was in a position to shoot the photo sequence (The Odds Against, 2004). Posting under his pen name Wretchard, Fernandez linked the AP story and an ABC News version of it, and quoted several passages from the story, including this.

> In a dramatic photo sequence one of the captives is shown lying on his side on the pavement, while a second is on his knees nearby in the street. The gunmen casually display their handguns as they shoot the two men. Both of the victims shown in the sequence wore traditional Arab headscarfs. In contrast, the attackers were bareheaded and apparently unafraid to show their faces. The entire sequence shows only two of the three victims lying dead after they were shot at close range. The final photo of the sequence shows a man standing near one of the bodies waving for help, as a U.S. Apache helicopter appears above the crime scene after the gunmen apparently melted away into the crowd.

As the title of his post suggests, Fernandez felt there was little chance of the photographer happening to be at the scene of a planned killing without having some connection to the incident. As evidence, he cited a similar photograph from the Vietnam War.

> Even with today's proliferation of compact photographic equipment, a legitimate photojournalist rarely gets the opportunity to capture an execution. Apart from the beheadings which are purposely recorded on video by the *jihadis* and from gun camera film, most footage of people actually being shot are taken by photographers in company with combatants who are ready to film an ambush. Those individuals are combat cameramen for their armies or embedded reporters. The most famous analogue to the Associated Press sequence of photographs is probably the Eddie Adams photo of the execution of Vietcong Captain Bay Lop by South Vietnamese General Nguyen Ngoc Loan. Adams owed that opportunity General Loan himself, who brought Adams along to cover what he believed to be a justifiable summary execution.

...It may have been pure luck, but it was surely the longest of odds that would have brought an Associated Press cameraman to the site of a surprise attack on two Iraqi electoral workers.

Two days later the online magazine *Salon* ran an opinion piece (Follman, 2004) with the photo which would later win a Pulitzer Prize, accusing "conservative bloggers" of taking "another cheap shot at the 'left-wing' media." Wretchard responded to the article in two posts. "Sixty Four Dollars" (2004) linked the *Salon* article, and maintained that "the photo itself raises more questions than any conservative blogger ever could." He quoted from another Associated Press story (Al-Obeidi, 2004) which had described the Haifa Street executions in this way:

> During morning rush hour, about 30 armed insurgents, hurling hand grenades and firing guns, swarmed onto Haifa Street, the scene of repeated clashes between U.S. forces and insurgents. They stopped a car carrying five employees of the Iraqi Electoral Commission and killed three of them. The other two escaped. The commission condemned the attack as a "terrorist ambush."

Wretchard then explicitly stated two questions about the provenance of the photo — one concerning the presence of the photographer at the scene, and the other concerning the vantage point from which the photograph was taken — and maintained the legitimacy of the questions he had raised.

> It was surely the most amazing of coincidences that placed an Associated Press photographer in a position to openly photograph an execution, where we are reliably informed, no less than 30 armed men were firing guns and hurling hand grenades.

> ...There may be a perfectly plausible explanation for everything, but for the record let me wonder:

> 1. How the Associated Press photographer happened to be at the attack site at the time. Was it on his route to home or work?

> 2. How he photographed the execution sequence in the midst of an attack by 30 persons from the middle of the major road (see the

photo provided by *Salon*).

Just asking. We need to go the "country mile" to reach the standard of proof that any responsible reader would need to form an opinion on the issues. The best way to do that is to ask questions and though one may wait in vain for the answers, one must ask them all the same in the same manner that *Salon* is asking questions about "conservative bloggers" who "suggest" that an "Associated Press photographer was complicit." You can hardly do one and not the other.

Later on the same day, "Haifa Street" (2004) repeated some of those points, but also took note of a passage in the *Salon* article which had described its author's off-the-record conversation with someone at the Associated Press. The anonymous AP source had offered this explanation of how the photographer had been at the site in time to photograph the shootings.

A source at the Associated Press knowledgeable about the events covered in Baghdad on Sunday told *Salon* that accusations that the photographer was aware of the militants' plans are "ridiculous." The photographer, whose identity the AP is withholding due to safety concerns, was likely "tipped off to a demonstration that was supposed to take place on Haifa Street," said the AP source, who was not at liberty to comment by name. But the photographer "definitely would not have had foreknowledge" of a violent event like an execution, the source said.

Wretchard found this explanation implausible.

Here was where the killers really lucked out. The AP photographer, though caught at unawares, who definitely had no "foreknowledge" of what was going down and at the worst expected a street demonstration, did not take cover, even as soldiers and Marines are trained to do when shooting starts. He was made of sterner stuff and held his ground, taking pictures of people he did not know killing individuals he did not recognize for reasons he would not have known about. This — in the midst of "30 armed insurgents, hurling hand grenades and firing guns" — as the Associated Press report says. And he continued to take photographs for a fairly long period of time, capturing not just a single photograph, but a sequence of them.

On *Little Green Footballs*, Charles Johnson added a question (Incident on Haifa Street, 2004) to those Fernandez had raised. He posted what had by that point become the defining photograph of the series — one election official on his knees, another lying on the pavement with a terrorist pointing a gun at his head — and included a caption showing the photo credit. Johnson took note of something he felt was unusual about the credit.

> At L[ittle] G[reen] F[ootballs], we have linked to (and shown) numerous pictures of *mujahideen* attacking coalition forces with all sorts of weapons. Every one of these photographs, from AP, Reuters, and Agence France Presse, has carried a byline for the photographer who shot it. AP stringers have never been shy about identifying themselves, even when standing a few feet away from terrorists. Yet, the caption for the photo above conceals the identity of the photographer. Why?

Johnson was less restrained in his speculation than Wretchard had been.

> Is it possible that this photo was not merely the work of an AP photographer who knew in advance of the attack — but was in fact, shot by an accomplice of the murderers who supplied the photo to the Associated Press? The propaganda value of the photo to the *mujahideen* is undeniable; it sends a terrifying message to any Iraqi who supports the upcoming elections.

With the controversy escalating in the blogosphere, the Associated Press made an on-the-record statement about the photos available through the *Poynter Online* journalism Web site (Stokes, 2004) the day after the *Salon* article appeared. The brief statement took the form of an e-mail to Jim Romenesko, editor of the *Romenesko* page on the *Poynter Online* site, and is reproduced here in its entirety; the bracketed words appear in the post, and are not this author's addition.

> From JACK STOKES, director of media relations, Associated Press: [This is a solicited letter regarding *Salon*'s "The Associated

Press 'insurgency'"] Several brave Iraqi photographers work for The Associated Press in places that only Iraqis can cover. Many are covering the communities they live in where family and tribal relations give them access that would not be available to Western photographers, or even Iraqi photographers who are not from the area.

Insurgents want their stories told as much as other people and some are willing to let Iraqi photographers take their pictures. It's important to note, though, that the photographers are not "embedded" with the insurgents. They do not have to swear allegiance or otherwise join up philosophically with them just to take their pictures.

Fernandez continued his *Belmont Club* commentary on the issue in a post titled with a quote pulled from the e-mail ("Insurgents Want Their Stories Told," 2004). He quoted the entire e-mail from the AP to *Poynter Online*, and pressed the question of the photographer's relationship to the terrorists (emphasis and punctuation as in the original).

In this regard, one hopes it is not impertinent to ask whether a photographer who <u>does not</u> "swear allegiance or otherwise join up philosophically with them (insurgents)" can take their pictures. Mr. Stokes might like to state whether the Associated Press photographer who took a sequence of pictures of an execution on Haifa Street, Baghdad is one of those "brave Iraqi photographers" to whom the insurgents are willing to entrust their stories. If so, at what point did the "brave Iraqi" photographer become aware that the story of the day was going to be the live execution of two Iraqi election workers?

Scott Johnson of the group blog *Power Line* posted an e-mail from one of its readers, in "On the AP and the Murders" (2004). The reader agreed it appeared that the Associated Press photographer had been told a terrorist act would occur on Haifa Street at a particular place and time; he described two prior incidents (an attempt to shoot down an airliner with a surface-to-air missile, and the killing of American contractors in Fallujah) in which he felt there was very good evidence that news organizations had been given advance notice of a terrorist attack so they could be at the site and record visual images of it. Of particular interest here, though, is the *Power Line* reader's interpretive comment on the tensions inherent in western news outlets operating in an unconventional war theater.

> The AP and other news agencies are in a difficult position. They would like to get information from both sides (as much to display their "neutrality" as anything). They do not desire to be seen by either side as partisans of the other — especially in the case of the terrorists, who, unlike the US military, would be likely to take violent action on such a perception. And they can't resist the idea of getting a scoop or prize-winning, career-building photograph. And news from inside the insurgency is rare and desirable. The insurgents sensibly (from their point of view) try to keep the circle of witting participants as small as possible, as late as possible. That they admit certain ostensibly "Western" journalists into their orbit is clear, and considering the risks this entails, it is telling.

On the next day another *Power Line* blogger, John Hinderaker, reviewed the two statements the AP had provided regarding the photographs (AP Admits Relationship With Terrorists, 2004), and took the position that the AP had essentially acknowledged having prior knowledge of some action planned for that location, and having existing relationships to the terrorists. He linked and quoted the statement from an anonymous AP source which been included in the *Salon* article (reproduced above), then followed it with his interpretation of the passage.

> So the AP admitted that its photographer was "tipped off" by the terrorists. The only quibble asserted by the AP was that the photographer expected only a "demonstration," not a murder ... . We'd like to ask some more questions of the photographer, of course, but that's impossible since the AP won't identify him because of "safety concerns." Really? Who would endanger his safety? The terrorists? They could have shot him on Sunday if they were unhappy about having their picture taken.

Hinderaker then linked and quoted the AP's on-the-record statement from *Poynter Online* (also reproduced above), and again followed it with his interpretation.

That makes the admission pretty well complete, I think. The AP is using photographers who have relationships with the terrorists; this is for the purpose of helping to tell the terrorists' "stories." The photographers don't have to swear allegiance to the terrorists — gosh, that's reassuring — but they have "family and tribal relations" with them. And they aren't embedded — I'm not sure I believe that — but they don't need to be either, since the terrorists tip them off when they are about to commit an act that they want filmed.

A week later, another blogger took issue with Fernandez's and Hinderaker's position that the AP must have had prior knowledge of a planned terrorist act. The post on *Dead Parrot Society* (Media Critics: Haifa Street Execution Photo Edition, 2005) seems to have played a pivotal role in this controversy, since its refutation was based largely on particular technical characteristics of the image; those characteristics became central to the controversy as it continued. Ryan, a journalist working for a mainstream news outlet, began the post by accusing the AP's blog critics of putting the press in a double bind (punctuation and emphasis as in the blog original).

We've gotten beyond silly things like "Look at [the] depths our enemy will sink to" and right to the heart of the matter: How is this another way the media has proved it's against the war? (For the curious, the rule is pretty simple: If we *don't* run graphic images, it's because we're afraid they'd show people the barbaric nature of the terrorists we face, thereby causing the public to support the war .... If we *do* run graphic images, it's because we want to spread the terrorists' message, and we hope they'll sicken people, thereby causing them to be against the war ... . Hey, nobody ever said it was *hard* to be a media critic.)

Ryan then began his examination of the image's characteristics, and challenged the other bloggers' assertion that the photographer must have been very close to the actual site of the street executions (emphasis in the original).

Do these writers *really* believe their characterizations of how the stringer got his shots? I can't imagine they do, not in a day where

[sic] a telephoto lens and a professional crop bring you right into a photo's face.

Ryan then showed two versions of the image in question, which he said had come from the Yahoo news feed; the second appears to be cropped by about one-third and centers on the gunman and victim. He then took up the question of the photographer's proximity to the shooter.

> So where was the photographer most likely standing when he got these shots? ... . If you were a professional photographer carrying professional equipment optimized for shooting pictures in a war zone (where you might not want to be right up close to the action), how far away could you have been and still gotten these shots? ... . I just spoke with a news photographer on our staff (for readers who don't know, I'm an online producer for a newspaper in Washington state). Judging by the perspective and clarity on the image above, he estimates that the photographer in Baghdad was using a 300-millimeter lens from about a block away. "From a very safe distance," he said.

Ryan also addressed the question Fernandez had first raised, about the likelihood a photographer would be in position at the moment of the attack (emphasis in the original).

> Even if it's totally random, given the number of insurgent attacks going on, what are the odds that at *some point* a photographer is going to happen to be there right when one occurs? On any given day, maybe not great. But over months, it's going to happen ... . The great, great likelihood here is that a professional news photographer, actively looking for a news photo, positioned himself near a very dangerous street, and ended up a block away, quite safe, for a matter of a few seconds while these shootings happened.

The award of a Pulitzer Prize to the AP for the photograph (LeSure, 2005; Breaking News Photography, n.d.) reignited the controversy a few months later. Both Scott Johnson of *Power Line* (The Pulitzer Prize for Felony Murder, 2005) and Ryan of *Dead Parrot Society* (Haifa Street Critics Are Back, 2005) posted recapitulations of their earlier arguments about the provenance of the image. Several days later Johnson followed up in a post (Murder on Haifa Street: An Update, 2005) describing his contact with a *New York Times* reporter preparing a short article about the controversy for its business section (Glassman, 2005). Johnson described how the reporter had sent him a link to a new statement from the Associated Press's director of photography (Lyon, 2005) about the photographer's movements on the day of the street execution, and asked for his comments on it.

> Mr. Glassman originally contacted me by e-mail, then spoke with me by telephone. In our telephone conversations he told me that the AP director of photography told him the photographer was 50 meters from the scene of the assassination; the AP has asserted elsewhere...that the photographer was 300 meters from the murders.

Johnson then posted his e-mail to Glassman, which referenced the earlier statements released by the Associated Press.

> My comment on the Pulitzer award to the AP cannot be understood outside the context of these AP-sourced statements or of John's [i.e., Hinderaker's] comments on these statements. One AP-sourced statement quoted by John said that the photographer was likely "tipped off to a demonstration that was supposed to take place on Haifa Street" but "would not have had foreknowledge" of a violent event like an execution. The other AP-sourced statement was from Jack Stokes — the AP's director of media relations — to Jim Romenesko responding to the controversy regarding this photograph. Stokes's statement suggested a collaborative relationship between AP photographers and terrorists who "want their stories told" and "are willing to let Iraqi photographers take their photos." Stokes's statement to Romenesko is crucial.

As a sidenote to this point in the controversy, Glassman's story (2005) described Johnson as having been satisfied by the AP's new statement about the photograph; Johnson's post, however, gives every indication to the contrary.

The detailed post continued with an analysis of the photograph by D. Gorton, a former *New York Times* photographer. Johnson described

Power Line's inquiry to Gorton, as an expert on news photography.

> In correspondence that we have not posted on the site, we sought the expert opinion of the prominent former *New York Times* photographer D. Gorton regarding the photograph. Mr. Gorton's analysis of the photo is consistent with our comments regarding the photo on the site and with our interpretation of the quoted AP statements.

Gorton's commentary on the photograph is thorough, including both the appearance of the scene and the technical characteristics of the image; the reader is encouraged to examine it in its entirety. As Charles Johnson of *Little Green Footballs* had done when the photograph was first published (Incident on Haifa Street, 2004), Gorton noted that the photographer was not credited by name, contrary to the usual practice (minor error in punctuation corrected; punctuation otherwise as in the original).

> Bear in mind that the Pulitzer Prize names the "Associated Press Staff." I would think that is the way that the AP entered the images into competition and thus started the controversy. If the picture was a "pick up" then it should have [been] labeled as such since meaningful control of the editorial function does not reach to "pick up" photos. Anyone, including a terrorist, can offer up pictures with a dubious or malicious provenance.

Of particular interest here are Gorton's thoughts on the photographer's proximity to the shooter, along the line Ryan had earlier developed on *Dead Parrot Society*. Gorton first explained the effect on the image of the camera lens's focal length, then made an inference about the distance at which the image had been made (punctuation as in the original).

> If I take a "normal" scene of a crowd with my 50mm lens on a 35mm camera and make a "normal" enlargement then the scene appears much as I saw it with the naked eye.

> But, if I rack up the enlarger to the ceiling and "blow up" a tiny portion of the scene, then that portion appears "compressed." People's heads are sticking out behind each other and the "head

sizes" are all very similar even though they are further away in reality. That's roughly what a telephoto lens does ... .

We do not have the original photo to make a judgment about. It is difficult to tell if the image has been enlarged, or if it has degraded through numerous duplications. However, assuming that this is the original dimension of the finished photo, I would estimate that the lens is the rough equivalent of a 180mm lens on a 35mm format. I would estimate the distance between 15 and 25 meters. The distance would be the same if the lens were "normal" [i.e., 50mm on a 35mm camera] but an enlargement of the print had occurred ... .

So, the assassination picture has all the earmarks of a planned image, indicating that the photographer had taken most of the considerations that I have written about above. It's also possible that a passing Iraqi, riding in the back of a pick-up truck, carrying a Nikon with a 180mm lens happened onto the scene, made a few snaps and dropped them off at the AP office in the Green Zone of Baghdad.

Johnson then indicated that Gorton reaffirmed his estimate of the photographer's proximity to the shooter after seeing an uncropped version of the image, quoting him as saying:

There is nothing about this alternate version that would trouble my initial analysis. It is common in the news photo business to make the image as direct and powerful as possible through enlargement of the original. I believe in my response to you that I pointed out that the picture appeared to be a "blow up."

Later on the same day, Johnson posted Gorton's thoughts about the Associated Press's new explanation of the photograph (A Postscript From D. Gorton, 2005). Gorton found several parts of the statement's account of the photographer's movements (Lyon, 2005) to be implausible or incomplete; again, the reader is encouraged to examine Gorton's comments in full. In particular, Gorton found it implausible that the photographer could have taken a hand-held shot with a long telephoto lens in the midst of a violent environment, from a distance long enough to assure his personal safety; he referred to this passage in the AP statement (Lyon, 2005):

> The photographer then walked toward the intersection where the executions would later take place to photograph the wreck of another recently burned car that he spotted nearby. Soon, he noticed about 20 people arriving and directing traffic away from the intersection, looking unofficial and "very unusual." Anticipating a problem, the car that had brought him there was put near a bridge for a quick getaway, if necessary. He left his photo equipment in the car and walked up to one of the people directing traffic to inquire about what they were doing. He was told "none of your business." He walked back to the car. That's when he heard an explosion. The concussion was powerful enough to break glass in the car.
>
> The photographer turned and saw the group holding two people at gunpoint on the street. One of the attackers was armed with an AK-47 rifle and another with a handgun. The photographer grabbed a camera with a 100-400mm telephoto lens set at 100mm and photographed the next events from beside the car. The gunmen shot two men in succession. The second shooting was obscured by passing traffic, with many passing cars now fleeing the area. The photographer got back in the car, which inadvertently went down a circular street that just went under the foot of the bridge and returned to the same intersection. He took the occasion to shoot several more photos from the car. Then he left the scene for good.

Gorton felt the AP's statement did not resolve the question of the photographer's proximity to the shootings, given the technical details it provided about the photographer's equipment and the sequence of events it described (punctuation as in the original).

> A 400mm lens gives a field of view of 6 degrees, in comparison to a (normal) 55mm lens which gives a field of view of 45 degrees. We have to make an estimate on the width of the field that was photographed. A 400mm lens on a normal 35mm back would yield a field of view of approximately 8.9 meters in width at 100 meters focus. A 180mm lens would give a similar field at around 40 meters. A typical Nikon zoom lens of 80-400mm weighs about 4 pounds in addition to the camera body, and is very difficult to handle at the 400mm setting without the use of a tripod. It also

retails in the United States for around $2,000. Quite a piece of gear to grab the moment your car is blown up, focus and shoot.

I believe that the more likely explanation is that the photographer was close to the scene, standing on part of his car, and using an intermediate setting in the zoom...perhaps as little as 150mm. Camera shake, not to mention nerves after an explosion, would likely preclude a handheld 400mm shot. A distance of around 30 to 50 meters (after examining the thumbnail of the original image) still seems reasonable.

I believe that the various stories that have been told, thus far, by the AP are confusing and at times contradictory. The details in the AP editor's note are at variance with other quotes ascribed to the AP of "300 meters" from the action, "100" meters and most recently "50" meters.

In the end, Gorton indicated that his personal concern in the matter was one of journalistic practice (minor spelling error corrected; punctuation as in the original).

I have worked with wire photographers from the AP as well as other news agencies. I found them, on the whole, the most talented, straightforward and best photographers around. None of this critique is meant to refer to them and their often dangerous and heroic work. This is about the edit staff of a wire agency and their handling of an Iraqi national "stringer."

Ryan, of *Dead Parrot Society*, had also been in touch with Gorton (Haifa Street Update III, 2005). In that post Ryan indicated he respected Gorton's opinion, describing him as "obviously an expert" and "a straightforward guy." By this point Ryan was more restrained in his overall assessment of the controversy, observing that it was unlikely to be fully resolved (emphasis in the blog original).

After reading Gorton's analysis several times over, he seems to be consistently stating that it is possible there was collusion involved in the photo. I think he's being careful to say you can't simply discount the theory ... . I'm not sure I can think of any piece of information, actually, that would definitively answer critics.

This example is of interest here in a number of respects. The controversy concerned the way a mainstream media outlet obtained information about events in a dangerous area; that is to say, the controversy concerned journalistic practice and not the factual accuracy or interpretive validity of a news product. The extreme emotionality of the image is likely to have heightened the attention to it, as is the immediacy of its connection to the frame of the text story it accompanied: Iraq is becoming unstable in the run-up to the election. Both the critics of the Associated Press, and the critics of those critics, took note of the implications of the image regarding policy questions about the U.S. presence in Iraq. As in similar controversies over the mainstream media outlets' newsgathering practices, the focus evolved in the ongoing interaction among bloggers.

Unlike other controversies which originated in the blogosphere and spilled out into the traditional media (such as the forged National Guard memos), this one remained largely confined to the online world. The mainstream media outlet which was criticized by bloggers responded first through an anonymous source to an online magazine, and then with a brief attributed statement to an established journalism Web site. When the AP proved somewhat evasive in answering questions about its stringer's relationship to the terrorists and his/her advance knowledge of the event, blog critics and blog defenders alike drew on the technical expertise of news photographers with no connection to the image in question. Only months later, when the photograph won a Pulitzer Prize and the controversy resurfaced, did the Associated Press issue a full statement, on its Web site, describing the provenance of the image.

As in other controversies, the opinion in the blogosphere was not uniform; some bloggers provided a defense of the AP, in the form of rebuttals to the blog critics. Some bloggers were satisfied by the AP's belated statement about the photograph; others felt the criticism stood unanswered. A good deal of the material in this controversy took the form of weighing evidence, much as a court would: the question of the photographer's position relative to the terrorists, as judged from the technical characteristics of the photographic image itself and the AP's account of events leading to the creation of the image.[38]

Mainstream journalists frequently attribute information to anonymous sources. There is some measure of debate about the practice, and the Society of Professional Journalists' ethics code (Society of Professional Journalists, 1996) is equivocal about it. The code does not require journalists to name their sources but does, however, encourage transparency. These two tenets apply:

Journalists should identify sources whenever possible.

Journalists should always question sources' motives before promising anonymity.

As one would expect, the practice has both an advantage and a drawback. While promising anonymity may aid a journalist in obtaining sensitive information valuable to the public at large — the whistleblower and insider scenarios — it can also create opportunities for manipulation or distortion by the source — the spin scenario. For that reason it is unsurprising to see uses of anonymous sources criticized by bloggers.

An interesting example of this variety of blog criticism concerns a *Washington Post* story (Roig-Franzia & Hsu, 2005) on the conflict between state and federal government after Hurricane Katrina caused extensive damage to the city of New Orleans in late August 2005. By the time the story was published a good deal of finger-pointing had already occurred regarding emergency preparations for the hurricane's landfall, and much of the story's copy pertained to the conflicting assertions about response failures and accountability. It included this passage:

A senior administration official said that Bush has clear legal authority to federalize National Guard units to quell civil disturbances under the Insurrection Act and will continue to try to unify the chains of command that are split among the president, the Louisiana governor and the New Orleans mayor. Louisiana did not reach out to a multi-state mutual aid compact for assistance until Wednesday, three state and federal officials said. As of Saturday, Blanco still had not declared a state of emergency, the senior Bush official said.

The passage contained what proved to be a factual misstatement — that the Louisiana governor had not declared a state of emergency as of September 3 — and *The Washington Post* published a correction, noting that the state governor had actually declared a state of emergency on August 26. The *Post*'s own media critic noted the controversy which had developed around this misstatement in his weekly roundup story (Kurtz, 2005).

> *The Washington Post*, like many news organizations, says it is trying to crack down on the use of anonymous sources. But the paper allowed a "senior administration official" to spin the story of the slow response to Katrina — with a claim that turned out to be false ... .
>
> Liberal bloggers have unloaded on *The Post*. Wrote Arianna Huffington: "Why were the *Post* reporters so willing to blindly accept the words of an administration official who obviously had a partisan agenda — and to grant the official anonymity?"
>
> *Post* National Editor Michael Abramowitz calls the incident "a bad mistake" that happened right on deadline. "We all feel bad about that," he says. "We should not have printed the information as background information, and it should have been checked. We fell down on the desk."

Although the paper had promptly corrected the factual error, its own media critic had questioned colleagues about the incident, and its national editor had expressed regret at having failed to check the statement by an anonymous source before going to press, a number of bloggers nonetheless harshly criticized the *Post*. On *Daily Kos* (Unprofessional, 2005), Armando questioned the rationale behind granting anonymity to the source. He also argued that the factual error was fatal to the story's frame, which was that conflict between local and federal officials had delayed the emergency response (emphasis in the original).

> Finally, why would you need a source to go anonymous on a fact that was a matter of public record?
>
> The point is simple — this was horrendously bad journalism. The

fact that Blanco DID declare a state of emergency was central to the story. The fact she DID declare a state of emergency completely undermined the story ... .

Here, *The Washington Post* had nothing but the word of a BushCo official — the false word. And they ran with the story anyway.

On *Eschaton*, Duncan Black (using his pen name, Atrios) likewise faulted the practice of withholding the identity of sources (*WaPo* Follies, 2005).

The joys of carte blanche anonymous sourcing. We're protected from knowing about the dishonesty and ignorance of our public officials. Oh joy!

In another post (Period, 2005), Black discounted the possibility that the administration official had been misinformed, and argued that *The Washington Post* should reveal the identity of the source.

The only possible punishment for lying to the press is that they tell the public that, indeed, you lied to them ... . So, our press feels that it's OK to let public officials lie to the public, under the cover of anonymity, with complete and total impunity provided by the information launderers at *The Washington Post*.

A curiosity about this case is that the bloggers addressed only one of the two anonymous sources cited in the story. The paragraph immediately preceding the one with the statement attributed to the senior federal official — which became the subject of much criticism — had itself contained a quote from an anonymous state official (Roig-Franzia & Hsu, 2005). The passage containing the statement from the anonymous local source reads:

The administration sought unified control over all local police and state National Guard units reporting to the governor. Louisiana officials rejected the request after talks throughout the night, concerned that such a move would be comparable to a federal declaration of martial law. Some officials in the state suspected a political motive behind the request. "Quite frankly, if they'd been able to pull off taking it away from the locals, they then could have

blamed everything on the locals," said the source, who does not
have the authority to speak publicly.

Oddly enough, this use of another anonymous source in the same
newspaper story did not provoke similar criticism.[39]

Another example of this variety of criticism concerns a *New York
Times* story on the investigation into the public disclosure of the name
of a sometime C.I.A. operative (Johnston & Stevenson, 2005). At the
time of the story's publication, the special prosecutor's inquiry into the
disclosure of Valerie Plame's identity in a 2003 syndicated political
column had generated a good deal of speculation about how her name
had become known to the columnist. As the special prosecutor had not
yet completed his inquiry and ongoing investigations are supposed to
remain confidential, this story was based largely on an anonymous
source. This can be seen in its lede:

> Karl Rove, the White House senior adviser, spoke with the
> columnist Robert D. Novak as he was preparing an article in July
> 2003 that identified a C.I.A. officer who was undercover, someone
> who has been officially briefed on the matter said.

Some bloggers took the position that the *Times* was being "spun"
by the White House. On *Liberal Oasis*, writer Bill Scher gave his post
the caustic title, "*NY Times* = Suckers" (2005). Scher linked the *Times*
story on the Plame investigation, and objected to its use of an
anonymous source.

> But more likely, the punditocracy will ignore the pattern that's
> emerging, and flock to today's *NY Times* report, claiming that Karl
> Rove didn't leak Plame's name to Bob Novak, but Novak told it
> to Rove. It is stupefying that the *NY Times* would print this story.
> It clearly comes from a single anonymous White House source, at
> a time when all White House officials are refusing to answer
> questions publicly. Basically, the *NY Times* is picking up where its
> own Judith Miller left off — giving the White House free ink to
> distribute its talking points.

Scher continued by elaborating on his assertion that this case of a mainstream outlet's use of an anonymous source was the spin scenario (deliberate manipulation of the journalist by the source) rather than the insider scenario (disclosure of accurate information too sensitive, at the time, to be attributed). He closed the post by reiterating the claim which some may find odd: that *The New York Times* was knowingly providing assistance to the Bush administration (emphasis in the original).

> And we know that nobody in the White House has been forthright about what happened, and willing to answer any questions in the public about it. They don't deserve the opportunity to make their case through self-serving leaks of selective info. Their credibility is shot.

> And since it is letting them, the *NY Times'[s] credibility is shot[,]* too.

On *Eschaton,* Duncan Black linked Sher's post and quoted several passages in the *Times* article making reference to the anonymous source. Black did not elaborate, other than to repeat the title of his post (Ridiculous *New York Times,* 2005) in its first sentence.

> ... someone who has been officially briefed on the matter said.

> ... the person who has been briefed on the matter said...

> ... the person who has been briefed on the matter said.

> The person who provided the information about Mr. Rove's conversation with Mr. Novak declined to be identified, citing requests by Mr. Fitzgerald [the special prosecutor] that no one discuss the case. The person discussed the matter in the belief that Mr. Rove was truthful in saying that he had not disclosed Ms. Wilson's identity.[40]

Bloggers sometimes argue that the mainstream press fails to run enough backgrounder or follow-up stories after spot news has been reported. As media criticism, this is a question of depth; the concern is that spot news alone often will not sufficiently inform the public about an issue. For the news outlets, this is an issue of allocation of newsgathering resources. No doubt the attention-getting value of spot news in a crowded media market is a factor in the news outlets' decision — "if it bleeds, it leads" has become something of a cynical axiom. Nonetheless, the need for relevant but less sensational reportage is apparent; bloggers sometimes fault the mainstream press in this regard.

Two good examples of this type of criticism can be found on *Rantingprofs*. A post titled, "The Sunnis" (2005) complimented *The Washington Post* for sending reporters out of Baghdad to gather a sense of Sunni attitudes toward a referendum on the proposed Iraqi constitution. Dauber linked one of three such stories the *Post* had run in the days preceding the vote (Fainaru & Shadid, 2005), but devoted her post to the need for similar background reporting (capitalization and punctuation as in the original).

> I'll say it again: we don't need good news for the sake of good news, we need fuller, broader, deeper reporting from Iraq, reporting that goes outside the limited range of the same tired reports on what blew up today in Baghdad and Mosul. I am not suggesting that the media should not report on what happens in terms of spot news. I'm suggesting there has to be more than that. And if in reading these three articles you thought, "wow, I didn't know X, or Y, or Z" or if you thought, "wow, I feel like I've got a better grip on things now than I did before," that would seem to prove the point.

"No Gloom or Doom" (2005) was Dauber's commentary on a later *Washington Post* story about the end of Ramadan in Iraq (Spinner & Sebti, 2005). The story was datelined Baghdad and began with a description of residents enjoying outdoor activities to mark the festival of Eid al-Fitr; near the end, it included a similar description of Mosul. Dauber took particular note of the passage concerning Mosul, and quoted from the story.

> But my larger point is that it isn't until very, very deep in the article that we get to this:
>
>> In Mosul, a northern city where violence has increased this year, residents said they could hardly recognize their

neighborhoods. Children frolicked in the streets, and families came together, visiting relatives. Iraqi police and army patrols kept a heavy presence in the city, which has been relatively quiet for 10 days, and shops, usually shuttered by the time the moon rises, stayed open until 11 on Wednesday night.

Muhammed Ibrahim, 22, a college student, said the recent constitutional referendum buoyed residents and made them feel safer about going outside during Eid. "Nothing happened so far. We hope this will last and they don't interrupt our happiness," he said.

Dauber then made her criticism explicit: such a change in conditions in Mosul, in the wake of the constitutional referendum, merited more extensive coverage.

That's a pretty big statement of change about a major city where reporting of violence has been pretty regular. Where's the major story reporting on the changes in Mosul?[41]

Writing and Editing

Often, blog criticism will focus on the creation of the news content as a text; it thus deals with the writing of the copy and the editorial oversight before the story is distributed. Such criticism may touch on the choice of source material to include or omit, the conflation of opinion and straight news reporting in one story, the suitability of a story's format or structure to the topic, or the editorial decisions about the trustworthiness of particular sources.

An interesting example of the first variety can be found on the eponymous blog of writer Michelle Malkin. Her post titled, "Cpl. Jeffrey B. Starr: What the NY Times Left Out" (2005) was a criticism of the reporter's choice of excerpt from a letter left by a deceased soldier. The story in question (Dao, 2005) was a lengthy series of profiles of soldiers who had been killed in action in the Iraq war, accompanied by a number of photographs, charts, and a timeline of events in the war; it was part of the extensive mainstream press material generated when the military casualties reached a total of 2,000. Malkin briefly noted the frame of the story, indicated by the headline's characterization of the 2,000 number as a "grim mark," but her criticism centered on the profile of one particular soldier. She quoted the *Times* story's reference to a letter left behind by Cpl. Starr.

> Another member of the 1/5, Cpl. Jeffrey B. Starr, rejected a $24,000 bonus to re-enlist. Corporal Starr believed strongly in the war, his father said, but was tired of the harsh life and nearness of death in Iraq. So he enrolled at Everett Community College near his parents' home in Snohomish, Wash., planning to study psychology after his enlistment ended in August.
>
> But he died in a firefight in Ramadi on April 30 during his third tour in Iraq. He was 22.
>
> Sifting through Corporal Starr's laptop computer after his death, his father found a letter to be delivered to the marine's girlfriend. "I kind of predicted this," Corporal Starr wrote of his own death. "A third time just seemed like I'm pushing my chances."

Those two sentences were all of the soldier's letter which was quoted in the *Times* article. Malkin described her contact with the deceased soldier's uncle, then reproduced his letter to her. Of interest here is that the letter included a larger excerpt of Cpl. Starr's letter, which his uncle felt put the quotation in a substantially different light from the *Times* story (syntax, punctuation, and emphasis as in the blog original).

> Last night, I received a letter from Corporal Starr's uncle, Timothy Lickness. He wanted you to know the rest of the story — and the parts of Corporal Starr's letter that the *Times* failed to include:
>
>> Yesterday's *New York Times* on-line edition carried the story of the 2000 Iraq US military death[s]. It grabbed my attention as the picture they used with the headline was that of my nephew, Cpl. Jeffrey B. Starr, USMC ... .
>>
>> Several months after Jeffrey was killed his laptop computer was returned to his parents who found a letter in it that was addressed to his girlfriend and was intended to be found only if he did not return alive. It is a most poignant letter and filled with personal feelings he had for his girlfriend. But of

importance to the rest of us was his expression of how he felt about putting his life at risk for this cause. He said it with grace and maturity.

He wrote: "Obviously if you are reading this then I have died in Iraq. I kind of predicted this, that is why I'm writing this in November. A third time just seemed like I'm pushing my chances. I don't regret going, everybody dies but few get to do it for something as important as freedom. It may seem confusing why we are in Iraq, it's not to me. I'm here helping these people, so that they can live the way we live. Not have to worry about tyrants or vicious dictators. To do what they want with their lives. To me that is why I died. Others have died for my freedom, now this is my mark."

What Jeffrey said is important. Americans need to understand that most of those who are or have been there understand what's going on. It would honor Jeffrey's memory if you would publish the rest of his story.

Malkin added a terse comment on the reporter's choice of words from the soldier's letter.

As for the *Times*, what do I always say? It's always more informative for what it leaves out than for what it puts in.

As have others, this post illustrates the interactivity between bloggers and their audience, and the essential contribution that interactivity can make to the media criticism. It is of particular interest here in that this post did not question the accuracy of the quotation which appeared in the mainstream press story, but rather, the reporter's choice of which part of his source document to include and the context in which the pulled quotation was couched.[42]

The preceding example of blog criticism concerned a mainstream journalist's judgment of available source material to omit from the finished story. A rather intriguing example concerns an editor's decision to insert material into a guest-written opinion piece. Mark Moore, an American professor of English working in Mexico, noticed an unusual editor's note prefacing an opinion column on *The New*

York Times Web site; he commented about this on his blog, *Mark in Mexico*, in a post titled, "*New York Times* Blows One — BIG TIME!" (2005; minor punctuation discrepancies corrected.)

> In an op-ed column in *The New York Times* today, Phillip Carter wrote, "Imagine my surprise the other day when I received orders to report to Fort Campbell, Ky., next Sunday," and "My recent call-up to active duty is the precursor to a 'surprise tour of Iraq.'"
>
> No, wait! That's not what he wrote, at all. And then the newsprint versions which had not yet been printed and the on-line version of the column [were] yanked and replaced...

Moore linked the online version of the piece (Carter, 2005a), and quoted the editor's note (syntax as in original).

> The Op-Ed page in some copies of Wednesday's newspaper carried an incorrect version of the below article about military recruitment. The article also briefly appeared on NYTimes.com before it was removed. The writer, an Army reserve officer, did not say "Imagine my surprise the other day when I received orders to report to Fort Campbell, Ky., next Sunday," nor did he characterize his recent call-up to active duty as the precursor to a "surprise tour of Iraq." That language was added by an editor and was to have been removed before the article was published. Because of a production error, it was not. The *Times* regrets the error. A corrected version of the article appears below.

It is useful to note that the version of the column archived by LexisNexis (Carter, 2005b) omits the editor's note entirely; at the time of this writing, the version available on the *Times* Web site (Carter, 2005a) does include it. Both versions describe the author of the piece, Phillip Carter, as "a lawyer and Army reserve officer who was recently called up to active duty for Operation Iraqi Freedom." Neither includes the text the note described as having been "added by an editor."

Many bloggers and *New York Times* readers found the editor's note to be insufficient explanation for copy which had been inserted into Carter's text. On *Daily Pundit*, novelist Bill Quick made his displeasure clear (NYT Caught Lying Again, 2005; emphasis in the original).

> The only thing you need to decipher this bit of self-aggrandizing code masquerading as a "correction" is to ask yourself, [a]n *editor* added these statements in *quotes*? Why? And they were supposed to be "removed" before the piece was printed? Why add the false quotes in the first place, then?

Political Animal is a blog attached to the *Washington Monthly* Web site. Kevin Drum saw the insertion as unprofessional behavior by editorial staff (Oops..., 2005). Drum caught another error in the author identification appended to both versions of the article (emphasis in the original).

> This is sure an embarrassing editor's note. I sometimes think that op-ed editors don't realize they aren't editing straight news. They should never even have *tried* to put those words in Phil's mouth, let alone allowed them to accidentally appear in print.

> Even now they don't quite have it right. It's true that Phil was "recently called up to active duty," but under the circumstances that still makes it sound like he was called up involuntarily. He wasn't. He volunteered.

The incident generated enough complaints that the *Times's* public editor devoted an entire column to it (Calame, 2005). He had spoken to Phillip Carter, and confirmed that the controversial passages had, in fact, been added to Carter's manuscript by the *Times* editorial staff. He also confirmed the persistent error in the author identification; Carter told him he had volunteered for active duty. In Calame's account of events, Carter objected to the insertions when asked for his approval, but the "production error," mentioned in the editor's note, came about in this way:

> In subsequent telephone conversations, Captain Carter told me, "I indicated I would pull the piece before having textual references added." David Shipley, the editor in charge of the Op-Ed pages, confirms the officer's threat. So the version of the article with the

suggested "surprise" phrases [i.e., the passages inserted by a Times editor] in the text was cast aside. It was then agreed that a reference to active duty would be included in the author identification that ran with the article ... .

So Captain Carter, who has contributed articles to several publications, approved the final version without the "surprise" phrases — a clearance that is standard practice on the Op-Ed pages. But then came the mistake that the editor's note called a "production error." The editor in charge of the piece accidentally discarded, or "spiked" in the paper's jargon, the cleared final version and instead put the previously rejected copy with the "surprise" phrases on the track for publication.

Calame went on to describe how Carter noticed the unauthorized additions to his column when it was posted on the NYTimes.com Web site, and immediately called the news desk to complain.[43]

The practice of providing pre-written text for constituent or op-ed letters has become a staple of the political arena. Political action committees and campaign organizations of all persuasions have adopted this technique as a way of generating favorable publicity for their cause. With either direct mailings or web pages, the advocates make available to their potential supporters pre-written letters or talking points which the supporters are encouraged to send to their legislative representatives or to newspapers. The odds are good that the reader has been exposed to such material on a number of occasions, and perhaps has even participated in such public relations campaigns when the material was consistent with his or her own viewpoint.

The practice has come to be known by the derogatory term, astroturfing. The etymology of slang terms is not always certain, but it would appear that astroturfing is a play on the metaphor grass roots, referring to a spontaneous expression of a sentiment shared among the populace. When the expression is deliberately stimulated through this sort of communication strategy, it will often be labeled by critics as astroturf. Needless to say, the exact point at which facilitation of participation in the political process becomes astroturfing seems to be highly influenced by the critic's personal viewpoint on the subject of the campaign! A more serious criticism, though, can be that the campaign has created a substantially inaccurate perception of public opinion, with a potential effect on a collective decision process.

The practice is of interest in this context in that, apart from any commentary on the immediate subject of the astroturfed letters, bloggers often question the editorial judgment of newspapers in running the letters. A detailed example can be found in Michelle Malkin's post, "Astroturf Alert: Another MoveOn.org Mail Blitz" (2005). She linked and quoted the talking points supplied by MoveOn through its Web site, concerning the controversy over the filibustered judicial nominations. Malkin then performed a test of the letter-writing campaign's impact.

> So, I did a little Nexis search to see if any letters to the editor using the MoveOn talking points have been published recently. Lo and behold, the astroturf is in full bloom! Here's a sample that slipped by the hawk-eyed letters editors of some of the nation's esteemed newspapers.

She followed this with several examples of the astroturfed letter appearing in regional newspapers. At the end of the post she linked to other bloggers who had likewise pointed out astroturf campaigns. It is interesting to note that she included a blogger with a political viewpoint diametrically opposed to hers.

On his blog, *The Daily Kos*, Markos Moulitsas had posted a substantially similar criticism (Stupid Papers and GOP Astroturf, 2004) during the closing months of the 2004 presidential campaign. The post is very brief, and Kos did not elaborate his media criticism beyond the post's bluntly-worded title. Just as Malkin had done with the MoveOn site, Kos quoted a passage from talking points provided by the Bush campaign organization. Rather than quoting from newspapers which ran astroturfed letters, Kos simply encouraged his readers to do their own search.

> Now google that entire phrase, and see the results. About 60 newspapers have run that letter ... .

As a political strategy, letter-writing campaigns predate

computer-mediated network communication. The exact nature of such campaigns seems to have been changed by the development of the online world, in a number of respects. The scope of an astroturf attempt can be vastly larger now, with regard both to geographic reach and the volume of letters generated; a perusal of such web pages will suggest this. The cost for organizations to run an astroturf campaign is lower, as is the cost for an individual to participate in it; this is to say that buying server space can be cheaper than a bulk mailing, and sending an e-mail can be less time-consuming than sending a letter. As the preceding examples show, the capability of modern search engines have forced a much higher degree of transparency onto a time-honored political strategy. Perhaps the most interesting point, in this context, is that there seems to be a tacit agreement among blog critics that mainstream outlets ought be more vigilant against astroturfed letter campaigns.[44]

A familiar criticism of the mainstream news media is that opinion and straight reporting are often conflated in a single story. The concern that the editorial distinction between interpretation and fact is being blurred by no means originated in the blogosphere, but such critique is evident in it. A concise example of this can be found on the group blog, *PoliPundit*, in a post titled "Pravda-Media Regresses to Sand Box Mentality" (2005). Jayson Javitz, an investment manager and lawyer, took issue with an Associated Press story (Benac, 2005) about a public exchange of insults between Representative Charles Rangel and Vice-president Dick Cheney. He quoted the lede of the Associated Press story; the "throwing stones" metaphor also appeared in the story's headline.

> There he goes again. The vice president has been throwing stones, and he's not the least bit sorry about it.

Javitz made his criticism with an economy of words. It is interesting to note the secondary orality (conventions of spoken language, represented in print text) in his comment.

> Okaaaay.
> Um, that's *not* an editorial.

That's actually intended as a news item ... .
Cute, huh?

The interviewing style of Deborah Solomon, a writer for *The New York Times Magazine,* drew a similar criticism. The piece in question (Solomon, 2005) was her interview of Jeff Gannon, a reporter for Talon News Service who had resigned in the wake of a controversy over his access to the White House press briefings and some embarrassing disclosures about his sex life. John Hinderaker, on *Power Line,* quoted a number of the questions Solomon put to Gannon in a post with a title implying his criticism (Is It Parody?, 2005). He prefaced the sequence with a sardonic comment of his own, aimed at Solomon, and closed with another (minor correction in capitalization).

> Solomon proceeds to show Gannon how a "real journalist" asks fair, unbiased questions:
>
> > Q. Or rather is [Jeff Gannon] the pseudonym under which you gained access to White House press briefings for two years, until your identity was revealed. Why do you think they let you in?
> >
> > Q. Are you suggesting that Bobby Eberle, the Republican operative who hired you to shill for his GOPUSA under the guise of his Talon News service, has special access at the White House?...
> >
> > Q. What are we supposed to make of the fact that before reporting for Talon News, you had never had a job in journalism and apparently earned your living running a gay escort service?
> >
> > Q. Do you find it hard to be a gay conservative in this country in light of the right-wing hostility to gay rights?
>
> You really couldn't make this stuff up.

Political science graduate student Brendan Nyhan essentially agreed about the tone of the questions, in a post on his eponymous blog (Deborah Solomon is Harsh, 2005).

Do Deborah Solomon's interviews in *The New York Times Magazine* make anyone else uncomfortable? ... I want a more aggressive press corps, but I still believe that interview subjects deserve respect, and some of her questions are basically personal attacks.

One of his readers drew law professor Glenn Reynolds's attention to a *New York Times* story (Becker & Sanger, 2005a) about the nomination of Paul Wolfowitz as president of the World Bank. Reynolds linked the story on the *Times* Web site and quoted passages from it in his *InstaPundit* post, adding emphasis to point to particular wording ("Elisabeth", 2005; emphasis and ellipsis in the blog original).

> President Bush said today that he would nominate Paul D. Wolfowitz, the deputy secretary of defense and one of the chief architects of the invasion of Iraq two years ago, to become president of the World Bank.

> The announcement, coming on the heels of the appointment of John R. Bolton as the new American ambassador to the United Nations, was greeted with quiet anguish in those foreign capitals where the Iraq conflict and its aftermath remain deply unpopular, and where Mr. Wolfowitz's drive to spread democracy around the world has been viewed with some suspicion ... .

> Despite the displeasure of some diplomats who had hoped that the administration would appoint a person without the almost radioactive reputation of a committed ideologue, they said that they expected Mr. Wolfowitz to receive the approval of the World Bank's board of directors in time for Mr. Wolfenson's departure in May.

Apart from adding emphasis to the quoted passages, Reynolds added only a terse comment, pointing out what he saw as a conflation of interpretation and factual reporting.

> And note that this article isn't even captioned "News Analysis" — it's supposed to be, you know, straight reporting.

As a sidenote to this example of blog criticism, there is something peculiar and, to this author, disturbing about *The New York Times* story in question. The link in the *InstaPundit* post pointed to a story on the *Times* Web site (Becker & Sanger, 2005a); this author followed the link and verified that the passages Reynolds had quoted in his post appeared verbatim in it. When this author searched for the story in the LexisNexis archive, the closest match he could find was a substantially different version of the story by the same authors, with the same dateline but the next day's publication date, and with a reworded headline (Becker & Sanger, 2005b). The language Reynolds had questioned did not appear in the LexisNexis version. When this author then looked for the story on *The New York Times* Web site using its own search engine (rather than following the link from the *InstaPundit* post), only the revised version (Becker & Sanger, 2005b) was available. The revised version contained no indication that it was a correction to the original version, or that the original story had been retracted.

By way of contrast, Cori Dauber paid a compliment to another *New York Times* reporter for a story about an Army enlistee preparing to serve in Iraq (Davey, 2006). The title of Dauber's post (Just the Story, 2006) gives a good sense of its thesis: the story is an exemplar of straight reporting. In its entirety, the post is this (syntax and capitalization as in the blog original).

> You can read this anyway you want, all the reporter does is tell the story of this brand new Army private about to go to Iraq, without, in my opinion, bias or agenda getting in the way.
>
> This is the Reddest of Red state families, and I'm sure to many of the *Times* '[s] readers this kid will seem tragically naive, but that's there if you want to see it, it isn't pushed into your face so that you're forced to see it as an inevitable interpretation.
>
> Isn't that what reporting should be? Here's what happened, here's what I saw of these people, now make of it what you will.[45]

While not as common, some blog criticism concerns the structure or format of mainstream news products. A blogger may take the position that the sequencing of factual information in a story does not reflect the relative importance of the facts presented; that is to say, the story does not follow the traditional inverted pyramid structure (News Style, n.d.; Porter & Ferris, 1988, p. 374) of placing the most important facts near the beginning and relegating less consequential facts to later in the story. In essence, this is a criticism of the journalist's execution of a standard structure. A more complex criticism, occasionally found on blogs, is that there is a fundamental mismatch between the genre of the story and the nature of the meaning it is meant to convey. In essence, this is an objection that there is a logical mismatch between the format and the content.

An instance of the first sort is when the blogger argues that the reporter or editor has "buried the lede," which is to say that the most newsworthy dimension of the story appears relatively late in the text. A straightforward example of this can be found on *Hoystory*, the personal blog of Matthew Hoy, a veteran journalist working as a page designer for a metropolitan newspaper. In a post titled "Finally" (2005), Hoy critiqued a *New York Times* story (Hernandez, 2005) reporting a "dirty trick" in a tight race for a Senate seat from Maryland.

The critique took the form of a fisking (Fisk, n.d.); Hoy reproduced passages from the *Times* story in sequence, and interlaced his own critical comments about them. As is common in fisking, the language was informal and blunt, imputing motives to the creator of the mainstream outlet's story. Hoy began by linking the story, and indicating his thesis that the format of the story was inappropriate for the news event it described (minor spelling error corrected; emphasis in the blog original).

> Today's *New York Times* finally runs an article on the Democratic Senatorial Campaign Committee's illegal accessing of Maryland Lt. Gov. Michael Steele's credit report, more than two weeks after the story first broke ... .

> The story is written as a horse race piece and not a hard news crime/scandal piece. You don't find out that there is a criminal investigation until the *seventh* graf. Talk about burying the lede.

Hoy then quoted the headline and lede of the story, adding his criticism to both.

The headline:

Democrats Are on Defensive in Maryland Senate Race

This headline is written to guarantee that you don't read any farther. It communicates nothing. It's boring. Dull. You probably don't want to read the story. The lede:

National Republicans, who face an uphill battle in their efforts to capture the open United States Senate seat in heavily Democratic Maryland next year, are trying to exploit potential legal problems that Democrats are now suddenly facing in that race.

Ah, you made it past the headline, let us see if we can put you to sleep before you go any further. "Potential legal problems?" Boring. Read no further.

The Republicans are seizing on a disclosure that two researchers at the Democratic Senatorial Campaign Committee improperly obtained the credit report of Lt. Gov. Michael Steele, a Republican who is considering a bid for the Senate seat.

Dang! You read the next paragraph. This is a soft-peddled lede. We've got to mention this, but we would rather you not think too hard on it. You see, they "improperly obtained the credit report." If this were Republicans we would've used the term "illegally."

Hoy continued to reproduce paragraphs from the *Times* story in sequence, adding his tart comments, such as these.

Have you forgot about the credit report yet? Good. See, nothing more to read here. It's just a he said/she said political thing. You can stop reading now ... .

This is the obligatory, who is this Steele guy and why is he running paragraph. You can stop reading now. Please ... .

See, this is really not important, because we here at the *Times* have been ignoring it for a couple of weeks. If it were important, we would've told you sooner ... .

> Why are you still reading this article? You see, everything is fine. The Democrats are terribly sorry about the whole incident, now go back to eating your breakfast. Is that an Einstein Bros. bagel? Are you going to eat it?...

> See, we talked to the prosecutor. Covering all our bases. Could you please stop reading now?

At that point in his fisking of the *Times* story, Hoy had arrived at the fact which he felt should have been the lede: there was an ongoing criminal investigation into a substantial violation of the law.

> It is illegal to obtain a credit report under false pretenses. The maximum penalty for doing so is two years in prison and a $250,000 fine.

> Ugh. Pretty serious crime, huh? If Republicans had done this, we certainly would've put this up higher.

Along a similar line, Cori Dauber questioned the sequencing of information contained in a *Washington Post* story (Knickmeyer, 2005c) about the role religion might play in an upcoming Iraqi election. The title of the *Rantingprofs* post makes the criticism apparent: "All the Good Stuff Gets Buried" (2005). She began by linking the story, and setting up the complaint that the reporter had not supplied crucial factual support for what Dauber understood to be the story's frame (minor spelling error corrected; emphasis as in the blog original).

> The *Post* follows up with a second article on preparations for the Iraqi elections today, by a different reporter, and the central theme of the article is the role religion is playing in electioneering ... . The point seems to be, therefore, that this is a bad thing, something we should not just disapprove of but be worried about, but she doesn't articulate *why* that's so.

> Islamic societies simply don't separate Mosque and State in the same way we brightline Church and State — not unless that brightline is imposed by a strongman imposing it from above. So the question isn't whether campaign arguments are being made by

clerics. The question is whether those arguments are being made in favor of hardline Islamic parties, anti-democratic parties, parties that would use the democratic process for anti-democratic purposes, like suppressing the rights of women or religious minorities. And whether that's the case or not is information the reporter does not choose to share with us.

Dauber went on to single out a descriptive passage which had been relegated to a subordinate position in the story.

> Look what's in paragraph 7:
>
> > At another Sunni mosque, in northern Baghdad, Aluned Hassan Taha used Friday prayers to ask insurgents to release four Western peace activists and humanitarian workers, including one American, kidnapped two weeks ago.
>
> A Sunni imam uses Friday prayers to have his congregation pray for Western aid workers? I'd say that's pretty big news, wouldn't you?

Dauber explicitly made the complaint that this story had buried its lede. She carefully elaborated on what she saw as the significance of information the reporter had chosen to place at the end of the story (emphasis in the original).

> And look what ends up in the very last paragraph:
>
> > While competition among factions has been intense, and occasionally violent, coalition-building will be the theme for the post-election period, according to a Western official who spoke to reporters in Baghdad on Friday. The Shiite alliance now in power is not expected to win a majority of seats and will probably have to seek allies to form a new government, said the official, who spoke on condition of anonymity.
>
> Shouldn't that be the very *first* paragraph, the lead, the *frame* for the story?...There's a saying that an election doesn't make a democracy. It's the second election that makes the democracy, the handover of power. And here this reporter is suggesting that those in power aren't going to be able to hold onto power.

> That's a stunning piece of evidence that, at the political level, the Iraq project is working, even with clerical participation.
>
> And it's buried.
>
> Worse than buried, it's just dumped out there with no explanation given[,] whatsoever.[46]

In the mainstream news media, a conventional way of reporting the popular opinion is through brief quotations from a number of ordinary people obtained in ordinary situations. These are sometimes called streeters, a shortening of man-in-the-street interviews. While obviously a staple of broadcast news, streeters also appear in print news stories. Usually there is little or no explanation provided about how the journalist selected those particular individuals to interview for the story; the tacit assumption would seem to be that they are a fair representation of public opinion in some general sense.

Cori Dauber has developed a critique of this convention over a number of posts. The logical basis for her criticism is that there is no warrant for the assumption that the prevalence of a particular opinion in the streeters of a news product matches the degree to which that opinion is actually found in the population at large. Put into the technical jargon of survey methodology, streeters are grab or convenience samples. Survey researchers take care to use random sampling in selecting their respondents to the survey questions; when the respondents are selected randomly from the population one wishes to describe, the relative proportions of an opinion or preference found in the sample can reasonably be assumed to be those in the entire population (for a readable explanation of this point, see Babbie, 1990, pp. 75-76). Reputable public opinion pollsters always use some form of random sampling to arrive at the familiar percentages of various viewpoints attributed to the public as a whole.

Dauber has observed that a distinct format of print news story has evolved, based around streeters. She dubbed this the "restaurant story"; hence the title of her critique of a *New York Times* story (Gettleman, 2005) about Iraqi civilians' attitudes toward an upcoming election. She began "The Return of the Restaurant Story" (2005) with a concise description of the story format, the logical deficiency inherent in it, and the inadequacy of it as journalism (emphasis as in the blog original).

> I've written before about what I like to call, "the Restaurant Story," a *New York Times* specialty.
>
> When the polls show attitudes that you don't like (that is, attitudes that go against the narrative you've been pushing), not to worry!
>
> Get out there and interview some people — preferably (when doing a domestic story) in restaurants.
>
> Then report (entirely accurately) that people hold different opinions on the matter at hand. Provide great quotes representing both sides. Maybe even provide more quotes from those whose opinions aren't in the majority (if we were to look at scientific polling data.)
>
> Just make sure you never, ever, report on how you decided who[m] to talk to, how many people you actually spoke with, or — and this is most important of all — how you chose which quotes to use.
>
> Doing that might make it clear that you're nowhere close to random sampling and nowhere close to random selection of quotes, that your quotes were selectively chosen, and couldn't stand up to the polling data. After all, the whole point is to provide people with something vivid and colorful to compare with those cold, impersonal numbers.

Dauber then applied this generic critique of the format to the particular example of it from *The New York Times* (Gettleman, 2005).

> Start (of course) with the guy who won't vote:
>
> > Hejaz Hazim, a computer engineer who could not find a job in computers and now cleans clothes, slammed his iron into a dress shirt the other day and let off a burst of steam about the coming election.
> >
> > "This election is bogus," Mr. Hazim said. "There is no drinking water in this city. There is no security. Why should I vote?"

Follow with the guy who will:

> Across town in the Shiite stronghold of Sadr City, a grocer
> called Abu Allah stood behind his pyramids of fruit and said
> that no matter what, he was going to the polls. "Even if there's
> a bomb in my polling place," he said, "I will go in it."

Explain the importance of the division:

> The biggest chasm seems to be between the most powerful
> groups in Iraq: the Shiites and the Sunnis. Every single Shiite
> interviewed for this article said he or she planned to vote.
> Though there are a few Sunni leaders running for office, all the
> Sunnis interviewed, except one, said they were going to
> boycott.

Dauber then pointed out the problem with the use of streeters to
support that summary interpretation (emphasis as in the
original).

> Note, now, that there is no indication of how the interviewees were
> selected, where they were found, who they were, what
> neighborhoods they live in (which matters), what their
> backgrounds are. The implication is that the *Times* just randomly
> grabbed Sunnis off the street — the way trained pollsters would.
> But while that's the implication the *Times* is trying to leave us
> with, there's no promise to that effect, and no particular reason to
> believe it's the case given that their findings are so radically in
> contrast with every single scientific poll that's been conducted.

> Not that you would ever know that if your single source of news
> was the *New York Times*. Which doesn't seem interested, near as
> I can tell, in reporting on scientific polls.

Dauber noted that, in this story, there was a qualified acknowledgment
that this way of gauging public opinion had inherent limitations.

They continue:

> Granted, the opinions of 50 to 60 people, all told, hardly
> constitute a scientific sample. But they are revealing.

This was an unsatisfying explanation, to Dauber (syntax and emphasis as in the blog original).

> Well, that's more of an admission than we usually get out of the *Times* about the nature of these articles, but in fact, *why should* we believe they're revealing? They might be *interesting,* but <u>if we're comparing an article such as this with a poll, I'll take the poll every time. At a minimum, it should be the obligation of the reporter at this point to inform the reader that polling data is publicly available.</u>

> No such admission appears to be forthcoming.

> Instead we get more quotes. And from those who aren't planning to vote — the side the polls say is the minority!

A brief mention of the scientific polls was placed near the end of the story, prompting a mildly sarcastic response from Dauber.

> But look! What's this?

>> According to a survey released this week in a Baghdad newspaper, two-thirds of respondents in the capital said they would vote in the election, which also includes provincial races. Half said they would cast their ballot for religious parties, half for secular. The poll did not break down results by sect or ethnicity.

Dauber concluded her critique by noting the subordinate position in which the mention of polling results was placed in the story, and that those results fundamentally contradicted the frame of the story (syntax and emphasis as in the blog original).

> <u>And it only took 50 (fifty) paragraphs,</u> and a discussion of ethnic loyalty in voting patterns. <u>No worries. I'm sure everyone who read that article made it down that far, and understood the implications immediately.</u>

> <u>But if a scientific poll says that two-thirds plan to vote, then the</u> *Times* <u>interviews really aren't that revealing at all, are they? And</u>

in fact it's difficult to see what the point of the entire article is, unless it's to say, well, sure there are these nifty polls floating around out there, but we think our man-in-the-street interviews are better, more informative, more predictive.

But if that's their argument — they should make it up front.

Dauber reprised and sharpened this critique in another post, a few months later (What to Do When the Polls Don't Go Your Way (2005). She linked a *USA Today* story (Slavin, 2005), reporting the findings of a nationwide poll of Iraqis on their views of the current situation in their country and their expectations for the future, in the wake of the January 2005 election. Dauber quoted the summary paragraph, near the beginning of the story, and followed with a terse comment on the poll's findings (emphasis added by Dauber in the blog original).

> The survey of 1,967 Iraqis was conducted Feb. 27-March 5, after Iraq held its first free elections in half a century in January. According to the poll, 62% say the country is headed in the right direction and 23% say it is headed in the wrong direction. That is the widest spread recorded in seven polls by the group, says Stuart Krusell, IRI director of operations for Iraq. In September, 43% of Iraqis thought the country was headed in the wrong direction and 42% thought it was headed in the right direction. The IRI is a non-partisan, U.S. taxpayer-funded group that promotes democracy abroad.

Wow. That's pretty positive, huh?

Dauber then linked her restaurant story post described above and reproduced some passages from it. She noted the appearance of a lengthy restaurant story (Worth, 2005) in that day's edition of *The New York Times* (syntax and emphasis as in the blog original).

> So, with yet another positive poll of Iraqis out, it was fairly predictable that there would suddenly be a piece centered on efforts to "sense" the feeling on the Iraqi street appearing in the *Times*. Just so long as those efforts didn't involve actual scientific polling methods.

Sure enough, today we get, "Many Iraqis Losing Hope That Politics Will Yield Real Change."

The piece starts with the requisite quote from the unhappy single Iraqi, and boy, kudos to the reporter, he really found himself a spectacularly unhappy Iraqi.

Dauber quoted the passage from the *Times* story describing the disgruntled Iraqi, then went on to note what she felt was a disturbing and counterfactual assertion by the *Times* reporter (syntax and emphasis as in the blog original).

What's amazing is what comes next. <u>It displays either a stunning lack of awareness of what's been going on in Iraq for, well, months and months, or is simply a bald-faced lie</u> — and a pretty damn[ed] bad one, since even if reporters for the *Times* don't have Google (which I admit, there are days I begin to suspect that) they have to know that their readers do have it.

He writes:

<u>Nothing like a scientific poll is possible yet in Iraq.</u> But as the national assembly's first brief meeting came and went, broadcast into thousands of Iraqi homes on television, a sampling of street opinion in two Iraqi cities found a widespread dismay and even anger that the elections have not yet translated into a new government.

Dauber refuted the reporter's assertion that rigorous polling was impossible in Iraq by linking five separate polls which had been conducted in 2003, 2004, and 2005; they included polls by Zogby International and *USA Today*/CNN/Gallup. She then addressed the reporter's contention, based on the streeters he had conducted, that the Shia were pessimistic (syntax and emphasis as in the blog original).

One could argue there flaws in these polls. But then they would be flawed scientific polls. Not non-existent scientific polls.

Back to the reporter:

<u>The interviews</u> — which included members of Iraq's major

religious and ethnic groups — indicated in particular a <u>striking sense of disillusionment among Shiites,</u> who make up 60 percent of Iraq's population but were brutally suppressed under the rule of Saddam Hussein.

Dauber noted that the reporter's contention was flatly contradicted by the IRI poll reported by *USA Today* (Slavin, 2005), and explained the disparity by the methodological weakness of the restaurant story format (syntax and emphasis as in the original).

> Now, it's entirely possible that those who were most excited about voting are the most angry that a government hasn't been formed. But in the IRI poll, they are also the most positive about the future.
>
> How to reconcile those two? Well, the poll data [are] fairly fresh, taken up until March 5th. Is it really possible that the Shia have become so frustrated with the extra week's wrangling that they've become disillusioned with the entire process and given up?
>
> Or is it more likely that that's why we put our faith in scientific polling, and not reporters wandering around on the street ... . Because <u>while the poll shows 62% are positive overall, 66% of the Shia in the south are positive.</u>
>
> That is not a "striking sense of disillusionment."[47]

The ethics code of the Society of Professional Journalists (1996) requires that newsworkers exercise due diligence in verifying the accuracy of information they put into their products. The first point under the code's "Seek Truth and Report It" tenet imposes this requirement:

> Journalists should test the accuracy of information from all sources and exercise care to avoid inadvertent error.

It seems fair to observe that, as a practical matter, under actual working conditions, this will often involve some assessment of the trustworthiness of particular sources. Publication deadlines and competitive pressures from other outlets are likely to limit the time in which the diligence can be exercised. It would be unreasonable to expect the mainstream journalists to be infallible in their judgments of potential sources' trustworthiness, but it would nonetheless seem perfectly reasonable to demand some baseline level of verification as a matter of good practice. As one would expect, mainstream journalists sometimes fall short of their profession's ideal in this regard, and bloggers sometimes criticize their lack of due diligence.

An especially difficult problem for journalists is the situation in which competing factual claims are made by sources in conflict with each other. In such cases, it may be a practical impossibility for the journalist to definitively resolve the disparity in those claims. Nonetheless, a blog critic may point out that reporter has tacitly accepted the veracity of one of the competing claims without adequately acknowledging evidence to the contrary.

A straightforward example of this sort of critique concerns a *Washington Post* story (White, 2005) about a suicide attempt by a detainee at the U.S. military prison in Guantanamo Bay. The reporter relied heavily on the detainee's lawyer as a source for descriptions of his experiences in custody; the story includes this passage:

> Dossari, 26, said U.S. troops have put out cigarettes on his skin, threatened to kill him and severely beat him. He told his lawyer that he saw U.S. Marines at Kandahar "using pages of the Koran to shine their boots," and was brutalized at Guantanamo Bay by Immediate Response Force guards who videotaped themselves attacking him.

The direct quote concerning desecration of a sacred text drew a pointed criticism from Cori Dauber in a *Rantingprofs* post titled "Here We Go Again: More Koran Desecration" (2005). She quoted the passage, adding emphasis to the quote about mistreatment of the Koran, then faulted the reporter for privileging the account of one of the parties in conflict (minor spelling error corrected; emphasis in the original).

> Here we go again. Did the *Post* confirm any of this, most especially *that* charge, before printing it? Where is the notation that there has already been a lengthy investigation into charges of Koran-desecration?

It's missing. The article as a whole and that paragraph in particular [are] nothing short of incendiary, and the reporter must know it. At the very least the reporter should have referenced the previous investigation, and acknowledged the fact that charges of Koran desecration seemed pretty clearly to be a conscious tactic ... .

Given the response the last time a charge like this was made in the press ... . did the *Post* attempt to confirm these allegations in Kandahar? And if so, what were the results?

Putting the charge in this article with no mention of previous charges ultimately proving false ain't the most responsible move[,] either.

The Post's comments thread includes a quip by another blogger, Jason Van Steenwyk. It is of interest here as an illustration of a common-sense fact check on the alleged desecration.

Heh. Must have been funny to watch those marines try to shine their boots. They're suede.

Dauber's comments in the preceding example made reference to the violent anti-American protests (*Newsweek* Backs Off Quran Desecration Story, 2005; Seelye, 2005) triggered by an earlier report in *Newsweek* alleging Koran-desecration at the Guantanamo facility itself. That controversy is no doubt familiar to the reader, as it generated an enormous amount of commentary in both the mainstream media and the blogosphere. Of interest here is the degree to which *Newsweek* verified the allegation, made by a single anonymous source, before publishing it.

The origin of the controversy was an item in the Periscope feature of *Newsweek*. In its entirety (Isikoff & Barry, 2005), it was this (capitalization and punctuation as in the original; emphasis added to the passage on which the controversy subsequently centered):

Investigators probing abuses at Guantanamo Bay have confirmed some infractions alleged in internal FBI e-mails that surfaced late last year. Among the previously unreported cases, sources tell NEWSWEEK: interrogators, in an attempt to rattle suspects, placed Qur'ans on toilets and, in at least one case, flushed a holy book down the toilet. An Army spokesman confirms that 10 interrogators have been disciplined for mistreating prisoners at Gitmo. These findings could put former Gitmo commander Maj. Gen. Geoffrey Miller in the hot seat. Two months ago, a more senior general, Air Force Lt. Gen. Randall Schmidt, was placed in charge of the probe in part so that Miller could be questioned. The FBI e-mails indicate that FBI agents quarreled repeatedly with military commanders, including Miller and his predecessor, retired Gen. Michael Dunleavy, over the military's more aggressive techniques. "Both agreed the Bureau has their way of doing business and DOD has their marching orders from the SecDef," one e-mail stated, referring to Secretary of Defense Donald Rumsfeld. Sources familiar with the probe say investigators didn't find that Miller authorized abusive treatment. But given the complaints, sources say, investigators say he should have known what was happening — and acted to try to prevent it. An Army spokesman declined to comment.

After the rioting had led to a number of deaths, *Newsweek* first printed an explanation of its decision to publish the item but did not retract the story. The editor's account of how the item went to press (Whitaker, 2005) illustrates the ethical complexities of reporting based on an anonymous source (emphasis added to the references to their source).

> Two weeks ago, in our issue dated May 9, Michael Isikoff and John Barry reported in a brief item in our Periscope section that U.S. military investigators had found evidence that American guards at the detention center in Guantanamo Bay, Cuba, had committed infractions in trying to get terror suspects to talk, including in one case flushing a Qur'an down a toilet. Their information came from a knowledgeable U.S. government source, and before deciding whether to publish it we approached two separate Defense Department officials for comment. One declined to give us a response; the other challenged another aspect of the story but did not dispute the Qur'an charge.
>
> ...[W]e believed our story was newsworthy because a U.S. official said government investigators turned up this evidence. So we published the item ... .

> Last Friday, a top Pentagon spokesman told us that a review of the probe cited in our story showed that it was never meant to look into charges of Qur'an desecration. The spokesman also said the Pentagon had investigated other desecration charges by detainees and found them "not credible." <u>Our original source later said he couldn't be certain</u> about reading of the alleged Qur'an incident in the report we cited, and said it might have been in other investigative documents or drafts.

While the editor expressed "regret that we got any part of our story wrong" in this statement, he nonetheless declined, at that point, to retract the story (Seelye, 2005).

> But Mr. Whitaker said in an interview later: "We're not retracting anything. We don't know what the ultimate facts are."

It may be worth noting, in passing, that the Periscope item repeatedly used the plural but the editor's statement used the singular, in describing the source on which the item was based. Much of the blog criticism of the item questioned *Newsweek*'s verification of the allegation, before publishing it.

Later on the same day, *Newsweek* did issue a formal retraction in the form of a press release (*Newsweek* Statement on Qu'ran story from Editor Mark Whitaker, 2005). The retraction is now appended to both the Periscope item (Isikoff & Barry, 2005) and to the explanation of its publication (Whitaker, 2005). The one-sentence retraction consisted of this:

> Based on what we know now, we are retracting our original story that an internal military investigation had uncovered Qur'an abuse at Guantanamo Bay.

Jeff Jarvis posted a short reflective essay on the ethical imperative of his profession (When the Story Gets in the Way of the Truth, 2005). He began the *Buzz Machine* post by noting the tragic consequences of the erroneous report.

> What a terrible lesson in journalism: about the danger of unnamed sources, about the risk of rushing a story, about the cynicism of

gotcha journalism, about the damage a wrong story can do. *Newsweek* quotes an unnamed source alleging that the Koran was desecrated at Guantanamo Bay and anti-American riots break out in Afghanistan, causing at least 15 deaths and other damage not so easy to add up.

Jarvis then addressed the decision to publish the item. He noted that *Newsweek*'s source, in the end, would not stand by his/her statement to them and there was no independent confirmation of the allegation; he connected the lack of verification to what he understands as the legitimate purpose of journalism.

> [G]iven the knowledge that such a report could only be incendiary, then why report it except to play one of two games:
>
> *Show-off* — in which the journalist delights in knowing something no one else knows and wants to tell the world before everyone else does, even if it's not assuredly true.
>
> *Gotcha* — in which the reporter thinks he has exposed something somebody wanted to hide.
>
> An incident such as this should force us to ask what the end result of journalism should be. Is it to expose anything we can expose? Is it to beat the other guy to tell you something you didn't know?
>
> Or is it to tell the truth? And if you don't know it to be true, is it reporting? ...
>
> I'm not saying that *Newsweek* lied. But they didn't know the truth before they said what they said.

Fellow journalist Joe Gandelman posted similar thoughts (*Newsweek* Apologizes, 2005) on *The Moderate Voice*. He attributed *Newsweek*'s decision to publish with only weak sourcing to competitiveness and pride (capitalization and emphasis as in the blog original; minor syntax errors corrected).

> A lot of this [i.e., the editor's statement about the publication of

the item] is CYA because, in the final analysis, *Newsweek* was WRONG and had not gotten the kind of iron-clad verification it needed ... .

Why was it [i.e., the item] run? ... . To be sure, anyone who has worked in the news media knows the intoxicating feeling of being onto a good story. If you have the facts you don't want to sit on them; you want to publish them as soon as possible so your employer is FIRST and BREAKS the story. It's a combination of a journalism and an ego thing. Being second to report a new twist on a new story isn't what competitive journalism is all about.

This combination of journalism plus reporter's ego becomes risky when the reporter's job is investigative journalism since being wrong can have more profound implications...

Gandelman added some further comments (*Newsweek* Uses "R" Word, 2005) after the formal retraction was issued (syntax and capitalization as in the original).

After issuing an apology that was basically a retraction, then insisting it wasn't a retraction, *Newsweek* has finally done it: it has USED the "R" word and issued a definitive retraction ... .

This is what SHOULD HAVE been done earlier...[ellipsis in original] with no qualifiers ... .

This is NOT a matter of ideology; this is [a] matter of quality journalism and appropriate corporate response to a quality-control issue.

The belated retraction led Cori Dauber to observe (Why Do They Hate Us?, 2005) that some in the mainstream press seemed too ready to accept detainees' accounts of events at face value (emphasis in original).

What is astonishing is that, this far into the war, the American press continues to be suitably skeptical of American government statements but appears, still, to be completely innocent of the fact that other parties also have agendas that might lead them to shade, distort, or utterly disregard the truth. Everyone else seems aware of the fact that al Qaeda training manuals include discussions of how to lie and manipulate, everyone else seems to be aware of the fact that disinformation is a part of the game. There have even been stories about this *in* the mainstream press, but reporters don't seem to be putting two and two together.

In other words, when *Newsweek* says that allegations like this have been floating around for awhile, that doesn't let them off the hook at all. They still needed tight sourcing, they should not have been any less skeptical of the claim — perhaps they should have been more so.

As support for her contention that terrorists made strategic use of disinformation, Dauber had embedded a hyperlink in that passage to a CBS story (By the Book, 2002) describing the contents of an Al Qaeda training manual obtained by the FBI in an investigation of the 1998 bombings of American embassies in Africa. Two other blog posts may be of interest, in this regard. On *InstaPundit* (*Newsweek* Has Retracted, 2005), Glenn Reynolds provided a link to translations of al-Qaeda training materials. On *Semi-Random Ramblings* (*Newsweek* Lied, People Died, 2005), Dave Price quoted a relevant passage from a translated manual (Lesson Eighteen: Prisons and Detention Centers, n.d.) available at that link (bracketed material in the original).

1. At the beginning of the trial, once more the brothers must insist on proving that torture was inflicted on them by State Security [investigators] before the judge.

2. Complain [to the court] of mistreatment while in prison.[48]

The issue of source trustworthiness is by no means confined to sensational, headline-grabbing stories. It has proven a chronic problem in straight news coverage of the Iraq war, since journalists have special concerns for their personal safety when gathering news in the field, and are subject to various limitations on the actions they can take to corroborate information others have supplied them. Their reliance on untrained or minimally-trained stringers, purported eyewitnesses whose allegiances are unknown, or local news outlets with sympathy for a particular side in the conflict force reporters and editors to make assessments of the trustworthiness of their sources. Even when reporters are able to observe the site of a news event for themselves, it may be difficult for them to check on the accuracy of the disparate accounts of events supplied by parties in conflict with each other. It is not surprising that journalists' assessments of source credibility would influence the news products; nor is it surprising that such implicit judgments would draw criticism.

This thorny problem can be seen clearly in a *Washington Post* story describing an air raid near Ramadi (Knickmeyer, 2005a). The lede of the story shows the fundamentally contradictory accounts with which the reporter worked, and illustrates how the issue of source credibility arises in routine, straight news coverage (emphasis added to source attributions of information).

> A U.S. fighter jet bombed a crowd gathered around a burned Humvee on the edge of a provincial capital in western Iraq, killing 25 people, including 18 children, <u>hospital officials and family members said</u> Monday. <u>The military said</u> the Sunday raid targeted insurgents planting a bomb for new attacks.

> In all, <u>residents and hospital workers said</u>, 39 civilians and at least 13 armed insurgents were killed in a day of U.S. airstrikes in Ramadi, the capital of Anbar province, a Sunni Arab region with a heavy insurgent presence.

> <u>The U.S. military said</u> it killed a total of 70 insurgents in Sunday's airstrikes and, in a statement, said it knew of no civilian deaths.

Cori Dauber noted the dilemma in "Resolving Competing Claims" (2005). She felt that the reporter had demoted an important piece of contextual information which might have helped the reader evaluate the relative merit of those competing accounts of the air raid.

> This is all about how to weigh evidence. Not until the end of the article do we read:

>> Ramadi serves as one of the bases and shelters for the insurgency. Iraqi and foreign fighters operate in a string of towns on both sides of the Euphrates River in Anbar province. They ferry weapons, recruits and money from neighboring

Syria into Iraq in the province.

> Never do we read that claims of civilian casualties are a classic propaganda ploy of terrorists and insurgents, or that doctors and hospital directors have been involved.

Dauber felt that, in such a situation, the reporter ought provide whatever additional evidence might be available to help the reader make an informed decision about the conflicting accounts (emphasis in the original).

> But the real issue is that what we are given is two sets of irresolvable and competing claims, with no evidence external to those claims that permit us to resolve the dispute ... . We are left with this "he said, she said" presentation that gives us no way to resolve the dispute, except that one side is more emotionally resonant, and therefore more sympathetic. The reporter gives us nothing, in short, that helps us. Giving us evidence that permits us to *choose* is not breaking neutrality, it's keeping us informed. If one side has a better claim on our support, we need to know that. Why else is the reporter there to inform us?

> Why else does the process have any meaning?

Dauber's criticism of the same reporter's work was sharper in "The *Post* Has Decided Who to Believe" (2005). The story in question (Knickmeyer, 2005b) described a brazen display of small arms by insurgents in Ramadi, intended to frighten Sunni tribal leaders who planned to meet with U.S. Marine officers. Dauber quoted the story's lede.

> Armed fighters claiming allegiance to Abu Musab Zarqawi took to the streets of a western Iraqi provincial capital Thursday in a fleeting show aimed at intimidating Iraqi Sunni Arab leaders taking part in dialogue with U.S. Marines in a stronghold of the insurgency, provincial officials, residents and other witnesses said.

> The scene — lean figures, many in masks and dark tracksuits lugging shoulder-mounted rocket launchers or wielding AK-47 assault rifles — reinforced what the U.S. military has acknowledged is the strong insurgent presence in the Euphrates

River cities and towns of Anbar province, an overwhelmingly Sunni area near the Syrian border. The appearance of the fighters dismayed many of the residents of Ramadi, the war-blighted provincial capital.

Dauber observed that the vivid wording produced the impression that the reporter had actually witnessed the movements of the insurgents, herself. It may be worth noting, regarding this point, that although the story described events in Ramadi, it was datelined Baghdad; the same was true of the story in the previous example.

Dauber commented that the headline appeared to be similarly definitive about the events; in effect, the reporter and editor had decided which of two conflicting accounts to believe (emphasis in the original).

Look at this headline: "Ramadi Insurgents Flaunt Threat." That, my friends, is a *statement of fact* to anyone skimming their newspaper. And to anyone about to read the article that follows, it tells them that the *Post* has already decided, in the dispute between two sides over what really happened in Ramadi yesterday, which of those two sides is more credible, or, at least, has the more believable position. Only in the subhead does a reader learn, "US Dismisses Reported Display of Force as Hype." Yet that too, takes the same side as the headline. Because, as you'll only learn from reading the following article quite carefully, the key word there is "reported." The US isn't so much dismissing the reports as "hype," as in "an exaggeration of an actual event." They're dismissing the reports as essentially "fake," which is a horse of another color.

The description of the military's comment on the report was well into the article (emphasis in the blog original).

Only in the fifth graf do we see this:

The U.S. military, which maintains Marine bases and thousands of troops on the outskirts of Ramadi, denied the accounts of unrest, saying that the city was largely calm Thursday and that insurgents were manipulating the news media. "Today I witnessed inaccurate reporting, use of unreliable sources, media using other media as sources, an active insurgent propaganda machine, and the pack journalism at its wors[t], " Capt. Jeffrey

Pool, a spokesman for the 2nd Marine Division, said in an e-mail to news organizations.

Boy, how bad do things have to be before a military spokesman spanks the press that baldly?

Dauber continued by singling out the following paragraph in the story, which she felt called the reporter's sources into question (emphasis in the blog original).

This is an absolutely stunning report:

Witnesses in Ramadi said they saw some of the armed fighters instruct a journalist for an Arabic-language news outlet to report that Zarqawi's group, al Qaeda in Iraq, had taken over the entire city.

Dauber noted other information in the story which likewise raised doubts about the accounts of insurgents taking control of Ramadi. She then summed up her criticism of the reporter's assessment of source credibility (emphasis in the original).

[G]iven how many outlets are basing their reporting on what happened in Ramadi yesterday, not on what *their* reporters saw, but on "eyewitnesses," the fact that Zarqawi's men were in the streets — and we now know telling at least some people what to say happened — gives *more* credibility to the US military's story, not less. Because I have yet to see a news organization whose reporting was based on a Western reporter's having been in the city at the time this supposedly happened ... .

That would be enough, you would think, for the *Post* to frame the story in terms of doubt and uncertainty.[49]

Error Correction

It would be unreasonable to expect mainstream journalists to be infallible; however diligently newsworkers might try to assure the accuracy of their reporting, it is inevitable that mistakes will be part of the copy. Just as it set a professional standard for accuracy, the ethics code of the Society of Professional Journalists (1996) also defines the appropriate course of action when an error is discovered in a news product. Under its "Be Accountable" tenet, there is a straightforward imperative for journalists.

> Journalists should admit mistakes and correct them promptly.

At first glance, that sentence would seem unequivocal. In the real world, its implementation has proven problematic for a number of reasons. The distinction between fact and interpretation is not always a bright line, as earlier passages here have illustrated; not all relevant facts are immediately accessible to journalists on deadline, and a certain degree of prospective interpretation is unavoidable as journalists arrange the currently available facts into a coherent story frame. In consequence, the notion that errors must be acknowledged and corrected is straightforward but determining when a particular bit of text requires that treatment, after a story has more fully developed, is not. Moreover, the relative prominence of the correction often becomes an issue. When an error has received extensive coverage, does the correction to the error require an equivalent amount of exposure?

The dilemma is compounded by the questionable practice of addressing an error with a rowback rather than an explicit correction. A standard journalism textbook (Mencher, 1991, p. 668) supplies this description:

> A story that attempts to correct a previous story without indicating that the prior story had been in error or without taking responsibility for the error.

The earlier chapter on blog criticism of accuracy noted a number of rowbacks, in passing. Rowbacks are far from rare, and a number of mainstream journalists themselves have sharply criticized the practice. One condemned rowbacks as, in essence, self-destructive behavior by journalists (Shearer, 2004).

> This technique — which avoids telling readers that the overall thesis or a major portion of a story is wrong — ought to be rooted

out of newspapers.

> Until papers aggressively report on their own and others' mistakes in coverage — usually honest mistakes that happen on daily deadlines — the public will continue to question our credibility or, at least, our willingness to be forthright about the stories we got wrong.

A former public editor of *The New York Times* described rowbacks as "a squirrelly journalistic dance step" (Okrent, 2004a), and described at some length the difficulties his newspaper encountered in trying to devise an appropriate corrections policy for opinion columnists (Okrent, 2004b).

When Cori Dauber first commented on a *New York Times* story about Iraqi civilians killed during an attack on a convoy in Baghdad, her major concern was that the reporter had failed to check the accuracy of witnesses' accounts of the incident. Her critique evolved into exposing a rowback of this reporting, after it became clear that the key witness upon whom the reporter relied had made a blatantly false statement and an independent military inquiry into the incident, using concrete forensic evidence and methodical investigative procedure, had proven the initial report to be almost totally inaccurate.

The *Times* story in question (Wong, 2004a) asserted, flatly, that American soldiers had fired on a car containing civilians after the detonation of a roadside bomb. The lede is unequivocal about the incident, as is the headline: "G.I.'s Fire on Family in Car, Killing 2, Witnesses Say."

> American soldiers on Monday night killed an Iraqi man and a boy and wounded four others in a car that was driving behind their convoy after a roadside bomb went off nearby, said witnesses, a police official and relatives of the family in the car. The soldiers, traveling in a convoy of two Humvees, opened fire on the family, which was riding in a dark blue station wagon, after the bomb exploded on Palestine Street about 300 yards from the Oil Ministry, witnesses said ... .

> "You want to know the truth?" said Lt. Muhammad Ali, an Iraqi policeman who was driving away from Al Kindi Hospital with several colleagues after taking one of the women there. "I'll tell

you the truth. The Americans did this."

In a *Rantingprofs* post titled "The Coverage of Civilian Casualties in Iraq" (2004), Dauber reproduced e-mail she had received from a reader which disputed that account of the incident.

The *NY Times* ran a story that after an I[improvised]E[xplosive]D[device] exploded near a convoy, Americans shot into a civilian vehicle and killed a father and son, and wounded others. The reporter, Ed Wong, quoted an Iraqi policeman ... .

The Army brought in an outside investigating team (as per S[tandard]O[perating]P[rocedure]), who concluded that the civilians were not shot by Americans, but were wounded by shrapnel from the IED. No Americans fired their weapons. The Iraqi policeman? When interviewed, the policeman quoted denied making the statement, and said someone else used his name. Another policeman admitted to using a different name, and says he did not see any shooting, but heard it on the radio.

Dauber's reader had forwarded e-mail from the Army unit's commander, describing the findings of the outside investigation. The e-mail from the commanding officer was lengthy and detailed, and included these passages.

Upon detonation of the IED, the MP patrol [i.e., the convoy which had been attacked by the explosive device] responded by moving rapidly away from the explosion site and proceeded to the Martyr's Monument for medical treatment of two wounded soldiers. No soldiers fired their weapons during the incident. A patrol from 1-36 Infantry, hearing the explosion, moved to the site and assessed that the IED had exploded between the second and third HMMWV's, hitting not only the U.S. vehicles but killing the two Iraqi males in the front seat of the Opel and injuring two passengers in the back seat. U.S. medics attended to the wounded before turning them over to Iraqi Police (IP) for transport to a civilian hospital.

...Upon interrogation, Lieutenant Muhammad Ali stated that he was not at the scene of the attack, but believed that another IP officer, Ali Hussein, who works in the same police station, used his name during an interview with a reporter that night as a vendetta [sic] to get him (LT Muhammad Ali) in trouble. Upon questioning, IP officer Ali Hussein admitted that he was the IP officer who gave the interview and that he told the reporter that U.S. forces had fired wildly after the IED explosion, killing the two civilians in the Opel.

He admitted he had no first-hand knowledge of whether the soldiers had fired or not, but repeated what he said he heard over the radio. When pressed why he had used a false name, he stated that he gave the name "Muhammad Ali" without thinking ... .

The 1st Armored Division surgeon attended the autopsy of the two dead Iraqi civilians and noted that there was no evidence of wounds caused by rifle or machine gun bullets. The wounds were irregular in shape and caused by shrapnel — pieces of which were removed from the wounds during the autopsy. There were no bullets in the bodies. Wounds to the two injured Iraqi civilians were likewise determined to have been caused by shrapnel. Likewise, visual inspection of the Opel station wagon revealed an irregular pattern of damage but no bullet holes, just what you would expect from damage caused by a large explosion. All the holes in the car were either too mis[s]hapen or too large for them to be bullet holes.

Dauber first raised a question about the reporter's reliance on purported witnesses to the events.

What I find frustrating about this is the assumption that witnesses have credibility if they are making charges against the US military. Was there any sense that relying on the word of an Iraqi policeman who hadn't been on the scene might be questionable?...Did anyone wonder if the Iraqi civilians might not have the purest of motives in a neighborhood where, clearly, somebody wanted Americans dead?

She then turned to the matter of correcting the record, noting that the findings of the Army's inquiry into the incident had not been reported.

And more to the point, why no follow up? These are incendiary charges at best. But the results of the investigation as Col. Mansoor [the unit commander] describes them seem fairly definitive to this relatively well-read layperson. Can you imagine the outcry if the *Times* reported allegations of suspected murder, but never reported the police investigation completely exonerated the person?

Dauber returned to this critique a month later, when the *Times's* public editor responded to correspondence from her readers and the unit's commanding officer (*The New York Times* Responds, 2004). She reproduced the letter from the public editor at that time, Daniel Okrent, in its entirety; it described his inquiry into the newsgathering leading to the story, then the way in which the error was addressed by the *Times*.

> The next day [after the attack], Wong received a telephone call from Brig. Gen Mark Kimmitt, the deputy chief of operations in Baghdad, who told him that a fresh report of the incident indicated that the victims were in fact killed by shrapnel. Mr. Wong immediately called the *Times'* Web site to update his story. One day after the initial story appeared in *The Times*, another carrying Mr. Wong's byline was published, under the general heading "The Iraq Struggle: Violence," and the specific headline, "Army Copter Downed West of Baghdad in Hotbed of Anti-U.S. Sentiment." In that story Mr. Wong included the following paragraphs:
>
>> Contributing to the tense security situation are claims from Iraqi civilians and police officers that American soldiers have killed innocent civilians. On Monday night, a policeman and victims' relatives said soldiers in Humvees had shot at a family in a station wagon at the site of a roadside bomb explosion in Baghdad, killing two people and wounding four.
>>
>> But General Kimmitt said in an interview on Tuesday that initial reports based on photographs of the scene show that bomb shrapnel was responsible for the deaths and injuries. The military is still investigating, he said.

Okrent noted that in the initial story the reporter had made only a brief mention of an unidentified soldier stating that the civilians had been killed by the bomb, while the story had featured the purported witnesses' account that troops had fired on the car. He also noted the obscure positioning of the correction, in a following story. He quoted the initial story's single sentence about the soldier's description of the event.

> A soldier at the scene of the Palestine Street violence in Baghdad said that the bomb had killed two Iraqi civilians and wounded two others and that all had been in the blue station wagon.

> This sentence would have been a more powerful counterweight to the assertions of the Iraqi policeman and the family members had it more clearly indicated that the soldier was specifically asserting that bullets, from American personnel or others, were not involved. And the following day's story would have served as a far more effective corrective had Gen. Kimmitt's comments not appeared in the sixteenth and seventeenth paragraphs of a story whose headline was about a downed helicopter outside of Baghdad.

Okrent then acknowledged the inherent deficiency in using rowbacks as a way of correcting errors in reporting; he noted that both *Times* readers and other news outlets were likely to have seen the erroneous initial report but not the correction.

> I believe the likelihood of readers who read through the first day's story actually encountering the pertinent paragraphs of the second story is very slight. Further, a search on nytimes.com for a story about the incident can lead one directly to the first day story, with no indication there even was a second-day story. This is also true in *The Times'* own internal database. Whereas formal corrections are attached to articles in electronic archives, second-day stories that correct or otherwise clarify an earlier article are not.

> Additionally, as Col. Mansoor [the unit commander] points out, many other American news outlets pick up stories from *The Times*; I find it highly likely that many of them did not see the clarifying paragraphs in the second article.

Dauber agreed with Okrent's analysis of the problem with rowbacks. She observed that this case was not an isolated instance, but a routine practice in war reporting.

The *Times*, like many outlets, publishes on many days, a "roundup" article that is basically a list of all events, good and bad, that happened the day before in Iraq. But the headline never indicates that it's a roundup piece; instead the headline cites only the most sensational of all the events listed. And my complaint has often been that if there is some kind of accusation against the military it will often be given a stand-alone piece one day, with the military's answer being folded into the roundup piece the next day, where no one would think to look for it.

It may be worth noting, in this context, that as of this writing the initial *Times* reporting of the incident (Wong, 2004a) has not been retracted, and the version available from LexisNexis carries no correction or editor's note. When retrieved directly from the *Times* Web site, the story bears the annotation "Clarifying Article Appended." The entire roundup story to which Okrent referred (Wong, 2004b) is simply added to the initial story (Wong, 2004a); the brief passage making reference to the erroneous reporting is placed deep in the roundup, as Okrent had noted, and enclosed in a row of asterisks. There is no indication on the "clarifying article" itself, when retrieved from LexisNexis, that it corrects an error in the prior day's reporting on the incident.[50]

Dauber had noticeably harsher words to describe another rowback in *The New York Times* (Keller, 2004), regarding the hearings of the 9/11 Commission. While she did not use the word *rowback* in "Squeeze Play" (2004), the substance of the critique is the same: the correction was given much less prominence than the original reporting (capitalization as in the original).

> After pronouncing in the strongest possible terms that the 9/11 commission had declared no ties between Saddam and al Qaeda on the front page and ignoring for days the fact that the commission Chairs were taking the administration's side against the press — the *New York Times* is finally forced to admit that the commission Chairs have weighed in against the press. And so they do. On page A-11.

Dauber did a detailed analysis of the brief roundup story's content, then emphasized what she saw as the *Times*'s lack of candor in acknowledging the problem with its earlier reporting on the Commission's hearings.

> So they finally admit that the commission chairs don't see a discrepancy between their position and the administration's on al Qaeda's links to Iraq, but they bury that admission by choosing very weak quotes to that effect, by burying the admission in a round-up article on what was said about the commission on the Sunday shows, and then by burying the article — and by never admitting that this was a controversy in the press or about the press.[51]

The controversy over President Bush's assertion in the 2003 State of the Union address, that the Hussein regime in Iraq had tried to obtain nuclear weapon materials, is no doubt familiar to the reader. Of interest here is the release, a year-and-a-half later, of two reports tending to corroborate that assertion. A *New York Times* story describing these reports (Stevenson & Johnston, 2004) drew the attention of bloggers. The lede of the story acknowledges how the new reports ran contrary to much of the prior reporting on the matter.

> Were those infamous 16 words correct after all?...

> But now two new reports have reopened the question of whether Mr. Bush was indeed correct when, on Jan. 28, 2003, he told the nation and the world, "The British government has learned that Saddam Hussein recently sought significant quantities of uranium from Africa."

> One of the reports was released on Wednesday by a British commission reviewing the intelligence used by Prime Minister Tony Blair in making the case for war ... . [T]he report concluded that the assertions by Mr. Bush and Mr. Blair about Iraq's attempts to acquire uranium were "well founded."

> The other report came from the Senate Intelligence Committee. It generally found extensive problems with the prewar intelligence assessments about Iraq's weapons programs ... . [b]ut it also contained some information that tended to bolster the view that Iraq had tried to acquire uranium from Niger and possibly one or

two other African nations.

While the story ostensibly dealt with the President's assertion in the State of the Union address, some bloggers noted its relevance to earlier public statements by a central figure in the controversy. The story prompted a terse comment from Glenn Reynolds on *InstaPundit* (Wilson-Lied Media Spin Update, 2004).

> *The New York Times* initiates another quasi-rowback with this story on the Niger/Uranium flap. But look at the headline, and note what's left out.

Reynolds linked to a lengthier post by retired investment executive Tom Maguire on *JustOneMinute* (What I Didn't Find in the *NY Times*, 2004). Maguire developed fully the point which Reynolds had implied (minor punctuation error corrected).

> With a Sunday piece ... Richard Stevenson and David Johnston of the *NY Times* tiptoe up to the issue of the *Times* reporting on the President's "16 Words."

> Our question, as noted previously — will the *Times* report on the news contained in the Senate report that Mr. Wilson gave "misleading information" in anonymous leaks to *The Washington Post*, and by extension Nick Kristof of the *NY Times*? Will they discuss his [i.e., Wilson's] flawed (but famous) op-ed piece, which the *NY Times* was surely pleased to have run?

Maguire had embedded links to the Kristof (apparently Kristof, 2003) and Wilson (2003) articles in that passage. He continued by sarcastically characterizing the way in which the current *Times* story dealt with the relevance of the new reports to Wilson's earlier public statements.

> And this passage from the *Times* could have been torn from the pages of *Pravda*:

>> The new reports also raised questions about one of the White House's chief critics over the issue, Joseph C. Wilson IV, a former ambassador sent to Niger in 2002 to investigate whether

> Iraq had tried to purchase uranium there. Among other things, the report pointed out that Mr. Wilson's official account to the C.I.A. noted that a former prime minister of Niger had told him that he had been approached in 1999 about meeting with an Iraqi delegation interested in "expanding commercial relations" between Niger and Iraq. The former prime minister told Mr. Wilson that he interpreted the approach to mean the Iraqis were interested in acquiring a form of uranium.

"Raised questions"? Would these two very talented reporters care to hint at just what questions were raised? I would need a decoder ring to know that this refers to Mr. Wilson's famous "What I Didn't Find In Africa" op-ed that ran in the *NY Times* a year ago.

As is common in critiques of rowbacks, Maguire also noted the relative lack of prominence given the story, compared to earlier reporting of Wilson's public statements (minor punctuation error corrected).

> Just a note about story placement in the Dead Tree [i.e., print] version — this appears on p. 14 of the Sunday *Times* main news section in a feature called "Washington Memo." Their front page section, "Inside," which highlights other stories, does not mention it, nor does the page 2 "News Summary" feature.[52]

The release of the Senate Intelligence Committee's report had also drawn Cori Dauber's notice. She posted a methodical critique of a *New York Times* story from a few days earlier (Risen, 2004) which summarized the Committee's review of the intelligence concerning a possible Iraq/Niger procurement. Her *Rantingprofs* post explicitly raised the objection (The Rowback of All Rowbacks, 2004) that the *Times* was correcting its earlier reporting on the public statements of Joseph Wilson without forthrightly acknowledging it. She began by stating what she sees as the press' obligation, when a story develops in an unexpected way over time (syntax and emphasis as in the original).

> Here's my position, and I think it's one that can be defended: <u>if a newspaper (or other media outlet) covers a story, and subsequent developments show that fundamental elements of that story as it</u>

was covered were essentially incorrect (in other words, we aren't talking about a correction, a situation where the paper got something wrong, but a situation where the situation developed, proving the original interpretation false) then that outlet owes it to its audience to provide that information with as much emphasis as the original story received.

If the original story was on the front page, you can't tell readers that new developments have shown that story false in a single sentence on page A-32 that makes no reference to the first story...

Because in an article in today's *Times* comes the Mother of All Rowbacks.

Dauber felt the story's headline and lede concealed a good deal of startling new information relevant to controversy (syntax, emphasis, and punctuation as in the original).

Today on page A-12, not on the front page, comes a story headlined, "How Niger Uranium Story Defied Wide Skepticism." Now, that suggests to the casual reader that this is a story about how the uranium story kept going despite skepticism about it. But, there was always skepticism about it, and it kept going for awhile anyway, so it looks like a somewhat historical piece, not a piece that presents relatively breaking news ... .

This is, in other words, a story about the history of the Niger story as we understood it when we picked up our paper this morning. there's nothing in this frame that tells the reader that the real news is that what the report says is also *that the Niger story didn't go south, that there's something new in the report, that in fact the news here is that the report says our understanding of the Niger story needs to do a 180 ...* .

Not until the 11th graf does the actual rowback even begin!

Dauber then quoted passages placed well into the story which constituted, she felt, substantial new developments in the story. She labeled these new facts, which disputed major points of prior reportage, "revised claims."

Instead of assigning a trained intelligence officer to the Niger case, though, the C.I.A. sent a former American ambassador, Joseph Wilson, to talk to former Niger officials. His wife, Valerie Plame, was an officer in the counterproliferation division, and she had suggested that he be sent to Niger, according to the Senate report. That finding contradicts previous statements by Mr. Wilson ... .

In his C.I.A. debriefing, Mr. Wilson reported that the former prime minister [of Niger] said he knew of no contracts with any so-called rogue nations while he was prime minister, from 1997 through 1999. But he did say that in June 1999, a businessman insisted that he meet with an Iraqi delegation to discuss expanded commercial relations with Baghdad, according to the Senate report. The meeting took place, but the prime minister said he never pursued the idea because of United Nations sanctions on Iraq ... .

Analysts at the C.I.A. did not believe that Mr. Wilson had provided significant information, so the agency did not brief Mr. Cheney about it, despite his clear interest in the issue, the Senate found.

She concluded the post with a tart comment.

So it's a rowback, but a grudging and graceless one.[53]

The debunking of an ex-Marine's stories of atrocities committed by American troops in Iraq is a complex and especially interesting case of error correction. Jimmy Massey, who served three months in Iraq and then was discharged for post-traumatic stress syndrome, came to national attention in 2004 when he began making public assertions that he and his comrades had deliberately killed civilians, including a number of children, and committed a variety of other atrocities. The Associated Press reported Massey's allegations (Crary, 2004; Duff-Brown, 2004; Diderich, 2005), as did *The Washington Post* (Struck, 2004) and *USA Today* (Hampson, 2005). The *Sacramento Bee* and *Modesto Bee* ran a feature interview with Massey (Rockwell, 2004).

The actual controversy over the coverage of Massey began when the *Saint Louis Post-Dispatch* published a comprehensive debunking of Massey's accounts of atrocities (Harris, 2005a; Harris, 2005b). The reporter himself and a photographer from the *Post-Dispatch* had been embedded with Massey's unit during the time most of the alleged atrocities were supposed to have occurred. Michelle Malkin quoted extensively from Harris's two stories in "An Anti-War Smear Artist Exposed" (2005), including this passage (emphasis added in the blog original):

> News organizations worldwide published or broadcast Massey's claims without any corroboration and in most cases without investigation. Outside of the Marines, almost no one has seriously questioned whether Massey, a 12-year veteran who was honorably discharged, was telling the truth.
>
> He wasn't.
>
> Each of his claims is either demonstrably false or exaggerated — according to his fellow Marines, Massey's own admissions, and the five journalists who were embedded with Massey's unit, including a reporter and photographer from the *Post-Dispatch* and reporters from the Associated Press and *The Wall Street Journal.*

On the following day, Malkin posted a long excerpt from an interview with Harris on CNN's "American Morning" show (Jimmy Massey: A Slanderer and His MSM Enablers, 2005). When asked how he was certain that Massey's allegations were false, Harris pointed out that he, himself, had been embedded with Massey's unit along with a number of other journalists. The transcript (Marine's Tales of Iraq Atrocities Debunked, 2005) includes this exchange concerning the press's failure to verify Massey's allegations (syntax and punctuation as in the original):

> COSTELLO: Yes, but Ron, if th[is] was completely untrue, I mean, this guy has made it into pretty big publications like "Vanity Fair." He's written a book that's bee[n] published in France.
>
> HARRIS: Oh, it's been published everywhere. Nobody — in not one publication or not one broadcast, is there any corroboration. It's just Jimmy Massey's story. Nobody ever called a journalists [sic] who were covering him. Nobody ever interviewed the [M]arines, which I did all of. Nobody ever checked his story. They

don't even have another source that says on background or another source who didn't want to be quoted. It's just Jimmy Massey's story.

At the end of the post, Malkin reproduced an query she sent to *The Washington Post* reporter who had written about Massey.

> Here's the e-mail I sent to WaPo reporter Doug Struck this morning. I'll let you know if I receive a response:
>
> Mr. Struck —
> On Dec. 8, 2004, you had a bylined piece in *The Washington Post* highlighting the testimony of Jimmie [sic] Massey, the former U.S. Marine staff sergeant who testified at a deserter's Canadian asylum hearing that his unit killed at least 30 unarmed civilians in Iraq during the war in 2003 and that Marines routinely shot and killed wounded Iraqis.
>
> The *St. Louis Post-Dispatch* investigated Massey's claims and debunked them this Sunday.
>
> Do you or someone else at the *Post* plan on following up?

Malkin continued to press the mainstream news outlets which had reported Massey's allegations for a response to Harris's debunking of Massey's claims (The Media and the Unhinged Marine, 2005). She noted a number of other bloggers who were also following the controversy, including Jim Hoft (*Gateway Pundit*), Laer Pearce *(Cheat Seeking Missiles*), and Christopher Fotos (*PostWatch*). Malkin had received no reply from *The Washington Post* reporter (Struck, 2004) and gotten only a noncommittal response from the editor of the *Sacramento Bee* (which had published Rockwell, 2004), but reproduced the e-mail she received from the *USA Today* reporter (Hampson, 2005) who had made mention of Massey's allegations of atrocities in a story about his return to home.

> I personally have no plans for a follow up. Our story was not so much about the veracity of Massey's claims — few if any of those mentioned in the *Post-Dispatch* piece were in our story — as the reaction in a small, patriotic town to its former Marine recruiter

coming back as a war protester. (We also went into Massey's psychological history.) Certainly, he had a lot of critics/opponents/skeptics in town even back then. So I don't expect we'll revisit the subject.

This led her to a cynical assessment of the mainstream news outlets' accountability.

All in all, the MSM's reaction has been a collective shrug.

Malkin had praise for two affiliated California newspapers several days later (The Massey Mess: "Error in Judgment", 2005). The editorial page editors of both the *Sacramento Bee* (Holwerk, 2005) and the *Modesto Bee* (Sly, 2005) had published what amounted to retractions of their feature interview with Massey (Rockwell, 2004). Malkin quoted the op-ed editor of the *Sacramento Bee* at some length, including these passages:

We should have done more to check the truth of Massey's charges before deciding whether to publish them. We didn't, and the responsibility for that is mine.

It was an error in judgment, and *The Bee's* readers are entitled to an explanation of how I made that error ... .

The problem is that we didn't go far enough. Before we published the story, we should have called the Marine Corps for [a] response. We also could have attempted to speak to other members of Massey's Marine unit, and to check whether any reporters were embedded with Massey's company. But we didn't ... .

It was clear in retrospect that we hadn't done due diligence with the Jimmy Massey interview.

The op-ed editor of the *Modesto Bee*, which had run a version of the same interview with Massey, made a similar apology to her readers.

We relied on our colleagues in Sacramento but should have done our own verification. Sacramento did confirm with Massey the responses in the commentary, but it did not seek a response from the Marine Corps.

Around the country, other media are guilty of the same failures ...

[W]e want to assure you that we have learned from this experience and will beef up procedures to prevent a painful repeat.

A full month later, Malkin noted the publication of a belated follow-up by the Associated Press itself (McClam, 2005). She quoted the story at length in "Jimmy Massey's Lies: The AP Finally Wakes Up" (2005), beginning with this passage concerning Massey's allegation that his unit had shot at a group of Iraqi demonstrators (punctuation as in the Associated Press story):

> In a lengthy telephone interview with the Associated Press, Massey repeated his claim that his unit — and he personally — fired on the demonstrators. He said four were killed. He said his original estimate of 10 was inaccurate.

> But reporters and a photographer who were embedded with the 3/7 say there is no evidence such a shooting happened — indeed, no evidence that the Marines confronted any demonstrators so early in the war.

> "There was certainly no organized protesting, no 'Go home,' anything like that," said Ravi Nessman, an AP reporter who knew Massey while he was embedded with Weapons Company. "When (the Marines) were driving into central Baghdad, they were cheered."

> "Things went bad much later," he said.

Malkin went on to quote the passage in which the Associated Press acknowledged its failure to check Massey's allegations with its own embedded reporter, which appeared near the end of the story.

> The Associated Press quoted Massey five times between May 2004 and October 2005 — four times directly, and once citing a CBC report in which Massey said his unit had committed "cold-blooded, calculated murder."

In each case, Massey alleged his platoon had killed innocent civilians or committed atrocities against Iraqis. Two of the five stories included Marine Corps denials of Massey's allegations.

"Clearly our stories should have included the firsthand observations of our own embedded reporter," said AP Managing Editor Mike Silverman.

To this admission, Malkin added a sarcastic postscript.

Thanks. Sherlock.

The Massey case is noteworthy in a number of respects, including the symbiosis of the mainstream journalist who first exposed the error and the bloggers who pursued it, and of the two op-ed editors who mentioned Malkin's work in their retractions of the Massey interview they published. Several ironies are apparent in this case, as well. The Associated Press did much to disseminate Massey's allegations, but neglected to check them first with its own reporter embedded with Massey's unit. Massey's allegations were ultimately debunked by another embed with first-hand knowledge of the unit's activities.

Perhaps the most striking irony of all, in the context of this section on error correction, is that as of this writing none of the stories mentioned above which reported Massey's allegations (Crary, 2004; Diderich, 2005; Duff-Brown, 2004; Hampson, 2005; Rockwell, 2004; Struck, 2004) bears an appended correction or editor's note. Neither does a feature in Massey's hometown newspaper (Schmerker, 2005), based in large part on the *USA Today* story (Hampson, 2005). In short, the Associated Press's belated investigation of Massey's allegations (McClam, 2005) was, itself, a rowback.[54]

CHAPTER 6

The Economics of Blogs

As the preceding chapters have suggested, a substantial number of individuals invest a considerable amount of effort in the creation of blog content.

At first glance this might appear to be economically irrational behavior on their part: comparatively high in cost and low in return on the investment. One way to make sense of this situation would be to blithely posit that the rational actor model of economic behavior is fatally flawed, in general, or for some reason does not apply to this particular slice of human activity.

While some have noted various limitations on the explanatory or predictive power of the model, it nonetheless seems obvious that people do, in fact, routinely base much of their action on a comparison of the costs and benefits of the action to themselves, however idiosyncratic their calculus may appear to others. What then to make of the bloggers, who invest so much time and energy in producing content which they then make available for free?

The key to this apparent paradox is two-fold: the special nature of information products as economic goods, and the characteristics of the communication channel through which the blogosphere is created. Like tangible objects, information has economic characteristics; those two types of economic goods have fundamentally different characteristics, however, which lead to fundamentally different production and distribution dynamics. Moreover, computer-mediated communication displays characteristics fundamentally different from other forms of mediated communication, such as broadcast and print. It is not so surprising, then, that the economics of the blogosphere do not simply mimic the economics of the legacy media. An examination of the goods and channel characteristics will be profitable here — pun intended — with an eye toward the communication behaviors which the channel facilitates, but does not determine.

Technological Facilitation

Information has value, as an economic good, but it is a different sort of economic good than tangible objects or hours of human labor. It goes without saying that blog content is information, and follows that blog content will share the fundamental economic characteristics of other information goods. The most consequential characteristic for our purposes here is that information goods tend to be non-rivalrous, in the sense that the owner of particular information can sell it or give it to another party, and still retain much or all of the good's value. This thought would seem nonsensical if one considered the information good to be the artifact which conveys it, but it is clear that the value of a movie on a digital video disk is the movie (i.e., the stream of motion image and sound) and not the plastic disk itself; likewise for the content of a paperback novel, a newspaper, or a scholarly book. One can enjoy the movie and dispose of the plastic disk without giving up the memory of the movie's plot or the entertainment experience it provided during viewing. Further, one can obtain additional value from this information good by discussing the movie with others, again without possessing the artifact which conveyed it. Clearly, tangible objects and human labor are intrinsically different economic goods; when one sells a car one no longer can drive it, and one cannot work the same hours for two different employers, simultaneously.

Regarding the channel through which information goods increasingly are distributed, the convergence of a variety of information-conveying artifacts into a common digital format is of consequence, also. Given that the economic value of information is the symbolically-encoded meaning — whether it be visual image, sound, or text — cost savings in either the creation of information product or its distribution will immediately affect the economic rationality of its creation and distribution. Put into less convoluted language, it becomes a more sensible choice to create a product with little expected monetary benefit when it only cost a few out-of-pocket dollars to create it. Moreover, just as information is distributed in symbolic form, the return to its creator can be symbolic, as well. In particular, the expressive reward to a blogger — the emotional satisfaction of having "said" something — can be substantial enough to repay that person's investment of time and effort.

A couple of technical features need particular mention, at this point. Hyperlinking is a capability included in HTML, the standard programming language of online documents; hyperlinking is the distinctive trait of hypertext. Authors of online documents can utilize this capability to provide their readers convenient access to other online documents. Most bloggers make extensive use of hyperlinking, both to other creators of online content and to their own archive. Hyperlinking has thus facilitated the development of a genre convention with significant consequences in costs and benefits to both bloggers and their readers, a point explored in more detail below.

Convergence is the term commonly used for the migration of what previously had been distinct media (e.g., print, audio, video) into a common, fungible digital stream. This has made the creation of multimedia content an enthusiast's home project, when not long ago it was a professional's studio enterprise. Bloggers routinely include visual images and sound in their work, in addition to text. At the producer's end of the value chain, the equipment used for word processing is capable of editing video, and at the consumer's end the equipment capable of accessing plain text is capable of accessing motion image and sound. The same observation applies: this has had significant impact on the costs and benefits of creating or consuming blog content.

Hypertext has proven to be an innovation with an unusually high potential for reinvention by the user (see Rogers, 1995, p. 17). This technology can be used to archive or retrieve documents, author documents alone or collaboratively, interact synchronously or asynchronously, and exchange messages privately or publicly, for instance. The content can be trivial or consequential; the document can include visual images or sound, or be plain text; its style can be utilitarian or ornate. In short, the technology facilitates a wide range of document characteristics, but determines none of them in particular. Given this striking characteristic of the channel through which content is distributed, it is unsurprising that hypertext has had such a wide-ranging, but largely unanticipated, impact on the media system.

None of this is to say that either the growth of information goods into a sizeable economic sector, or the technological innovations which made convergence a trend, or even the public and private investments which built the necessary distribution infrastructure over which those information goods travel, in any way determined the content now available in the blogosphere. It is crucial to recognize these as facilitating the emergence of the blogosphere, but neither causing it to emerge nor dictating its content. It follows that the actual blog content exists because human beings wish to create it and human beings wish to consume it. And if, as this author believes, the blogosphere is rapidly maturing into a full-fledged social institution, it is solely because it creates significant value for people living in the social system.

Cost/Benefit Ratio

For a blogger and his/her reader, the personal comparison of costs and benefits of the activity matter. Both the act of producing blog content and the act of consuming blog content are entirely voluntary; unless one makes the unreasonable assumption that bloggers and their readers are mentally defective in some way, it seems obvious that they perceive the benefits to outweigh the costs. Lest this seem a trivial observation, there are some who have suggested that bloggers are something less than rational actors; "salivating morons" (Lovelady, quoted in Rosen, 2005), "high on the perfume of many 'hits'" (Engberg, 2004), "too stupid" (Zerbisias, 2004), and "borg-like" (Rall, 2005) are a few of the more caustic characterizations. This author hopes the examples in the preceding chapters are more than enough to refute that dismissive understanding of bloggers, and by extension, their audience.

Given that bloggers and readers are rational actors engaged in information transactions they perceive to be beneficial, it is worthwhile to consider the costs and benefits to both producers and consumers of blog content. There is no easy way to employ monetary values in this. Information products are different from other economic goods; unlike other information goods, even, there is no purchase price for a piece of blog content. It would be misleading to say the content is cost-free, however, just because the creator does not buy raw materials and the consumer does not pay for the final product.

An economic analysis of blogging and blog reading is useful at the micro level in understanding the participant's motivation and intent, and at the macro level in discerning some major features of the blogosphere as a social object. The most obvious cost is time and effort, for the parties in the transaction. Time and effort are a variable cost, for both; a prolific blogger will incur higher costs, as will an avid reader of blogs. There are a number of channel features and related genre conventions which help mitigate this particular cost, and are worth noting. It will be convenient to first consider cost-savings for the reader.

The system of uniquely naming online documents, the URL, makes the practice of permalinking (Permalink, n.d.) possible. Quite simply, a permalink is the URL which leads directly to a specific blog post, in its archive. Bloggers routinely embed hyperlinks when they refer to related posts on their own or another blog; if the hyperlink led to the blog's home page, the reader would still need to search the site for the particular document. Permalinking every post, as they accumulate in the blog's archive, saves the reader a considerable amount of time which would otherwise be required to search for a specific item. Some consider permalinking to be a defining feature of blogs, distinguishing them from other online document formats (see Blog, n.d., on this point).

Another genre convention which the channel facilitates is the trackback (Trackback, n.d.). Should a reader wish to examine other bloggers' reaction to a given post, the list of trackbacks, usually placed at the end of a post, will contain the permalinks of those posts mentioning it. Both permalinks and trackbacks are blog conventions facilitated by the technical capabilities of HTML, the standard programming language for online documents, and URLs, the standard document management system in cyberspace. Trackbacks offer a functional approximation of the scholarly practice of citing others' work. For the author they offer support; for the reader they offer additional depth. They are of interest here in that trackbacks can save considerable time for a reader interested in exploring a given topic or issue.

The blogroll (Blogroll, n.d.) is yet another available time-saver for a reader. Many blogs include a table of hyperlinks to other Web sites the blogger feels are worthy of the reader's attention. The practice is not uniform; some bloggers offer only like-minded material, while others organize their blogroll into categories, including other bloggers with entirely different perspectives. This sort of blogroll is roughly analogous to the literature review or state-of-the-discipline articles found in academic journals; it lists major authors, clustered by their point of view. Again this is a genre convention facilitated by the channel, which offers a reduction in the reader's investment of time.

In short, there are a number of genre conventions, made possible by the technical capabilities of the channel, which offer time savings to the blog reader. In more overtly economic terms, these are cost-reduction mechanisms for the consumer of blog content. There are corresponding cost-reduction mechanisms at the producer's end of the value chain, as well.

While weblogs, as a genre of online document, began as personal pages, group blogging (Group blog, n.d.) has become common. In this form of collaboration, a small number of bloggers all contribute their independently-authored posts to a single blog, on a regular basis. *Power Line*, *Red State, Daily Kos, Volokh Conspiracy*, and *Dead Parrot Society* would be examples of blogs on which more than one individual's work appears. A blog needs to provide a steady supply of fresh content to attract and retain its audience, just as mainstream media outlets do. In a group blog the cost of time and effort for the creation of content is shared among a number of individuals; hence, the cost for each is reduced.

The practice of guest blogging is related. A guest blogger is a person who is invited to contribute content to a blog for some length of time; the understanding, however, is that the guest does not enjoy joint ownership of the blog site in the way group bloggers do. Guest blogging is common when a blogger wishes to take some time off from writing for his or her blog without letting the site become dormant. In short, group blogging and guest blogging are both ways of reducing the cost of time and effort for individual bloggers while maintaining freshness and currency in a blog's content, or enhancing the depth and quantity of material on it.

Common to both the producer and consumer of blog content is

that there is no fixed schedule for its production or consumption. This activity is asynchronous computer-mediated communication; either party can engage in it independently of the other without increased cost or loss of value to either. This is in contrast to broadcast media, where the producers of content must work within set production schedules and the consumers must either attend to the broadcast at a set time or record the material in some way. In short, the cost of coordinating physical actions with others has been reduced to zero, for both the producers and consumers of blog content.

As in the case of other information workers, bloggers need source materials for their product; the raw material for producing an information good is information, in other words. Digital convergence has reduced the cost to access source materials, as more and more have become available online at little or no charge. Moreover, bloggers commonly include readers' comments in the posts, either by quoting e-mail from readers or in enabling comments threads following the text of a post. The interactivity facilitated by the channel has thus become an additional source of raw material for the blogger.

Time and effort are the primary variable costs for the blogger and the reader. Channel characteristics have significantly mitigated those variable costs in the ways noted above. There are some fixed costs which should be noted, as well.

The most obvious fixed cost is the computing machinery required to produce or consume blog content. Certainly the availability of relatively powerful and inexpensive personal computers facilitated the emergence of the blogosphere; it is difficult to imagine the blogosphere developing if participants had to have an account on a university workstation, for instance. The versatility of the personal computer effectively reduces the share of the fixed cost allocated to blogging or blog reading; owners use the machinery for a variety of other tasks, and most likely purchased the machinery for those tasks in the first place.

For the consumer of blog content, a simple personal computer and an Internet account is the extent of this fixed cost; by fixed, we mean that that the marginal cost of consuming another unit of blog content — in plain language, the additional expense of reading another blog — is zero. With heavy competition, the price of Internet access has diminished and the availability of the service become widespread.

A producer of blog content faces a somewhat larger investment, in the form of server space for the blog and the software application for authoring the content. Blog hosting services such as Squarespace (http://www.squarespace.com), TypePad (http://www.typepad.com), and Blogger (http://www.blogger.com) have dramatically reduced the cost of server space; open source software such as WordPress (http://wordpress.org) has reduced the cost of the blog-authoring application. It is worth noting that the server cost is not entirely fixed for the producer, since blogs with high traffic incur higher fees. The key point here is that the cost of the computing machinery, either for the consumer or producer, is at most only a minimal barrier to entry into the marketplace and varies relatively little with the amount of product consumed or produced.

Convergence has mitigated the person's physical location as a limiting factor on participating in the content marketplace. It has often been noted that one of the most interesting characteristics of computer-mediated communication, in general, is the way the channel reduces the constraints time and space place on the interaction. In this case, bloggers need not live in a metropolitan area, as many writers in traditional print media do, as a practical matter. A corresponding cost-reduction applies to the consumers; they do not need to go anywhere, physically, to obtain a tangible artifact conveying the content. In short, physical space likewise plays little role in a cost/benefit analysis of blogging and blog reading.

Certainly the population of personal computers, in itself, could not enable the blogosphere; the network over which the content is distributed was expensive to build and is expensive to maintain. In this cost/benefit analysis, the distribution infrastructure is a public good. This is not to dismiss the considerable cost of the network, but to note that the cost has been completely displaced from the blogger and the blog reader. The network itself over which the digitized content travels is not a cost the individuals must consider, as rational economic actors choosing to produce or consume blog content. In essence, the distribution infrastructure is a sunk cost at the social, rather than individual, level.

In sum, the major variable cost for both the producer and consumer of blog content is the time and effort spent engaging with the material. Blog content is a nontangible information good, so the main cost in its production is likewise nontangible. The associated fixed costs are the personal computing machinery and server space, both of which can be modest. The largest variable cost associated with blogging is the network itself, which is a sunk cost borne at the social level and not experienced directly by the individual producer or consumer. In consequence, the barrier to entry into the blog content marketplace is virtually nil, and hence the competition for audience attention virtually perfect.

Thus far the analysis has concerned outlays; the returns must be considered, as well. On the consumer's end, the benefit is the enjoyment of the blog content, whether as entertainment, stimulation, surveillance of one's environment, or social interaction. Such gains have been thoroughly studied in the literature concerning the uses and gratifications of mass media (see Katz, Blumler, and Gurevitch, 1974 for a concise overview); here we are considering the gratifications as an economic benefit to a rational consumer of blog content. The gains to the producers need further explication, since the monetary rewards are relatively limited.

There seems little doubt that the primary, and immediate, benefit to a blogger is the expressive reward, the satisfaction of having put his or her perceptions and feelings into a form that can be shared with others. That this gain cannot be directly measured in monetary units in no way diminishes its value; certainly there are a great many things of value to humans which cannot readily be priced, and a great many activities humans engage in for the intrinsic enjoyment of them. For instance, the act of creating a work of art — whether textual, visual, auditory, physical, or kinetic — offers far more expressive reward than financial to most people. It is worth noting, further, that money is best thought of as a medium of exchange, rather than an absolute metric of a good's total value (see Friedman, 2002, p. 37 ff. on this point). Since blog content is an information good, which behaves differently from physical goods in the first place, it is not so surprising that the non-priced part of this good's value might be the most consequential, or that the act of producing it is a gain in itself.

Bloggers often mention the expressive reward they obtain. A number have pointed to the 9/11 terrorist attack as the impetus for their blogging; Jeff Jarvis described how blogging provided an emotional release for him in a *Buzz Machine* post titled, "To Witness"

(2005).

> On September 11th in New York, I didn't know what I was: witness, reporter, survivor. I stayed at the World Trade Center to report after the first jet hit. My wife remains, well, disapproving of that decision, but that's because, as it turned out, the danger was far from over. I, too, disapproved of my decision when I was enveloped by the cloud of destruction.

> But danger apart, I knew I had to report. A few days later, I started this blog to continue remembering and witnessing.

Scott Johnson, one of the *Power Line* bloggers, described his enjoyment of the autonomy blogging offers in a television interview (Interview With Scott Johnson, 2004).

> We started the site over Memorial Day weekend in 2002 with — really with 9/11 in mind, wanting to cover events relating to the war and political items related to the war without the kind of, oh, lag time that's involved in submitting 750-word columns to editors and waiting to hear if they are of interest to them. So we appreciated the freedom that a site on the Web afforded us and the ability to pursue our interests at leisure.

A psychotherapist who uses the pseudonym Neo-neocon concisely expressed a similar appreciation of the autonomy blogging affords her (in the comment thread of "Condescension and Leaving the Political Fold," 2005).

> The beauty of a blog is that the blogger writes about what he/she wishes to write about.

Computer engineer Steven Den Beste has since discontinued posting on his blog, *USS Clueless*, but wrote an interesting essay describing the expressive reward in terms of aesthetics (Art — An Unintentional Manifesto, 2001) and linking his blogging to his profession (emphasis in the original).

> My own tentative definition of art is that it is a means of communication. (Of course, as an engineer I look for the function

of anything: something *is* what it *does.*) ...

I like to think that *USS Clueless* is art, though I would never pretend that it is great art. If I have a message, it is this: if you know how something works, it is even more beautiful. Knowledge is wonderful. I try to understand what I see; I don't like mysteries, and I don't take anything for granted ...

To me a "miracle" isn't something inexplicable; it's something extraordinary and complex.

I look at what everyone looks at, but I apparently see what few see. I've been trying to let you all see through my eyes, to communicate my way of looking inside things. That's why I don't link to things unless I have something to say about them. My purpose is to find things which have aspects most don't see.

Here is my message: *The universe is immense and endlessly fascinating,* and the more you know about how it works, the more fascinating it becomes.

While it is a substantial benefit to a blogger, it would be false to assume that the expressive reward of creating blog content is the only return on a blogger's investment of time and effort.   There are a number of other revenue streams which should be noted. For some, the blog is in effect a sketchpad on which to develop work which will later have more overt professional value. One academician who blogs told this author (s)he often uses blogging as a way of informally prototyping ideas or analyses which are later incorporated into more traditional publications. An elaborate example of this development process can be found in the blogging of Michelle Malkin and Brian Maloney on the financial troubles of the Air America network (including Inside Air America, Part 1, 2005; Inside Air America, Part 2, 2005; and Inside Air America Extra, 2005), leading to their *New York Post Online* op-ed on the topic (Maloney & Malkin, 2005). Another good example would be Michael J. Totten's extensive blogging of his travels in northern Iraq and Afghanistan (for example, The Utah of the Middle East, 2006); Totten told this author he planned to later draw on this material in writing a book about the experience.

This repurposing of content — blog material into traditional media material — can work in the opposite direction, as well. Bloggers who also publish in other outlets sometimes link those publications, refer to them, quote from them, or reproduce them in their entirety. This practice can be seen on *Policy By Blog, Power Line, Andrew Sullivan, Michelle Malkin, ProfessorBainbridge*, and *InstaPundit*, for instance. In economic terms, the benefit is the same: the content producer obtains additional value from a given investment of time and effort.

It also seems apparent that blogging may perform crossmarketing, by raising a blogger's name recognition in another mass media channel. The blogs of radio personalities Hugh Hewitt and Tammy Bruce would be examples; on their blogs, they frequently refer to their radio broadcasts or link to transcripts of them. This corresponds roughly to the way academicians expend a good deal of effort writing books which will sell in very limited quantities to very narrow audiences and produce small royalties for them, at best. Despite the modest immediate return on the work to create them, the cumulative professional value of published books is large for academic authors, and hence the book royalties alone do not constitute the total return on the investment in them.

There are also relatively modest — for most bloggers, presumably — amounts of cash return available through the sales of logo merchandise and advertising space on blogs. An online mail order company called CafePress offers a surprisingly extensive line of logo merchandise such as coffee mugs, T-shirts, and other soft goods for a number of bloggers, who link to their own virtual "shop" on the CafePress site (http://www.cafepress.com). This sort of niche marketing is, of course, common outside the blogosphere.

The appearance of advertisements on blogs is familiar from earlier mass media channels; it is well-known that advertising on broadcast and print media reduces the purchase price of the product. Blog content in this respect is similar to terrestrial broadcast content, which can be distributed to consumers without charge because of the revenue generated by commercials. It is not surprising that the blogosphere has evolved its own advertising agencies, which place ads on blogs in return for payment to the bloggers; Blogads (http://www.blogads.com) and Google AdSense (https://www.google.com/adsense/) are good examples. Just as traditional advertising agencies compete on the basis of their ability to deliver desirable demographics for the advertiser, so do blog advertising agencies (see Blog Readers are Shockingly Influential, 2005, for instance).

An interesting, perhaps amusing, feature on some blogs is the virtual "tip jar." Readers who feel so moved can click this button and make some cash payment, of a size they determine, to the blogger. This is in the tradition of street performers; there is no formalized price for their product, but consumers can nonetheless offer some compensation for their enjoyment of it. In economic terms, this is about as purely voluntary a transaction as one can imagine.

To summarize its cost/benefit ratio to an individual, blogging is economically rational activity for people who enjoy working with ideas, expressing them in a distributable form, and engaging others in discussion of them. It likewise is economically rational activity for readers who find merit in blog content and obtain corresponding benefits from exposure to it. For both the producer and consumer of blog content, the greatest benefit is the intrinsic enjoyment of the interaction and engagement with the material. Time and effort are the most consequential variable costs of producing blog material, and of consuming blog material.

Since blog content is an information good, manufacturing and distribution costs are strikingly different from the production of physical goods. For the producer, raw material costs (i.e., source material) are minimal and distribution cost (i.e., server space) is modest. For both the producer and consumer, the machinery (i.e., a personal computer and Internet service) is a sunk cost amortized by its use for a variety of other tasks. The distribution infrastructure (i.e., the Internet itself) is a public good; its actual cost — which is substantial — is thus displaced from both the producer and consumer. Beyond the modest sunk costs, the marginal cost — apart from time and effort — to either the producer of a unit of blog content or to the consumer of that unit is essentially zero.

The Value Chain

Most physical goods go through some number of parties between their origins and their consumption; each of these intermediaries adds some component or feature to the good, or facilitates its progress toward the consumer. This string of transactions en route to the end user of the good is referred to as the value chain. Most information products have a value chain of some sort, as well; a book manuscript most likely has passed from the writer, to an editor, to a printer, to a distributor, to a retailer, and finally to its reader. Usually there are other intermediaries who are not directly in the line of hand-offs of the good or do not alter the good itself, but perform some essential facilitation of those transactions or transformations. For a book, it might be the agent who connects the writer and the editor, or the trucking company which transports the book from the printer to the distributor.

For mainstream media news products in particular, the value chain appears considerably shorter — real world events to news outlet to public — but we should still be aware of the various functional units in the news outlet itself (say, reporter to copy desk to editor) or divisions in a broadcast outlet (say, programming executives to writers to on-air talent) as intermediaries between the real world and the audience. Certainly the information product is affected by each of those actors, from its origin to its consumption.

The blogosphere clearly operates quite differently from the mainstream media. The real-world-to-reader value chain can be as short as one link: a single blogger. Or the chain can grow surprisingly long, with bloggers linking to others' work and adding material of their own. It would be tempting to simply say that the impact of the blogosphere on the news media marketplace is one of disintermediation — the shortening of the value chain — but that would not always be accurate. The starting point of a blog post is often a mainstream media product with a value chain of its own, and the post in question may well have incorporated the contributions of a number of other bloggers in some way. On the other hand, a post may consist solely of an eyewitness account of an event, or only of visual images created by one blogger. The distinguishing attribute of the blogosphere's value chain, then, is its variability: the complexity of a given blog post's value chain tends to fit the complexity of its subject matter.

Again, the channel characteristics of computer-mediated communication facilitate this flexibility. Hyperlinking is a convenient way to add value to a post in the form of supplemental material or factual evidence. It does not violate the property interest of the creator of the other material; the practice is considered fair use, as a matter of common practice. Glenn Reynolds has made this use of his *InstaPundit* material explicit, in his terms of use page (http://instapundit.com/tos.php).

> Permission is granted to read, quote, cite, link to, print out or otherwise use *InstaPundit* content, so long as you comply with the terms below.

> ...All quotations from *InstaPundit* will include credit to *InstaPundit* or to Glenn Reynolds and, wherever practicable, a hyperlink of the form *http://instapundit.com* ... to the site.

Hypertext linking, a feature of HTML, allows bloggers to draw on other sources in a way that traditional media do not. The hypertext links are inherently more powerful than simply citing or briefly quoting another author's work, as is done in the print media, in that hypertext links allow the reader immediate access to the supplemental materials in their entirety. It thus facilitates a value-added process, in that the value of a given unit of blog content can greatly be enhanced by embedding links to other material. It has become routine, even expected, for a piece of media criticism in the blogosphere to contain links to the subject of the critique, and often to other blog commentary on it. The channel feature, hyperlinking, facilitates the addition of value: a reader of the post can quickly and conveniently access the source material or supplemental evidence, while this added value cost the blogger very little effort and no money. A post can incorporate comments from readers, be updated with corrections or newly-available information, or link to other posts related to the topic.

The genre conventions of the blogosphere have clearly evolved to take advantage of the flexibility in its value chain, facilitated by the channel characteristics. Bloggers have no time or space constraints imposed by the channel itself, the way print and broadcast journalists do; there are no column inch requirements, or time slots into which the content must be fitted. Bloggers can post one-line or even one-word comments on a topic (with a link to the subject of their comment), or they can explore the topic at some length. They can append updates or corrections as appropriate; the material becomes incorporated into the post itself and immediately accessible to the reader. Moreover, a single unit of blog content can incorporate a variety of media: text, sound, still image, motion image. Unlike a television producer, for instance, a blogger can choose to employ motion image and sound, or not. Unlike a newspaper reporter, a blogger can rely primarily on text, or not. Unlike either, a blogger can acknowledge and correct an error in the same document which contained the error. In short, bloggers make their content available through a channel which lessens or entirely eliminates certain constraints which are inherent in the traditional mass media channels and reflected in the content genres distributed through them. The blogger, as the content creator, has far more latitude, technically and stylistically, than journalists operating in traditional mass media channels.

The Media Marketplace as an Ecosystem: Symbiosis

At this writing, the long-term relationship between blogs and the mainstream media is just beginning to become visible. This is, of course, to make the assumption that the blogosphere is emerging as a lasting social object, and is more than a passing cultural fad. In this author's judgment view there is already sufficient evidence to warrant that perspective. Another assumption, here, is that bloggers make a genuine contribution to the public sphere, and are not merely parasites on or saboteurs of the existing media system. The question will be taken up more fully in a later chapter, but this author is satisfied on that point, as well.

In some respects the relationship appears to be a straightforward competition for audience attention, between the legacy press and the upstart blogosphere. This might explain a lack of cordiality on both sides, towards the other. While it is true that one can find examples of bloggers complimenting mainstream journalists and mainstream journalists acknowledging the work of bloggers, so far these are occasional courtesies rather than characteristic of their relationship. Indeed, there would not be much individual or social need for the blogosphere to fulfill, if it had no issues with the mainstream press. Nor should one take note only of the bloggers' blunt critique of mainstream journalists; more journalists have had caustic words for bloggers than the examples cited earlier. In short, bloggers have and often will castigate mainstream journalists, and mainstream journalists have and often will return the favor.

It seems fair to describe the mainstream media as an oligopoly. That is to say, a relatively small number of mainstream media outlets supply content to a relatively large number of consumers. While there have been obvious changes in the composition of this oligopoly over the years — fewer newspapers and more broadcast/cable outlets, for instance; increased chain ownership, for another — the high barriers to entry have kept this market sector an oligopoly. Put plainly, few people are able to gather the capital necessary to begin competing in the traditional media market, or have a realistic expectation of generating enough revenue for ongoing operations once they did.

Seen as a sector of the news marketplace, the blogosphere offers certain economic advantages to a content entrepreneur. The barriers to entry are extremely low, and the channel more flexible in its technical capabilities than any other. Bloggers do not incur the burden of regulatory compliance which broadcasters face, even though a blogger's content is available worldwide. We should not overlook the disadvantages the blogosphere entails, though. The revenue streams for most bloggers are modest, perhaps erratic. Switching costs for bloggers' readers are nil; substituting a different blog is considerably easier than changing a newspaper subscription or a cable service. Audience loyalty is thus based only on current satisfaction with the content, and no other extrinsic economic factors. It seems clear that neither the traditional media nor the blogosphere enjoys a decisive overall advantage over the other in a head-to-head competition for audience attention. Rather, the traditional media and the blogosphere have different relative advantages and disadvantages as content producers in a news marketplace which lately has become less of an oligopoly for the entry of the latter.

Perhaps this is a good explanation for something which would otherwise be puzzling. Taken as a cohort, the mainstream media exhibit a high degree of isomorphism (DiMaggio & Powell, 1983); within this sector of the news marketplace, outlets tend to resemble each other in their organization, their functioning, and their products. In contrast, the blogosphere exhibits a high degree of differentiation (Caves & Williamson, 1985); blogs tend to be idiosyncratic, in style and content both. This is understandable if one sees the mainstream outlets as aimed at a mass audience and blogs as aimed at niches, as a consequence of their distinctly different economic characteristics.

This last point suggests that attending only to the ways in which these two social objects compete obscures the subtle and complex way they have begun to influence each other, or even complement each other. This is to say that on closer examination the relationship appears to be accidentally symbiotic more than ruthlessly competitive. Mainstream media outlets have begun experimenting with incorporating blogs into their operations, in a variety of ways (Oxfeld, 2005). A major journalism education organization has advocated what they call "citizen journalism," based largely on features of the blogosphere (Outing, 2005). One major newspaper has run columns by a blog critic of it (see My Second "Outside the Tent" Piece, 2005). Several news and commentary magazines have incorporated bloggers into their online presence: Andrew Sullivan's *Daily Dish* on *Time* (http://time.blogs.com/daily_dish/), Kevin Drum's *Political Animal* on *Washington Monthly* (www.washingtonmonthly.com/), and the *Blog Row* on *National Review* (www.nationalreview.com/) are examples.

The Rathergate scandal described in an earlier chapter prompted a good deal of reflection about journalism as a profession; since it was the blogosphere which exposed a serious factual error in the reporting of a major mainstream outlet, it is not surprising to find evidence of the symbiosis between the two in those reflections. Andrew Sullivan, a prolific writer with much experience in both the mainstream media and the blogosphere, described the value of corrective feedback to professional journalists (Sullivan, 2004).

> The blogosphere is a media improvement because the sheer number of blogs, and the speed of response, make errors hard to sustain for very long ... . And the essence of journalistic trust is not simply the ability to get things right and to present views or ideas or facts clearly and entertainingly. It is also the capacity to admit error, suck it up, and correct what you've gotten wrong. Take it from me. I've both corrected and been corrected. When you screw

up, it hurts. But in the long run, it's a good hurt, because it takes you down a peg or two and reminds you what you're supposed to be doing in the first place. Any journalist who starts mistaking himself for an oracle needs to be reminded who he is from time to time.

John Hinderaker, a lawyer by profession and one of the *Power Line* bloggers who helped expose the forgeries, described the blogosphere as a decentralized, networked knowledge base (To Our Readers, 2004). Of interest here is the collaboration of bloggers and their readers, indicating a softening of the boundary between the producer and consumer of information goods.

> The power of the blogosphere (more properly, the [I]nternet) does not lie in a handful of bloggers with well-read sites. It resides in the hundreds of thousands, or millions, of smart, well-informed, engaged readers who, collectively, have amazing knowledge and expertise in just about any area you can think of. What is new is the ability to bring together these disparate sources of knowledge, analyze them, and disseminate them in real time. We [i.e., bloggers] help to do this, but on a big, fast-breaking story like this one, the real impetus comes from our readers ... .

Paul Mirengoff, another contributor to *Power Line*, detailed the feedback loops operating on bloggers, themselves (But Who Checks the Bloggers?, 2004). Two points are of particular interest here. The blogosphere is not monolithic, so there are internal feedback loops within it. Moreover, the mainstream media act as a check on the blogosphere.

> A story that we run can be checked, in the first instance, against its sources, which we cite and, if possible, link to. Next it is checked by our readers. They are quick to correct us because they don't want us left hanging out to dry, and we can't thank them enough for this ... .

> The next level of review comes from other conservative blogs. Conservative bloggers perform a great service by gently pointing out possible weaknesses in stories that are making the rounds, or at least warning folks not to get too enthusiastic too soon...

If the conservative side of the blogosphere falls down on the job, there's always the liberal side. We don't spend much time arguing with our liberal counterparts — life is too short. But on a story as big as the CBS one, we had to respond to the inevitable liberal counterattack ... .

Finally, on a story like this, the MSM comes into play. In order to remain credible, our version had to stand up to the document examiners and other experts used by the MSM, including CBS. In addition, it had to withstand the scrutiny of their investigative reporters.

As illustrated in the examples described in earlier chapters, bloggers hound mainstream journalists to more fully realize their avowed professional standards, particularly those concerning accuracy and error correction; mainstream journalists, in turn, demand that bloggers be as accountable for their content as the professionals in the news industry, if they expect to be taken seriously. Both provide a feedback loop on the operations of the other, without seriously threatening either's existence. It is not so surprising, then, to see a number of bloggers whose work also appears in mainstream outlets, and a number of mainstream journalists who also blog. Still, this would not suggest that the two sectors will eventually merge, as that would entail a loss of their respective advantages.

In this light, the two social objects are structurally opposed in the sense of providing checks and balances on each other's influence in the public sphere. Yet this opposition does not necessarily lead to a simplistic win/lose competition, since both operate in an ecology of media production and consumption, and the product quality of both can be better for it. The inherent symmetry of the relationship is apparent in this, and it is that symmetry which shows the relationship to be symbiotic in its essence.

CHAPTER 7

Blogs as
Alternative Media

If the term is used loosely, alternative media refers, by definition, to all material in the blogosphere since it is, as a social object, an alternative to the mainstream media. This chapter will construe the term more narrowly, and use the term to refer to blog content which mimics established genres in the mainstream media, but is not explicit critique of particular mainstream media products. The key distinction here is that, as alternative media, these blog posts are not links in a value chain including our mainstream media — as critical posts would be — but instead a bypass to that chain, or a supplement to that chain.

There is a great deal of material in the blogosphere which consists, essentially, of the author's personal responses to the political turmoil of the day. While this material can be interesting or amusing, the posts tend to be short and spicy in their language but relatively limited in their substantive content. It would appear that such material primarily offers socioemotional value to the author and reader — in the form of an affirmation of their political identity — more than factual information, analytical insight, or intellectual challenge.

Of interest in this chapter is straight news reporting provided by non-journalists, or — as many have come to call them — citizen journalists. An interesting variant is photoblogging, corresponding to the pictorial features commonly found in the mainstream press. Also of interest here are the essays, perhaps philosophical or reflective in tone, on such broad topics as self-governance or history. Some blogs specialize in a particular content area, such as the milbloggers (the armed services) and the blawgers (the legal system), or apply a particular perspective to contemporary events, such as the psychbloggers (social psychology); in these, the bloggers bring their specialized expertise to bear on the issues of the day.

This material is best considered as alternative news content, in the sense that the products are not so much reactions to pieces created by the mainstream media and best considered in relation to the mainstream product, but complete and self-contained alternatives or supplements to the products supplied by the traditional media. That is to say, one can find straight news reporting, essays, policy analyses, personal reflections, and editorials in the blogosphere, just as such genres of information product are supplied by mainstream media outlets. One might wonder what such blog material offers a reader, beyond what is already available in ample supply from the mainstream media. It appears that the major advantage is one of perspective; bloggers can sometimes offer specialized expertise, pictorial or documentary evidence, eyewitness accounts, translations of foreign-language news, or heterodox analyses not generally available from mainstream outlets. To the extent that the mainstream media are largely characterized by isomorphism while the blogosphere tends toward differentiation, a point raised in the preceding chapter, this can clearly be a broadening or deepening of the news products available to the public. While a skeptic might object that serious journalism is a job for professional journalists, in effect suggesting a blanket dismissal of the amateur reporting and editorializing done by bloggers, it is worth noting that bloggers' lack of acculturation into the prevailing norms and practices of the journalism industry also offers the possibility that they will bring fresh insights into the media mix available to the public at large, or will provide coverage of events ignored by the mainstream media.

Reporting

A good example of straight news reporting can be found on the group blog, *TigerHawk*, in a post titled very much like a typical headline: "Lt. Gen. David Petraeus Speaks at Princeton" (2005). Other than occasional passages in which the author — a medical equipment executive who uses the pseudonym, TigerHawk — refers to himself in the first person or injects a brief personal comment, the lengthy post is written very much in the straight news voice common in the mainstream press. For instance, the first paragraph contains the usual who-what-where-why-when-how elements of the lede in a mainstream press story.

> The festivities surrounding the 75th anniversary of Princeton University's Woodrow Wilson School For Public and International Affairs continued yesterday with a speech by Lt. General David Petraeus (M.P.A. '85, Ph.D. '87). General Petraeus has recently returned from Iraq, having served as the Commander, Multi-National Security Transition Command and NATO Training Mission. Before that, he was Commanding General of the 101st Airborne Division during its year in Iraq.

> The advertised topic of General Petraeus' talk — which was not covered by the mainstream media — was "A Soldier's Reflections on Iraq," but it turned out to be a quite specific briefing on the present condition of Iraq's military and special police, which General Petraeus had been charged with organizing and training through the completion of his tour … .

The post continues with a thorough summary of the content of Petraeus's speech and the following question-and-answer session, including a good number of verbatim quotes.

An interesting difference between typical blog reporting of an event and the traditional inverted pyramid story format of the mainstream press is that the blogger usually follows the actual chronological sequence of the event, instead of resequencing quotations and descriptions into the reporter's judgment of their relative importance. Moreover, the blogger does not work under the time or space constraints felt by all mainstream journalists; in this case, TigerHawk provided a lengthier and more detailed account of the speech than one would expect to find even in a local newspaper. Clearly a blogger cannot avoid making some judgment of what to include and what to omit, any more than a professional journalist can. Still, the blog reporting can be a more transparent account, in the sense that the story format itself does not impose such constraints on the writer.

A similar thought applies to photoblogging: news industry conventions about the visual quality of images — lighting, composition, focal length, depth of field, for instance — need not constrain a blogger in the way these attributes are a concern of professional photojournalists. Freelance writer Shelby Murdoc made good use of blogs' ability to include visual images in a pair of *Murdoc Online* posts showing the damage from Hurricane Katrina. Both contain very little text; the content is the images themselves, as is the case with mainstream media pictorial features. In terms of visual aesthetics, they are snapshots taken with consumer-level equipment through the window of a small airplane flying over the area. The first post (Pictures From the Air, 2005) showed the extensive damage to the towns of Pass Christian, Gulfport, and Biloxi, immediately after the hurricane passed; as is often found in photoblogging, it opens with a brief explanation of the provenance of the images and why Murdoc chose to post them.

> While almost all of the attention has been on New Orleans, the fact is that [H]urricane Katrina (thankfully) turned and didn't hit the city directly. While this was fortunate for the 100,000 residents stranded in the city, it didn't bode well for those in the other cities and towns along the Gulf Coast of Mississippi and Alabama. They took a direct hit, and it's important that we don't forget about them. These pictures were sent in by a reader who works with the spouse of the photographer, who is in the Air Force Reserve.

The balance of the post is a series of about two dozen images. Murdoc added a brief caption to each, indicating its location and sometimes noting something of particular interest about it. For instance, he followed a picture of a totally destroyed highway bridge with this terse comment:

> This is Highway 90 east of Biloxi. No relief coming that way.

This post contains an interesting example of the value-added process noted in the preceding chapter. Murdoc explained that he had identified the locations shown in the pictures by comparing them to Google Earth satellite images of the region. He was able to match a Google Earth image quite closely with one of the aerial pictures, and created a before-and-after juxtaposition of the marina in Pass Christian.

Several months later Murdoc posted a followup about the damage to the area in "Gulf Coast Photos" (2006). He explained that another reader had sent him a number of current pictures taken from the ground; these were of debris which had not yet been cleared. Again, he indicated that his motivation for posting the images was to provide a sense of the severe damage in an area which had gotten less mainstream press coverage than New Orleans.

> Even though the plight of the residents of Mississippi and Alabama who were hit by Hurricane Katrina never received a lot of attention while everyone watched New Orleans, even though what little coverage there ever was has faded away, the wreckage is still there and there are still people in a bad way.

> Don't forget them.[55]

A number of bloggers have provided continuing coverage of the Iraq war in the form of their own direct observation of the area, much in the vein of the traditional overseas correspondents. Freelance writer Michael J. Totten used his eponymous blog as a journal of his travels in northern Iraq. The style of the writing is informal and personal, but Totten clearly intended to convey a factual sense of the places he visited provided a large number of still photos with the text. He did not tour the combat theater, but instead focused on civilian life in Iraq, post-Hussein. An interesting attribute of this extensive body of material is that Totten often mentioned, or showed in an image, mundane details of daily life; again, this can be seen as a higher degree of transparency in conveying the situation than the conventions of the mainstream media will allow. Paradoxically, the informal and overtly subjective stance of the bloggers may position them to create more objective content (in the sense of less coloration introduced in the process of conveying reality over time and space; see Cooper, 2006b, p. 1064 on this point) than professional journalists, who must operate within the industrial and format conventions of their respective media. In material such as this, the value chain is very short; only the blogger intermediates between reality and the reader.

A couple of examples will serve to illustrate these points. In a post titled, "The Safest City in Iraq" (2006), Totten elaborated on his overall impressions of Dohok with description and pictures of a supermarket there.

In Dohok everything changed. There I kept thinking: *This is Iraq?* It doesn't look like Iraq at all. (But it is Iraq, so I guess it does look like Iraq.) More important, it doesn't feel like Iraq. There is no terrorism and no fighting — none whatsoever — in Dohok. There are too many Peshmerga checkpoints between the war zone and the city. You could go there on holiday (if you want) and feel just as relaxed as you would in a medium-sized city in Canada. The people are friendlier, though, so you might even feel more at ease.

My American friend Sean LaFreniere recently e-mailed me from Denmark. "Is it true they have laser scanners in supermarkets in Kurdistan?" he asked me.

Well, yeah. Iraqi Kurdistan has serious problems that will take a long time to fix. (Very little electricity unless you own a generator, no ATMs, corruption in government, etc.) But most Americans would be shocked, I think, to discover just how prosperous, modern, and *normal* it is, at least on the surface.

Yes, they have laser scanners in supermarkets. A supermarket in Northern Iraq looks more or less like a supermarket anywhere in North America.

Totten included a series of snapshots of the exterior of a supermarket and items on its shelves. He closed the post with several pictures of a residential area, which he described in this way:

I asked my driver and translator to take me to a typical nice residential neighborhood, and specifically *not* a neighborhood where the elite live. I just wanted to see an average middle class area in Dohok, off the main streets, so I could show Americans and Europeans what it looks like.

We pulled off the main drag and into the neighborhood closest to where we were when I asked. We didn't cross the city to get there. It's just where we happened to be when I said I wanted to get out of the car and take pictures of where we happened to stop. This is what it looked like, a typical middle class neighborhood in Dohok, Iraq.

Totten provided a similar description of ordinary life in Suleimaniya, in "The Utah of the Middle East" (2006). Again, he interspersed a good number of still images of residential and commercial areas of the city.

Somewhere around 800,000 people live in the city today. Three years ago only half as many lived there. Like any city that undergoes rapid urban migration, most of the newcomers live on the outskirts. Unlike in most Third World cities, the people who live on the outskirts don't live in shanties or slums. Their part of the city is actually more prosperous than the old urban core.

I'm not cherry-picking these photos. I spent almost a week in the city. Every neighborhood I saw, from one end of Suleimaniya to the other, looked either lower middle-class or amazingly wealthy...

Real poverty, of the grinding Third World variety, did not appear to exist. If it does exist, it is very well hidden, at least in the cities. (The countryside is still primitive.)

While in Suleimaniya, Totten toured the compound which had been the local headquarters of the secret police during the Hussein regime. In "The Head of the Snake" (2006), a phrase he said Hussein had used to refer to Suleimaniya, Totten provided a number of disturbing pictures of the facility, which since had been turned into a museum. The captions were brief, and included his own emotional reactions to the site.

Dozens of people were packed into single caged cells. This one, pictured below, needed to have blood scrubbed off the walls before it could be opened to visitors ... .

The hardest thing to see was the cell used to hold children before they were murdered. My translator[,] Alan[,] read some of the messages carved into the wall.

"I was ten years old. But they changed my age to 18 for

execution."

"Dear Mom and Dad. I am going to be executed by the Baath. I will not see you again."[56]

Other bloggers chose to report on the war theater itself, as embeds with combat units. In contrast to the contemporary "hotel journalism" coverage supplied by the mainstream media, there is an emphasis on detailed description of events in their chronological sequence. On the other hand, these reports are mostly limited to the blogger's direct observations or to immediately accessible sources. Bill Roggio's description of an uneventful night patrol (The Hounds of Husaybah, 2005) illustrates this type of blog reporting (minor punctuation errors corrected).

> I joined up with the 4th Mobile Assault Platoon, call sign Jackal 4, for a zero-dark-thirty patrol ... . The patrol sped off in full blackout, piloted by drivers with night vision goggles. The Jackals escorted a Civil Affairs Group (CAG) to and from Hue City. The "440 District," named after the number of buildings in the neighborhood, was paid a visit, as were neighborhoods in the north and south of the city, and a remote desert region with buildings and walls scattered about.

> At night the streets of Husaybah often appear as [a] series of mazes quite mean by American standards. The houses are surrounded by ramshackle walls; rubble, trash, abandoned cars and fifty gallon drums are strewn along the roadways. All are potential hiding places for IEDs [improvised explosive devices]. Since Steel Curtain [an earlier combat operation], four IEDs have been uncovered, but it's unknown if these are bombs missed in previous sweeps, or ones newly deployed. Staff Sergeant Strong believes insurgents are attempting to reenter the city and resume attacks on the Coalition.

> No IEDs or insurgents were encountered during the early morning's patrol. The only takers were the myriad of Husaybah's dogs, who howl loudly and seem ever present. The jihadis ceded the night to the hounds of Husaybah and the Jackals of 4th Platoon.

While most mainstream outlets would not have run a story in which "nothing happened," this kind of reportage is arguably quite valuable to a reader at some distance from the area, forming a sense of the progress of the war from available media reports on it. Again, blog material often is a useful supplement to material provided by the mainstream media.[57]

Michael Yon also embedded with a combat unit in a war-torn area of Iraq. While he describes his extensive material as an "online magazine" and his lengthy posts as "dispatches," his work nonetheless displays the essential attributes of blogs, including reverse chronological order in displaying stories and permalinks for each. Yon's style contrasts somewhat with Roggio's in that he provides many visual images of warfare, and often includes his own reflections on events, using the first person to refer to himself. For instance, he offered this provocative comment (Prelude, 2005) on the overall trend he observed in Mosul, the tendency of news outlets to emphasize violence in their reporting, and his own presence in a combat zone (punctuation as in the original).

> Unfortunately, the "Sunni triangle" is a region churning with an insurgency that shows no sign of letup. But by focusing on the flames, the media does not give the world a fair or accurate representation of what's happening for most Iraqi people, or for most of the Coalition forces. I, too, have spent most of my time in Iraq in these dangerous provinces, so even these dispatches might indicate that Iraq has more problems than is actually the case.

> Yet even here in the warring provinces, progress is clear. I have endured many tedious meetings with agendas focused on roadside trash, local business development, or Iraqi police training. These normalities do not make good news.

> Though "the media" zooms in on the flames, viewers are equally complicit. After all, who among us is more likely to tune in or read about another successful Iraqi adopt-a-highway initiative, when the other option is dramatic footage of the fighting that our people face every day inside these jagged borders?

> And so it is. I am with the 1-24th Infantry Regiment of the 25th

Infantry Division, whose soldiers are fighting some of the most serious insurgency battles in Iraq.

Yon's material often includes vivid descriptions of combat. In "Gates of Fire" (2005) he described a "surge" operation, intended to surface insurgents and kill or capture them. He saw his unit's commanding officer wounded during a foot chase of insurgents who had abandoned their car.

> The car chase ended, but the men fled on foot up an alley. We approached in the Strykers and I heard Kurilla [the commanding officer] say on the radio, "Shots fired!" as he ducked for a moment then popped back up in the hatch. Kurilla continued, "Trail section clear the car and clear south to north! I'm going to block the back door on the north side!"
>
> About fifteen seconds later our ramp dropped. We ran into combat...
>
> There were shops, alley, doorways, windows.
>
> The soldiers with LTC Kurilla were searching fast, weapons at the ready, and they quickly flex-cuffed two men. But these were not the right guys. Meanwhile, SSG Konkol's men were clearing toward us, leaving the three bad guys boxed, but free.
>
> Shots were fired behind us but around a corner to the left.
>
> Both the young 2nd lieutenant and the young specialist were inside a shop when a close-quarters firefight broke out, and they ran outside. Not knowing how many men they were fighting, they wanted backup. LTC Kurilla began running in the direction of the shooting. He passed by me and I chased, Kurilla leading the way.
>
> There was a quick and heavy volume of fire. And then LTC Kurilla was shot ... .
>
> With his leg mangled, Kurilla pointed and fired his rifle into the doorway, yelling instructions to the soldiers about how to get in there.[58]

A very interesting way bloggers can supplement the coverage of our mainstream media is by making foreign reporting accessible. A post on *Iraq the Model* provides a concise example (Iraqi Tribes, 2006). It consisted of an excerpt from an Arabic-language publication, based in Lebanon, reporting the arrest of terrorists in the Anbar province of Iraq. The post in its entirety is this (ellipsis in the original; syntax and punctuation as in the original):

> From Dar al-Hayat (Arabic):
>
> > The Anbar tribes' campaign to rid the province of Zarqawi's terror organization, al-Qaeda in Iraq is in its 2nd day and so far, 270 Arab and foreign intruders have been arrested. ...
> >
> > Usama Jad'aan, the leader of Karabila tribes in Qaim told al-Hayat that "the operation will continue to eliminate terror elements according to a quality plan" and added "270 Arab and foreign intruders have been arrested, in addition to some Iraqis who were providing them shelter".
>
> Sheikh Jad'aan added "the operation is conducted in coordination between the tribes and the minister of defense Sa'doun al-Dulaimi and since we arrested hundreds of terrorists, I don't expect the operation to take a lot of time".

Power Line posted correspondence from one of their readers (On the Mosque Bombing, 2006), who supplied a translation of Arabic-language reporting on the bombing of a mosque in Samarah (capitalization, punctuation, and syntax as in the original).

> The following is my translation of a headline and news published by the Iraqi Arabic newspaper "Aswataliraq" on February 23.
>
> "Iraqis of Samarah start rebuilding bombed Shrine ... [elipsis in original], and demonstrate for national unity."
>
> "Local police further reported that thousands of local residences [sic] formed a demonstration, which headed to city hall. Demonstrators were chanting 'Not Sunni Not Shiite... [elipsis in original] one one national unity.' The demonstration dispersed by noon without incidents ... .

The following is my translation of a headline and news published by the Kuwaiti Arabic news agency KUNA on February 23.

"Iraqis form local Shiite committees to protect Sunni Mosques in Basra and the south."

"Large (peaceful) demonstrations broke out again today in Basra, protesting the heinous attacks on a Shiite shrine in Samarah. Over 100,000 protesters participated chanting condemnations against the attacks and calling for self-restraint and following religious instructions (from leading religious references) for calm. Sheik Abdul Husein Almuhamdawi (a religious leader in the province) said; 'Local national Shiite committees have been formed to protect local Sunni mosques from over zealous [sic] individuals'..."

The reader, Haider Ajina, went on to comment that American news coverage had given a misleading sense of the public reaction to the bombing.

This bombing in Samarah has brought more unity amongst Iraqis than any other incident since the stampede on the Kahdumiah bridge... Iraqi political parties, community leaders, religious leader, political leaders all are strongly condemning this bombing and asking for national support and help for the people of Samarah. This outpouring of compassion, support and help is what is not being reported.

An Iraqi journalist provided a similar viewpoint on the aftermath of the bombing of the mosque on his blog, *24 Steps to Liberty*. In a post titled "We Are All Misinformed!" (2006), Omar likewise described his distress at the contrast between western reporting of the popular feelings about the event, and the public statements made by many Iraqi political and religious leaders (syntax and bracketed as in the original; ellipses added by this author).

I was shocked today when I read the news in the foreign newspapers. No one emphasized the marvelous cooperation and solidarity between the Shiites and the Sunnis in Iraq yesterday after the bombing of one of the most respected and visited holy sites in Islam, the Askariyah shrine, which is in Samarra city north of Baghdad ... . [Just so you know, in the 9th century there weren't Shiites and Sunnis yet. There were Muslims, who were fighting each other over power. And later on they invented Sunnit and Shiite parts of Islam ... . Yesterday, the attack upset and angered Sunnis and Shiites equally.] ...

The first reaction to the bombing which "targeted a Shiite" shrine came from the Sunni residents of Samarra. The first demonstration to condemn the attack was held spontaneously by Sunnis in the area where the shrine is. Almost all Sunni leaders went on TV to condemn the attack and show solidarity and unity with the Shiites.

Omar provided quotations from a number of local news reports of leaders condemning the bombing and calling for calm. He closed the post with a personal comment on the selectivity of the reporting in the western press (syntax as in the original).

I was amazed how only the provocative and civil-war-style quotes were published today in the newspapers. Almost no newspaper showed how great, it appeared to us, the solidarity among Iraqis was yesterday ... . All what I am saying is that the news made Iraqis look like if they were fighting each other widely in the streets, which is not true. The news only made Iraqis sound like barbarians killing each other. There are barbarian Iraqis, like other people in the world, I am not saying all Iraqis are perfect and compete with angels in their manners. But why when anything good happens, they show the bad side of it too in their stories, but when any bad thing to happen, they only write about it and not the good sides around it?[59]

Essays

Many thoughtful essays appear in the blogosphere. In these longer posts, the blogger brings some personal experience, network of contacts, or professional expertise to bear on a topic of the day. Over time, some blogs have come to be associated with a particular topic area or perspective. For instance, milbloggers concern themselves with the armed forces; *Mudville Gazette, Baldilocks*, *Countercolumn*, and *Citizen Smash* are examples. Blawggers focus on law and the legal system; *Althouse, ProfessorBainbridge, Volokh Conspiracy,* and *Overlawyered* are examples. Psychbloggers write about social psychology; *Dr. Sanity* and *ShrinkWrapped* are examples. Whether a category name has developed or not, the common attribute of these essays, as alternative media product, is that the bloggers use their special knowledge or viewpoint as the basis for their commentary.

For example, psychiatrist Pat Santy posted a provocative essay on the distinction between shame and guilt cultures on her blog, *Dr. Sanity.* The post (Shame, Guilt, the Muslim Psyche, and the Danish Cartoons, 2006) analyzed the violent response in the Islamic world to a Danish newspaper's publication of cartoons depicting the prophet Mohammed. Santy began by contrasting the two emotions, at the individual level.

> Guilt is about actions or behavior; while shame is about the self. There is an important psychological difference in saying to someone that their behavior is bad; as contrasted with saying that they are bad. The former leads to guilt; the latter to shame ... .

> Most psychological theorists (Erikson, Freud, Kohut) see shame as a more "primitive" emotion (since it impacts one's basic sense of self) compared to guilt, which is developed later in the maturation of the self. It should be noted that without the development of guilt there is no development of a real social conscience.

Santy then extended the distinction to the level of cultural attributes.

> A guilt culture (i.e., the West) is typically and primarily concerned with truth, justice, and the preservation of individual rights. As noted earlier, the emotion of guilt is what keeps a person from behavior that goes against his/her own code of conduct as well as the culture's. Excessive guilt can, of course, be pathological.

> In contrast, in a typical shame culture (i.e., Arab/Islamic culture) what other people believe has a far more powerful impact on behavior than even what the individual believes. The desire to preserve honor and avoid shame to the exclusion of all else is one of the primary foundations of the culture.

This led Santy to her analysis of the hostile reaction to the Danish cartoons, a response which struck her as requiring explication in light of the routine publication of cartoons denigrating Jews in the Arabic press. She embedded links in the post which led to other online documents containing images of cartoons, so the reader could examine them independently (emphasis in the original).

> There is no shame involved in insulting or denigrating other cultures for Muslims. Therefore such insults are acceptable. That is why there is a disconnect between the disgusting cartoons that are incredibly offensive to Jews and Christians and/or the West (see here), yet at the same time, they angrily DEMAND on threat of violence that even the most mildly offensive cartoons (i.e., the Danish ones here) be immediately repudiated.
>
> SHAME MUST BE AVOIDED AT ALL COSTS. Everything else is secondary. Contradictions are irrelevant; logic and reason unimportant. HONOR MUST BE RESTORED, and this can only be done at the expense of those who originated the "insult."

Santy then argued that the West's response to the Islamic world's anger could also be understood in this light, but that apology would not be sufficient to resolve the conflict since its roots lay in the foundational cultural difference.

> Meanwhile, in our guilt culture, we obsess about how we might have hurt their feelings and some of us (not me) actually desire to make amends and apologize. This is laudable and very sensitive. It underscores the sense of tolerance that has evolved within Western culture. However well-meaning, IT WILL NOT WORK, particularly in the long-run. Making an apology for having "shamed" someone in such a culture is merely a sign of weakness from their perspective (since you are shaming yourself by admitting guilt), and hence only escalates the self-righteousness and demands that follow; and it does not ameliorate the next insult when it inevitably (and usually unintentionally) comes.

Another psychiatrist, Perry R. Branson, drew on his experience as a psychoanalyst to preface a comment on press coverage of the war on terror. The *ShrinkWrapped* post (The Information War, 2006) began with an anecdote from Branson's practice.

> Many years ago, a patient told me a story. She was trying to impress me with the power of her mother's personality and how her mother's hair trigger temper made everyone reluctant to challenge her. She recalled a summer at a lake in the country; her father would stay with them on the weekends and work in the city during the week. Her mother had found and rented the cabin and would not tolerate any criticism of their accommodations. One weekend night when her father was at the lake, there was a terrible rain storm; the roof began to leak. When her father mentioned the leak to her mother, her mother screamed at him that the cottage was fine, there was no leak, and he should go to sleep, whereupon her father dutifully rolled over and went to sleep, with the ceiling dripping on him throughout the night. There was never any further mention of the incident.

> And the most interesting aspect of the story?

> When my patient told me this story, she suddenly realized that though she had not thought of it for years, she had been, to that moment, uncertain whether or not the roof had really leaked.

Branson then began to connect this anecdote to media effects on public opinion. He noted two important dimensions of human consciousness evident in it.

> I mention this story for two reasons. First, it is important to recognize the importance of "authority" in shaping perceptions; second, the plasticity of perception and memory requires constant vigilance to safeguard reality.

Branson quoted Walter Cronkite's famous editorial comment in a CBS News broadcast, following the Tet Offensive in the Vietnam War, stating that America had become "mired in stalemate" and urging the U.S. government to withdraw from the war. Branson argued that Cronkite had been mistaken in taking that position, and cited as evidence a passage in the memoirs of a North Vietnamese general describing the severe losses they had in fact suffered in the battle. Branson noted that Cronkite's words had great influence in shaping the public's perception of the war situation (punctuation as in the original).

> Cronkite was not anti-American, however, his error was instrumental in turning a terrible defeat for the North Vietnamese into a disaster for America. By virtue of his unassailable authority, he turned himself into the best weapon the North Vietnamese Communists would ever acquire.

Branson then compared the dispiriting effect of Cronkite's broadcast on the public perception of the Vietnam War to current press coverage of the Iraq war. He outlined a provocative typology of public figures he felt were harming Western interests in a serious conflict.

> It occurred to me that while many people have assumed that the MSM [mainstream media] have "chosen sides" and are in opposition to the West, there is really no particular evidence for such a claim. How is it that so much of the MSM reporting is inaccurate, slanted, partially accurate, and seemingly almost designed to damage our war efforts, not only in Iraq, but throughout the entire sphere of the Information War against Islamic fascism?
>
> For now I would suggest there are four main groups of individuals who are actively involved, often without their conscious knowledge, in the Information War, whose work tends to damage the interests of the West:
>
> 1. The Anti-Americans: There is a small cadre of overt Anti-American, far left extremists...
>
> 2. The Sympathizers: ...These are people who think the use of American military power is never justified, unless it is not in our national interest...
>
> 3. The Opportunists: ...They often appear to have no idea how their actions damage our country and our war effort.
>
> 4. The Useful Idiots: Finally, the largest group consists of those who believe they are serving the public interest as they understand

it, but through short-sighted concentration on the immediate and the fuzzy thinking engendered by an adherence to political correctness, tend to frame their perspective in ways that are inimical to Western Civilization...

The most valuable and powerful weapon these people have is their authority.[60]

Sometimes there is a direct connection between the blogger's profession and some policy issue; the blogger uses his/her work as a vantage point on the issue. One example of this is a post on an art historian's blog, *Elephants in Academia.* The art professor, who uses the pseudonym Academic Elephant, objected to a bill pending in the Arizona state legislature which would compel higher education institutions to provide alternative coursework when a student found the regular coursework personally offensive in some way. She began the post, (Picture of the Day: Do I Offend?, 2006), with an image of a 16th century painting by Titian, "Venus of Urbino." The painting is a reclining nude.

Is this a great painting? Yes. Does it deserved to be studied in any course dealing with Renaissance art and/or culture? Yes. Is it provocative? Yes. Deliberately so.

But is it offensive? ... I say no. However, if you're my student and we're in the great state of Arizona, you get to make the call.

Academic Elephant linked the text of the bill; she then supplied an image of a substitute work by Titian, "La Schiavona," which is a standing portrait of a woman.

Well, Titian did lots of paintings of ladies with clothes on, so how about this? But it's not quite the same, now, is it?

Academic Elephant saw the bill as an "egregious example of political correctness run amok," a political intrusion into education which would have a negative unintended consequence.

Furthermore, it's an opportunity to further eviscerate the Western canon for not adhering to our contemporary social mores. In a world governed by legislation like this, students can remain inoculated from any contamination by the imperialism, sexism, racism and violence that color much of Western history. But the problem is that they would then be insulated from the past itself, and so be cut off not only from the unsavory bits but also from the great achievements of the past … .

Liberals might claim to be offended by what, from a 21st century viewpoint, is the blatant sexism of this objectification of a woman. Conservatives might be put off by the overt sexuality of the painting. In either case, it would be my job to engage their interest and explain why, when considered as an object of its own time, this is a great painting. Simply substituting the less challenging La Schiavona would be a cop out for all of us because there is no equivalent to the Venus. It's a watershed in western painting in terms of technique and composition. The treatment of the female nude would never be the same after this … .

Intellectual discourse in academia will only be impoverished by such political bias, be it liberal, conservative, or, in this case, a little of both.

Academic Elephant felt that students should examine the syllabi of courses they were considering taking, and that this would adequately protect them against the harm the bill was intended to address. She closed the post with a witty challenge.

As a footnote, the Duke of Urbino ordered this portrait of his mistress to ornament his bedroom the year after he married a very different woman. When it came time to take delivery of the coveted painting, however, he had to borrow money from his mother to get Titian to release it because the Duke was short on cash and other eager collectors were sniffing around the masterpiece.

Now tell me you don't want to study it.

Warren Meyer, who operates a number of recreational facilities in public parks under concession contract, used his own business as the basis for an essay on the economic impact of minimum (Case

Studies on the Minimum Wage, 2005). Meyer began the *Coyote Blog* post by disclosing his personal interest in such legislation (minor spelling errors corrected).

> OK, I will begin this post with what I guess is, for some, a damning admission: My company pays many of its employees minimum wage. I believe that I have a very honorable relationship with my employees, but for many, particularly on the left, the fact that I pay minimum wage puts me at the approximate moral level of a forced labor camp guard ... .
>
> I want to present four case studies from my own business as to what happens to workers and consumers when minimum wages go up.

Meyer then summarized the demographics of his work force, and described the compensation he provided them.

> To run our campgrounds, we mainly employ retired people. Of my 500 workers, well over half are over 60 years old, more than 150 are over 70, some 25 or so are over 80 and a few are even over 90!...
>
> Most of my employees travel the country in their RV. They take most of the year off, but many like to work over the summer to make a little money and to pay for their camping site. I give many of them a free or subsidized campsite, worth about $500+ a month, plus all their utilities and then pay them minimum wage for the hours they work. Many are thrilled with these terms — so many that I have a waiting list now of over 300 names of people who are looking for this type work.

He listed several reasons the minimum wage jobs were attractive to this cohort, contrary to the argument some of have made that minimum wage jobs are always undesirable.

> They value the amenities that come with the job, including living for free in a beautiful outdoor setting ...
>
> They have other means of support, so the money is incidental ...

They get to work with their spouse as a team ...

They would have a hard time getting hired by anyone else. Very few employers will hire new workers in their sixties, and certainly not older than that.

Meyer then listed effects that various state minimum wage laws had on his operations. In each case, he described in detail how an increase in the minimum wage law had an unanticipated negative impact at a particular campground.

Case 1: The jobs just go away ...

Case 2: The jobs get outsourced to contractors ...

Case 3: The jobs get automated away ...

Case 4: Prices go up to customers ... .

Meyer closed the post by noting that his business was not, itself, threatened by increases in minimum wage laws, but the laws would eventually discourage him from offering these jobs (minor errors corrected).

I'm not going to cry that my business is doomed by minimum wage increases, because it is not. As you can see above, we have many options for dealing with these changes. What I fear may be doomed, though, is the special relationship our company has always had with older, retired workers. For now, the business model is OK, but there is a point, somewhere between about $7.00 an hour and $10.00 an hour, where rising minimum wages will push us to look for other ways to staff our parks rather than our traditional use of live-on-site retirees. And that would be sad for everyone ... .

It is astounding to me that people still want to believe the notion that minimum wages don't affect employment ... . If the government set a price floor for gasoline, say at $3.00 a gallon, would anyone out there argue that people wouldn't use less gas? But when we try to raise the price floor on labor, the media and politicians with a straight face try to argue that businesses won't use less labor.[61]

Some blog essays are reflections on the meaning of historical events to the author. Perhaps this variety of blogosphere content is the most traditional, since weblogs originated as personal journals maintained in the public arena of cyberspace. The language is sometimes quite emotional, and it would seem that this material shows most clearly the expressive and socioemotional rewards of blogging for the writer and the audience. The comment threads on such posts often grow long, as readers respond to the content of the post and share reflections of their own.

A psychotherapist who uses the pseudonym Neo-neocon has offered a good deal of this material on her eponymous blog. The relevance of her professional training to her blogging is often apparent in these. She described the impact of the Kennedy assassination on her worldview, in "A Mind is a Difficult Thing to Change" (2005).

> I think it must be difficult for anyone born afterwards to understand the profound shock inherent in Kennedy's assassination. Those of us who'd grown up in the 50s were well aware — perhaps hyper-aware — of the threat of atomic war...but I think I can speak for most of us when I say that something on the order of Kennedy's death was almost literally unthinkable, right up till the day it happened.

Neo-neocon described being sent home from high school when the assassination occurred, and crying for days at the news (emphasis in the original).

> What was I weeping for? Many things, including Kennedy's wife and children. But I think it was really lost innocence — my own — that I was weeping for. Despite the atomic fears of the 50s, and then the Cuban missile crisis, our sense was that all threats would come from outside. We had a sense of security *within* this country, a sense of internal personal safety from our own countrymen, that was as powerful as it turned out to be false ... . It seemed that the world had opened itself up to chaos.

> We had heard of assassinations before; after all, there was Lincoln.

But that was fusty old history, not reality. But now the two intersected, and now — even though we would never have described it that way — now we, too, had entered history.

An Iraqi physician named Ali Fadhil posted a very interesting example of this sort of essay on *Free Iraqi*. Intensely personal in its language, "What Independence Means For Me" (2005) began with Fadhil's understanding of the word as a child (syntax and punctuation as in the original).

> When I was a kid the word independence meant almost nothing to me. It was mainly because I rarely heard the word given any real importance in our media. The reason was that we got our independence through the cooperation between the British and the constitutional monarchy they helped establish in Iraq. That wasn't something the "nationalists" who ruled from 1958 were interested in presenting to the public in any good way.
>
> Instead the terms that got more focus and were considered to be more worthy of sacrificing for were things like, "the revolution", "the historical leadership" and "the holy battle against the Zionists and imperialist Americans".
>
> So frankly speaking I don't think I understood what independence meant, and it certainly didn't mean anything good to me when I grew up to realize all the horrors of Saddam's regime and that I was living a life that [was] worth nothing. In fact I don't think I was living at all.

Fadhil then touched on the turbulence of post-Hussein Iraq, and the historical context which fostered that turbulence.

> It was later down the road through these last two years that I started to think a bit differently. It was because of the problems in Iraq that emerged mainly from ethnic and sectarian differences. I started to see that Iraq was never a nation. It was never united and was instead unified by force against the will of many of its components; by the British in the beginning and by the national governments later ... .

Thus the need to establish Iraq as a nation, independent and united became a necessity and a human cause. This goal is still far from being achieved but we are working for it. I can see many Iraqis putting all their efforts to bring this nation to life.

The post concluded with good wishes for Americans as they observed their independence day.

Happy 4th of July America and thank you for all your help and sacrifices, not just for us Iraqis but all free people that you helped them get their freedom, and thank you for being the symbol of freedom that gives hope to all oppressed people around the world.[62]

CHAPTER 8

The Blogosphere and the Public Sphere

As is to be expected after a technological or social innovation in communication occurs, there has already been a great deal of rumination about the influence of blogs on the public's discussion of issues, events, and policy questions. It would be an interesting project — but beyond the scope of this work — to analyze the major viewpoints on blogs and the public discourse, with an eye for the social group in which those viewpoints are the conventional wisdom: say, among news professionals, among academicians, among bloggers, and in the general public. Here, it is enough simply to note that the estimations of blogs' impact and value, potential or already realized, range from laudatory (e.g., Bennett, 2005; Hewitt, 2005; Leo, 2004) to derogatory (e.g., Engberg, 2004; Rall, 2005; Parker, 2005; Zerbisias, 2004). There are two major bodies of work in the scholarly literature on human communication behavior which will be helpful in bringing some clarity to this tumult. To that end it will be useful to approach the question of blogs' impact on the public discourse with regard to both quantity (as the participation in the discourse) and quality (as the value of the contributions to the overall good).

Over the course of a number of works, Jürgen Habermas painstakingly built the case for a level playing field in public talk about issues and events, and outlined features such a discourse would need to embody. This body of work is essentially normative, a conceptual exploration of an ideal public sphere. Elisabeth Noelle-Neumann identified a social dynamic in which individuals who disagree with what they take to be a majority opinion find themselves reluctant to give expression to that disagreement. In contrast, her body of work is essentially descriptive, an empirical inquiry into an existing public sphere. While much different in their scholarly foundations, their derivation, and their implications, both of these well-known works offer insights into blogs as a feature of the social landscape.

The connection between these seemingly disparate theories, the ideal speech situation of Habermas and the spiral of silence of Noelle-Neumann, is that both deal with public discussion of issues of public concern. In Habermas we find a description of a beneficent communication environment in which this discussion can take place, an environment in which there is institutional support for a constructive discussion — that is, a practical means by which individuals can take part in the discussion — and group norms for speech acts which foster participation in that discussion space. In Noelle-Neumann we find the effects which individuals' perceptions of that discussion space tend to have on their own willingness to contribute to the discussion. It will be useful to first summarize the main ideas in these two bodies of work which offer insights into the blogosphere: Habermas, regarding the blogosphere as a discourse, and Noelle-Neumann, regarding blogs as a mass communication medium.

The Ideal Speech Situation

Habermas's notion of a practical discourse — the substantive public discussion of some issue — boils down to group decision-making by a process of argumentation. One characteristic in particular is crucial to this process: that there be no coercion bearing on the interested parties, other than the relative strength of the arguments themselves. His expectation, under that condition, is that any self-interested behaviors (such as manipulation, intimidation, or misrepresentation, for instance) will effectively be cancelled out, resulting in a "cooperative search for truth" (1990, pp. 88-89).

What might at first glance seem to be a naively optimistic — or otherwise problematic — view of actual human motivations and behaviors in a dispute, gets mapped onto a concise set of operating rules, which Habermas (1990, p. 89) credits to Robert Alexy (1990, pp. 166-167). Those operating rules for an ideal speech situation can be paraphrased along these lines: (1) Anybody can participate in the discussion; (2) Every participant can raise any question, make any assertion, or express any feeling; and (3) No interference with another's participation is allowable.

By themselves, these rules would seem to invite chaos; is any string of words which anybody wants to inject into a discussion allowable, under the rules for an ideal situation? The short answer is no, because there is a qualifier — which, for the sake of parsimony, disappeared in this author's paraphrase — attached to the first rule. Any competent speaker (1990, p. 89) can participate; competent speakers are those who make comments falling into three defined classes, regarding their potential effect on the discussion (Habermas, 1990, p. 137, ff.; Farrell, 1993, p. 189, ff.). These three classes do impose constraints on the participants, and thus maintain some degree of order in the discussion. A constative concerns truth, in the sense of statements about real things in the real world. Assertions of fact or disputes about fact would fall in this category. A representative concerns the feelings of the speaker, and expressions of sincerity or intent would fall in this category. A regulative, as the label suggests, has to do with the acceptability of particular behavior, in this case, participation in a discussion. We can see a rough correspondence, then, between the constative and representative categories and the second rule, and the regulative category and the third rule. So while the three discourse rules, taken in isolation, are inadequate as a norm for an ideal discussion, this classification of competent speech acts provides sufficient additional constraint on what people might do in the discussion space.

In sum, the discussion is open to all who wish to join it, and to whatever constructive contribution they might wish to make to it. Hopefully the discussion will lead to a "rationally motivated recognition" of the best ideas (Habermas, 1975, p. 107), the quality of which is "grounded in the consensus of the participants through argumentation" (1975, p. 105). Regarding the overall beneficence of the collective decision process, "equal consideration [is] given to the interests of every individual in defining the general interest" (1990, p. 203). In effect, the ideal speech situation is Darwinian: the fittest ideas prevail, because they are based on the strongest arguments, which are the arguments most persuasive, and hence most acceptable, to the participants.

This model is very much in keeping with two famous passages in United States Supreme Court opinions. Justice William Brennan's majority opinion in the *Times v. Sullivan* case (1964) rested largely on what he described as "a profound national commitment to the principle that debate on public issues should be uninhibited, robust, and wide-open." It seems fair to say that this passage has since been accepted as a regulative, itself, regarding the way public issues will be addressed in the public discussion space. Participation is presumptively open, as the large number of First Amendment decisions have repeatedly affirmed. Correspondingly, restrictions on speech are relatively few and require strong justification of some sort. In short, the operating principle Brennan affirmed is very much in keeping with the three discourse rules in Habermas's ideal.

The conception of a reasoned consensus as the outcome of the discourse — or, at least, the acceptance of any decision finally reached — brings to mind Oliver Wendell Holmes's dissent in *Abrams et al. v. U.S.* (1919). This opinion is the source of the marketplace of ideas metaphor, although those exact words do not themselves appear in the dissent. Of interest here is Holmes's thought on how a public debate can best arrive at truth, a topic Habermas has also considered at length. In dissenting from the majority opinion that the Espionage Act of 1917, as amended in 1918, did not infringe on the First Amendment with its prohibition of language disparaging the government, Holmes wrote that "the ultimate good desired is better reached by free trade in ideas — that the best test of truth is the power of the thought to get itself accepted in the competition of the market." Clearly this is the kind of argumentation leading to a mutual recognition of the best ideas, which Habermas identified as the goal of a public discussion. The slang expression, "I'll buy that," meaning "I accept the truth of that," is a reminder of the pervasiveness of Holmes's metaphor.

Nonetheless there are a few issues with Habermas's conception of an ideal speech situation which will be relevant to our analysis of weblogs, and we should note them at this point. One question concerns the overall beneficence of the discourse. The first rule holds that the discussion must be open to participation, so that whatever decisions are reached will take all stakeholders' interests into account. As an ethical matter, this would seem intuitively obvious. But as a practical matter — a real operating rule for a real discussion in the real world

— the question of the boundary of the "communication community" (Habermas, 1975, p. 105) will inevitably arise, unless one considers every discussion *prima facie* to be open, on an equal footing, to every human being on the planet. This is not just a matter of logistics or networking, either, as the legitimacy of the discourse — that is, the degree to which it is binding on real people in the real world — relies on its openness to participation, and its ability to extend beyond the confines of its immediate time and space limitations (as in Habermas, 1990, p. 202). Since computer-mediated communication has largely erased time and space as practical constraints on individuals' ability to take part in discussions, whatever they might have to contribute to it, the question of whether a discourse's legitimacy is a function of its inclusiveness becomes all the more salient.

Related to this is the notion of consensus, which provides the philosophical grounding for whatever decisions might be reached through the discussion. It is the consensus, reached through a process of argumentation, which validates those decisions, and which, in effect, creates the value of the decisions (as in Habermas, 1975, p. 105). If the real-world communication community cannot simply be bounded by the human-ness (as opposed to inanimate-ness or animal-ness) of the participants, then perhaps the boundary is effectively created by the members' acceptance or rejection of particular ideas. In that case, the consensus and the boundary are tautological; those who accept the consensus are members of the community, and those who do not, are not.

Moreover, what to make of a persistent issue about which no consensus forms, or about which (given the nature of the matter to be decided) no consensus could form, for logical reasons? Examples of such issues are plentiful; abortion, capital punishment, welfare programs, and warfare would be obvious illustrations of important yet highly polarized issues suggesting no easy route to a consensus. Are there multiple communication communities, in that case? As a conceptual solution, that answer would seem to undercut the entire purpose of Habermas's ideal speech situation; we would simply go off in our own corners and talk among ourselves. And perhaps that is exactly what we often see happening, in the real world.

A similar tautology appears, regarding the qualifier on the first rule. To be a legitimate discussion, the discourse must be open to all competent participants. How would we recognize a competent participant? His or her speech acts — contributions to the discourse, in other words — would fall into the three categories of legitimate speech acts. Very well, then: speech competence, which is the threshold for participation, and conformity with those categories are tautological. But if every possible speech act falls into one of the categories, there is no need for the categories; anything can be said by anybody at any time. In this case, we have no protection against the discourse becoming chaotic. On the other hand, if those categories allow for speech which calls the categories themselves into question, we may have on our hands the conceptual problem of an infinite regress.

In fairness, Habermas's model may simply have hit the limit of how logically elegant a theoretical ideal can be, or, more likely, the limit of how ideal a truly practical discourse can be; both he (2001, pp. 102-103) and Alexy (1990, pp. 180-183) seem to acknowledge this limitation. But the question of how close a functioning, real-world discussion space can come to the ideal of "equality, universality, and lack of constraint" (Alexy, 1990, p. 166) will remain. Who, exactly, must be included, and who can legitimately be excluded? This is a question at the heart of mainstream media's scorn for the "guy sitting in his living room in his pajamas," a former CBS executive's caricature of bloggers (Are Bush Memos Authentic?, 2004; Fund, 2004). If they are competent, the bloggers' speech must be taken as seriously as that of the professional journalists; only if bloggers are not competent can they legitimately be ignored.

The Spiral of Silence

Noelle-Neumann's goal, over the course of empirical work, was to explain what seemed a strange quirk in people's expressive behavior. Even when living under a regime which vigorously protected their right to express opinions on the public questions of the day, there were circumstances under which people would be quite reluctant to do so, either verbally or with such visual devices as buttons or bumperstickers. She named this social dynamic the spiral of silence (1993), since the model includes both ongoing social interactions and individual actions.

The essence of the spiral of silence model is that people make comparisons of their individual perspective on a public issue, and their sense of the general public opinion on that issue. Needless to say, they are aware of their own opinions; they base their idea of public opinion, as a collective mindset, on mass-mediated news reporting. When those two opinions diverge significantly, a built-in fear of isolation or exclusion leads an individual holding a minority opinion to refrain from expressing it (1993, pp. 201-202). This comparison is not a snapshot, or static comparison, however; people derive a dynamic sense of which opinions — or behaviors — are gaining or declining in acceptance among the general population from their own exposure to mass-mediated content. This comparison, in turn, influences their own expressive activity; they become more ready to give expression to their opinions, in both public and private situations, when they see a rising trend in the fit between their opinions and that of the general public, and more reluctant when they see a declining trend (1993, p. 202). In short, an individual's expressiveness is influenced by his/her agreement or disagreement with what seems to that person to be the dominant opinion. As Noelle-Neumann puts it, colorfully, "feeling in harmony with the spirit of the age loosens the tongue" (1993, p. 26).

In essence, Noelle-Neumann is pointing to a social control mechanism, although not a kind of control which has been deliberately built into the social system, or one which is instantiated in law or regulation. Hence, the paradox that people living under a social system which guarantees their rights of expression may often feel inhibited about expressing themselves. Put another way, this model explains a subtle and decentralized pressure to conform, to be nonassertive in one's expressions, and Noelle-Neumann says flatly that this form of indirect social control is, in fact, more powerful in shaping people's actual expressions and behaviors than such overt controls as law and regulation (1993, p. 130). In short, individuals' desire for social acceptability, and the benefits which come from social acceptability, may tend to outweigh their expressive needs. Noelle-Neumann is careful to point out that this is not a simplistic causal model; it is not the case that people's expressive behaviors are determined by others. Rather, there is a tension between conformity and individualism, the need to be accepted by others — or, at least, to avoid becoming isolated (see 1993, p. 6 on this point) — and the need to be a human agent, in one's own regard (1993, p. 41); clearly, individuals differ in their personal negotiations of this tension, but nonetheless this is the crucial point of contact between the individual and society as a whole (1993, p. 229).

It is also important to note, in the spiral of silence model, the role of mediated communication. Ordinary people do not conduct their own opinion polls or any other kind of scientific measurements of general public opinion. Rather, they form a native sense of public opinion from the mediated information to which they are exposed. While people certainly learn about others' thinking through their face-to-face interactions in the daily routine, mediated content is the greatest source of individuals' sense of events beyond their own observation, and likewise, of public opinion beyond their direct experience (1993, p. 217). Hence, the fidelity of those media products to the actual opinions held by members of the public is of consequence in this dynamic public/personal calculus; along that line, Noelle-Neumann mentions some interesting examples of perceived public opinion distorted by news reporting. It is here that the ongoing discussion of media bias has relevance.

We should likewise take note of some issues with the spiral of silence theory, which will be relevant to an analysis of weblogs. An individual's fear of isolation, perhaps even outright stigma, is the driving force behind the scaled-up social dynamic of the spiral of silence. While Noelle-Neumann provides a good amount of evidence for accepting this fear of isolation as an inherent trait in human beings, we need to note that individuals will differ markedly in this trait. That is to say, there are obviously individuals who are at the conformist end of the scale, in terms of their personal need for social acceptance, and others who are clearly at the nonconformist end of it. Moreover, there are plentiful examples of celebrities who gained some measure of their notoriety by deliberately exhibiting some sort of nonconformity. Ironically enough, we can think of their social acceptance (manifest as celebrity) as being the product of a calibrated degree of nonconformity! The point here is that this trait ought not be overestimated, as a determinant of people's behaviors, even as it seems a strong explanation of a particular influence on their public expressions.

Another caution to be observed is that mediated content is

probably not the only influence on an individual's sense of public opinion. In the media effects literature, the two-step flow (Katz & Lazarsfeld, 1955, p. 309 ff.; Lazarsfeld, Berelson, & Gaudet, 1968, pp. 151-152) was noted early on: the influence of mass-mediated content on an individual is, itself, mediated by people with whom that individual is in face-to-face contact. Moreover, a certain degree of skepticism about the accuracy of opinion polling, as reported in the news media, seems to have set in, among the general population. At the least, we should keep in mind, in thinking about blogs as a social system feature, that the analytical move from the level of individual human being to the level of the society as a whole is not always a simple, unproblematic move.

The Quantity Question

In short, Habermas and Alexy generated a theoretical ideal of a communication environment, one which combined institutional support for arguing about public questions with a shared understanding of the speech acts which are allowable in that environment. Here, we are thinking of weblogs as the technological facilitation of a practical means by which individuals are able to join in that argumentation, and the blogosphere as operating according to group norms which inhibit participation very little, if at all. In Noelle-Neumann there are empirically-derived insights into the effect the existence of such an environment might have on the content of the argumentation in it.

If Noelle-Neumann's spiral of silence theory accurately describes a tendency in the communication behaviors of individual people in the real world, this tendency clearly has the potential to retard any social evolution toward Habermas's ideal speech situation. That is to say, if individuals have an interest in a discussion but are still unwilling to give expression to their thoughts for fear of social stigma, the discussion as a whole falls short of that ideal. And while there may be no coercion in a structural or institutional sense, and there even may be a legal guarantee of their right to participate, this behavioral tendency — rooted in human nature, according to Noelle-Neumann (1993, p. 202) — will clearly inhibit the vigorous assertion and interrogation dynamic the ideal discourse is predicated upon. Even allowing that Habermas's ideal is more useful as a vision statement than as a performance benchmark for actual public discussion, a spiral of silence dynamic clearly degrades the quality of a discussion.

This concern is a matter of degree, regarding the source of the inhibition. If individuals are reluctant to participate in a discourse because they have no substantive contribution to make to it or are indifferent about the question under discussion, the discourse is not degraded by their silence, nor are their rights to participate in any way infringed. But if they want to talk about their own stake in the issue under discussion — a representative — or if they have a serious question to raise or serious assertion to make — a constative — or if they have an objection to another's conduct in the discussion — a regulative — and are yet inhibited by their fear of isolation as a consequence of their speech, the discourse is therefore suboptimal.

Weblogs are beginning to mitigate the spiral of silence dynamic, and in that way, taking us a bit closer to the ideal speech situation. One way they do this by reducing the fear of being isolated. Given the extraordinary range of opinions expressed in the blogosphere, a blog reader is likely to find views more or less congruent with his or her own — as well as views posing challenges to his or her own. In itself, this counteracts a human's inherent fear of isolation; a reader is likely to come away from the blogs with the perception that there are other people out there who have similar questions or perceptions about the events of the day. In short, blogs reduce the inhibitory effect of public opinion contrary to an individual's personal viewpoint, by making evidence readily available through hyperlinking and blogrolling that one, in fact, is not alone in that viewpoint. And this is the essence of the blogosphere's challenge to the mainstream media; the conventional storylines and frames of the established journalists no longer constitute the master narrative of current events; heterodox narratives are viable, now.

Regardless of the quality of the material in the blogosphere — quality measured by such important characteristics as factual accuracy, logical reasoning, critical insights, or ethical concerns — the sheer diversity of thought in the blogosphere will blunt the inhibitory effect of perceived isolation on an individual with a viewpoint on the issues significantly different from the mainstream media's portrayal of public opinion. Certainly the quality of the material matters, both to the individual and to the public! But the point here is that the wild frontier ethos of blogs, in itself, encourages participation in a discourse. We should keep in mind that the Habermas/Alexy rules for an ideal discourse do not themselves address the quality of the speech acts made in it; rather, those rules stipulate broad participation and a very high degree of freedom of expression, with the expectation that, operationally, bad thinking will be winnowed out and good thinking will prevail, under the conditions of an ideal speech situation. Further, the legitimacy of the discourse as public decision-making is predicated on the willingness of stakeholders to give expression to their own interests in the issue. Once again, blogs move us closer to the ideal simply by reducing the inhibitions on participating.

In short, blogs offer readers a much wider range of thinking than is available in the traditional outlets. Readers can choose material which either challenges or affirms their personal views on issues and events. The heterogeneity of the material washes out the relative conformity of "public opinion" as presented in the traditional channels. Put another way, blogs, by altering the media mix, have the potential to alter individuals' perception of the general public opinion. For a reader with a viewpoint differing from conventional public opinion, exposure to blogosphere material can counteract the personal fear of isolation, and thereby lessen the reluctance to give expression, in one form or another, to that heterodox viewpoint. In that way, blogs can help an individual negotiate the tension between conformity and agency.

Another way the blogosphere moves us closer to the ideal discourse is by providing institutional support for it, albeit a nontraditional kind of institutional support. Apart from individuals' willingness to enter a discussion, they need a practical means to do so (see Habermas, 1990, p. 209 on this point). It seems clear that blogs, as a social system feature, support the three discourse rules quite nicely. The first rule concerns the openness of the discourse; anybody who wishes can create a blog or read material on others' blogs. Internet connections are readily available, the necessary computing machinery is affordable to the vast majority of people, no license or credential is required, and no physical travel is needed in order to contribute. The second rule concerns the content one can contribute to the discourse; apart from the recognized limitations on the First

Amendment — such as libel, creating a clear and present danger, or copyright infringement — the content is, quite simply, whatever the author wishes to post. The third rule concerns interference with another's participation; apart from such mischief as hacking another's site or creating denial of service attacks, no interference is possible.

Lest virtuality seem inadequate as institutional support — cyberspace has no bricks and mortar buildings, no paneled meeting rooms, no government agency overseeing it, no titled officials administering it — it is helpful to recall Anthony Giddens's notion of social structure as interrelated rules and resources (1984, p. xxxi), which both enable people to act and are created by the actions they take. In a discourse, speech is action. The blogosphere is a medium, an existing resource which people can make use of to create their speech acts. At the same time, the blogosphere is the outcome of those speech acts. This is the property Giddens refers to as the duality of structure (1984, p. 25 ff.), and which he sees as inherent in the social system, across the board. While the blogosphere is virtual, it is no less a real social system feature than any other institution we have traditionally associated with the public sphere.

Moreover, the consequence of the blogosphere's technological facilitation of a discourse (i.e., provision of institutional support for it), is that every individual can contribute to the collective sense of the public interest (as in Habermas, 1990, p. 203) more powerfully than before. Clearly the very low barriers to entry — money, technical skill, geographical constraints, temporal constraints — open the public sphere up to greater participation. Political commentary, broadly available to the general public, is no longer an oligopoly of the intellectual elite, as can be readily seen in the extraordinary variety of opinion available to anybody with a humble modem connection.

Habermas is mistaken in thinking that the ideal outcome of a discourse is a genuine consensus. It seems unlikely that a group of people could routinely arrive at a genuine consensus — a rational, unforced consensus — when those people are heterophilous (see Rogers, 1995, pp. 18-19) with regard to attitude, talent, preference, motivation, theological belief, or existential viewpoint. As a practical matter, there is hardly anything that everybody would agree on in a large, complex social system such as ours in the United States. It is difficult to image how that "rationally motivated recognition" of the best decision would coalesce when a consequential issue plays against such a variegated cultural context. Therefore the goal of a discourse is better thought of as stakeholder-neutral behavior norms and equity in the available resources for the argumentation, without the vain expectation of achieving an actual consensus on the decision. In that respect, the rules Robert Alexy derived from Habermas's theoretical explorations would seem to form a workable environment, one which would generally be perceived as fair, and hence perceived as legitimate. Again, to think of actual consensus as a realizable end goal or to measure the beneficence of a discourse by how well it produces the appearance of consensus is a profound conceptual mistake. Indeed, Habermas himself has criticized the 20th century world on the grounds that the public sphere, including the traditional mass media, often induced the appearance of consensus without substantive agreement on the issues (Goodnight, 1992, p. 247, 249). Rather than thinking of the public discourse as either a completely rational and free exchange of ideas leading to universal agreement or a subtly coercive social control mechanism which deftly subordinates some players and privileges others, we would do better to recognize the inherent tension in that dichotomy which seems unavoidable in a real social world populated by human beings (as Noelle-Neumann, 1993, p. 220 ff. reminds us).

The key attribute implicit in Habermas's conception of a public discourse is procedural neutrality. For it to be truly possible for anyone to raise any question or make any assertion, regarding a public issue, the rules for participating in the discourse must apply uniformly to all participants. Given the foundational importance of the First Amendment in the United States' social system, and the strict prohibition against legislative interference in speech, we should construe rules in this context to be mean customary behavior or, perhaps, social acceptability, since overt regulatory controls are few and limited. And in the vein of the critical studies perspective — which includes Habermas, himself! — we should also take note of structural disparities which might effectively inhibit the participation of some individuals or organizations and their ability to bring certain ideas or viewpoints into the discourse. Clearly, a social stigma which inhibits expression of minority viewpoints — the spiral of silence dynamic, in other words — is a structural disparity which damages the rational argumentation of positions on public questions (see Noelle-Neumann, 1993, p. 228 on this point). In this light, the benchmark of the discourse can be seen as the neutrality of the group norms with regard to the content of the speech and the identity of the speaker.

Habermas's overall project was to think through modern social organization with the intent of identifying improvements. Goodnight (1992) put it in dramatic terms: the public sphere is broken, in essence has become dysfunctional as an actual group decision-making space but facile at producing a Potemkin village version of it, and the long-term goal of Habermas's theorizing about an ideal speech situation was aimed at rebuilding a genuinely participatory and rational process by which questions of the public welfare can be constructively addressed. Ironically, the occasionally chaotic, largely unmanaged — and perhaps unmanageable — sometimes far-from-equilibrium thrashing of ideas in the blogosphere has led to the beginnings of a realization of Habermas's ideal discourse in the real world.

The Quality Question

While ensuring that the public sphere is open to participation and that there are no undue barriers to people actually entering it are important considerations regarding the legitimacy of the decisions made in it, these conditions cannot in themselves guarantee that the decisions reached in that space will be wise. For that reason the quality of the speech acts themselves needs to be addressed, as well. It would be foolish to pretend that every thought expressed in the blogosphere was insightful, factually accurate, rational, or ethically motivated — but then again, it would be foolish to pretend that about the content distributed by the traditional news media, or about debates in Congress, either. It will be helpful to address the issue of quality from three separate directions: with regard to the speaker, to the reader, and to the media system as a whole.

Competence
Given the scathingly negative estimations of the blogosphere which have been expressed in some quarters — the characterization of

bloggers as "salivating morons" (attributed to Lovelady in Rosen, 2005) or "parasites too stupid to realize they are killing off their hosts" (Zerbisias, 2004), for instance — it is worth noting that the three types of speech acts Habermas and Alexy saw as constructive in a practical discourse are in ample supply in the blogosphere. The typology of media criticism illustrated in the preceding chapters can be mapped onto the Habermas typology of competent speech acts quite readily.

- accuracy: constatives
- framing and agenda-setting/gatekeeping: representatives
- journalistic practices: regulatives

The Habermas/Alexy criteria for speaker competence are only minimally restrictive, which is in keeping with the intent of having a maximally open discourse. As noted earlier, the criteria verge on a tautology. A speaker whose expression falls into those categories is competent; a competent speaker is allowed to contribute just about anything to the discussion. Perhaps pure flaming — rude *ad hominem* or *ad feminam* attacks on a person, with no substantive meaning other than derogation — would fall outside the categories of constatives, representatives, and regulatives, and thus indicate an incompetent speaker who need not be taken seriously in the discourse.

But two things seem obvious, then. First, although the term flaming originated in the realm of computer-mediated communication, that sort of speech act certainly occurs in real life as often as in virtual life, and occurred in real life before virtual life existed; hence, the existence of flaming (i.e., incompetent speech) in the blogosphere does not disqualify the blogosphere, in itself. Second, it is clear that a large proportion of speech acts in the blogosphere are constatives, representatives, or regulatives, however heterodox the assertions they make or problematics they raise may be; hence, the authors of that content are, by definition, competent speakers who have a legitimate place in the discourse. In short, those who would broadly exclude bloggers from the public discourse, or maintain that the blogosphere is not a legitimate component of the public sphere, have no grounds for doing so.

Cocooning

A different sort of concern pertains to the consumers of blogs, those readers who come to rely on the blogosphere as an alternative to the traditional news media. It is possible that some readers will "cocoon" themselves with their use of blogs; that is to say, some users will choose to expose themselves only to content they expect to be congruent with their existing viewpoints, only attend to commentary or news information which they expect to reinforce their own predispositions on issues. Those predispositions will not be tested by contrary evidence or argument, simply because the user is not exposed to any. The worry, here, is twofold: the discourse as a whole will become shallower because the readers' understanding of issues will become one-dimensional, and that the larger discourse community (i.e., the general public) will fragment into small niches of like-minded readers with little interaction among them.

The first would seem, on the face of it, to be a harm which blogs are likely to bring about. We should note, however, that there is nothing truly different about this concern with the introduction of blogs into the media mix. A person who relied on only a single source in the traditional media, as a matter of habit — say only National Public Radio, or only CBS News, or only *The New York Times*, or only *National Review* — would be cocooned in exactly the same fashion as a person who only attended to *Red State* or *The Daily Kos*. In short, this is not an effect of blogs, but rather, a longstanding concern about the public discourse. Indeed, critical theorists bemoaned the "manufactured consent" produced by the traditional, mainstream media long before hypertext was devised.

In fact, there are features of the blogosphere which would tend to mitigate the cocoon problem in ways that are entirely new. Blogrolls are a common feature; they consist of a collection of hyperlinks to other weblogs, usually formatted as a table running down the margin of the page. While it is true that some bloggers only provide links to like-minded sites, many bloggers do provide links to material with noticeably different points of view from their own. The blogrolls on *Belgravia Dispatch, OxBlog, Balloon Juice, TigerHawk,* and *Gay Patriot* would be good examples. Further, we should note that the convenience, to the readers, of hyperlinks to other content sources is far greater than the mere availability of a different newspaper downtown, or the technical capability of recording and later viewing another network's newscast at a later time. The reader's ability to obtain more sources of news and commentary has not been diminished; if anything, the ability to do so has been made easier and far more convenient.

Moreover, the common blog practice of critiquing another outlet's material brings that other material into a reader's consciousness, out of necessity. The style of rebuttal called fisking, in particular, reproduces excerpts of a text the blogger disagrees with. The reader is incidentally exposed to that other material; should those ideas happen to be persuasive to the reader, a hyperlink typically leads directly to the other text. There is no comparable feature in the traditional media. While a newspaper or television broadcast may occasionally credit a report from another outlet, it does not typically reproduce substantial portions of that report nor provide instant access to it. If anything, blogs may actually mitigate a reader's tendency to cocoon, simply as a technologically-enabled feature of the genre. It is clear, even in the early stages of the blogosphere's evolution, that many serious blogs do expose their readers to multiple points of view, if only to critique them.

Some critics of the blogosphere have pointed to the occasional blogswarms (a relatively large number of bloggers posting on a particular topic, with a relatively high degree of congruence in their viewpoints) as an indicator of shallow thinking, rush to judgment, or conformity. While it certainly is possible that bloggers can be shallow, impulsive, or mindlessly imitative, the existence of blogswarms now and then is not sufficient to support a blanket characterization of bloggers in those terms. If it were, then one would likewise have to dismiss the mainstream media outlets for the frequent episodes of pack journalism, and for the routine echoing of each other's reporting.

We should, however, note two potential problems related to the blogosphere. One is the problem Noelle-Neumann referred to as pluralistic ignorance (1993, p. 169), the condition in which people come to have a substantially distorted sense of the general public opinion. In the spiral of silence dynamic, an erroneous perception of consensus may inhibit some individuals' participation in a public debate. It is conceivable, at least, that blog cocooning might be a contributing factor to pluralistic ignorance, but again, this is not a concern which first arose with the appearance of blogs. Noelle-Neumann's empirical work identified times when the traditional media seem to have contributed to a condition of pluralistic ignorance. Rather than leading readers to inaccurately perceive themselves to hold a minority opinion — that is, underestimate the degree to which their own points of view are prevalent among the general public — blog cocooning is more likely, if anything, to lead readers to overestimate the degree to which their opinions are shared by others.

Some observers have worried that the cumulative effect of individuals cocooning (in the sense of buffering themselves from exposure to viewpoints inconsistent with their own predispositions) could be a general polarization of groups toward the extremes of the opinion spectrum (for example, Sunnstein, 2002, pp. 185-186), possibly leading to some sort of overall social breakdown. This concern rests on empirical findings that homogeneous groups tend to migrate to the extreme of their shared viewpoint (Sunnstein, 2002, p. 176).

While the doomsday scenario cannot be dismissed out of hand, it seems less likely that the blogosphere will suppress viewpoint heterogeneity, across the entire discourse community, than it will foster it. Two dimensions of the blogosphere are especially relevant here, considered from the point of view of an individual consumer of mediated news and opinion. One is that the convenience of hypertext linking increases the chances that an individual will at least be exposed to opinions challenging his or her own; even if a person tends to reject those opinions, at least he or she is aware of their existence. This is apparent when one considers the greatly increased choices of content available through computer mediation compared with the restricted choices available through the traditional mass media. The second concerns the individual's sense of belonging or being isolated, with regard to viewpoint — a perception which Noelle-Neumann found to often be inaccurate. The direction of the inaccurate sense of popular opinion is crucial to the individual's choice to be silent or to participate in the discourse, since it is perceiving oneself to be in the minority opinion (i.e., an out group) which leads one to withdraw from the discourse. In contrast, if blog cocooning gives a reader a somewhat inaccurate sense that his/her opinions are mainstream, that reader will be more comfortable with giving expression to those opinions, rather than less comfortable. In sum, if blogs loosen readers' tongues, it is a beneficial effect rather than a harmful one to the public discourse as a whole.

The second problem is perhaps a more serious concern associated with cocooning. This is the possible fragmenting of the communication community (presumably, the entire public) into narrow affinity groups which have little interaction with each other, or — worse — do not recognize each other as competent speakers or fellow stakeholders, at all. Should this happen to a significant extent, the harm to a system of representative democracy seems obvious: the political process by which conflicts are supposed to be negotiated degenerates into a spoils system for interest groups. If we take as axiomatic, for the purpose of examining this concern, the Habermas principle that the legitimacy of the political process rests on the decisions being "grounded in consensus of the participants through argumentation" (1975, p. 105), then it would seem any further impetus from the blogosphere in this direction could be a negative effect, indeed. The longstanding influence of special-interest lobbyists and single-issue advocacy groups on the legislative process is strong evidence that the problem predates blogs, but that in itself does not reassure us that blogs will not exacerbate the existing problem.

Perhaps the key to analyzing this concern lies in the conception of the communication community, itself. As noted a little earlier, the concept verges on tautology when pushed into service as a normative ideal. The goal of the ideal discourse is to foster a consensus (on a particular set of ideas) among the members of the communication community. The ideal communication community would include anybody potentially affected by the decision made in the discourse. The membership of the communication community is thus bounded by their interest in participating in the discourse, which implies at least some degree of concurrence (at least with regard to the group norms for participating — regulatives, in other words) with the consensus which appears to be evolving. In metaphorical language, showing up to play the game implies acceptance of the rules of the game, even though one retains the option to challenge the referee's decision as one sees fit.

As a practical matter, there is no person who can possibly read everything written about every issue — be open to every speech act in the discourse, in other words. And likewise, there is no person who can actively participate in every debate which might conceivably affect him or her — contribute speech acts to the discourse, in other words. To put it bluntly, everybody cocoons to some degree as a matter of necessity, if only to cope with the problem of information overload. It would seem more useful, then, to think of the communication community as bounded not by a population (i.e., a particular collection of people) but by an ongoing dynamic of argumentation. If so, the benefit of the blogosphere would clearly outweigh any potential harm. The blogosphere is available to anyone with an Internet connection, and enables anyone to participate either as a reader or a speaker in that discourse. Moreover, debates which develop in the blogosphere are tending to diffuse into the mainstream media, further enriching the argumentation dynamic as a whole. In short, while it might seem at first glance that the blogosphere might contribute to a fracturing of the communication community through individuals' tendency to cocoon, in practice it will tend to mitigate any such problem rather than exacerbate it.

Again, it is a conceptual mistake to believe that an ideal discourse will necessarily lead to consensus, and that an ideal communication community will in time consist of group of like-minded altruists. The disadvantages of groupthink or forced conformity include the possibility of the community drifting toward an extreme point of view as social acceptability comes to outweigh decision quality. Regarding many issues about which reasonable people have substantial and heartfelt differences, it is unlikely that a true consensus would ever evolve. The short-term appearance of a consensus is likely to be false, an appearance driven largely by social acceptability rather than the actual merits of an idea or perspective. Put another way, the appearance of a consensus, paradoxically, may better be taken as an indicator of orthodoxy — which is to say, an indicator of a violation of the rule against coercion, that any perspective may be critiqued freely and any perspective may be articulated freely. Rather, an optimal discourse will produce, regarding issues of substantial controversy, a dissensus of respectful disagreement which is not tainted by the constraints of social acceptability but informed by the force of better argument and evidence. Put another way, the outcome of a healthy discourse is more likely to be a plurality or majority, rather than a consensus. That of course implies that the decision will not be uniformly pleasing to all parties with a stake in it; nonetheless, a true plurality decision is more socially beneficial than the false appearance of a consensus.

Bias

It is also worthwhile to consider blogs in light of the longstanding issue of media bias. This has been a contentious debate, with at least as much heat as light, in both scholarly circles and the popular press. For our purposes here, we can think of media bias as some sort of systematic distortion in the reporting and interpretation of events and public policy decisions (Cooper, 2006b). In simplest terms, bias is manifest as a routinized mismatch between the mediated depictions of reality, and reality itself. While that sounds simple enough on the face of it, the arguments have been — and are likely to be! — endless, about exactly what an undistorted portrayal of reality would be (Cooper, 1994). And in itself, this interminable debate would be a fair illustration of an issue that is unlikely to result in a genuine consensus, a collective recognition of the most compelling combination of argument and evidence, in the foreseeable future. Given that there is no consensus about media bias in the traditional news outlets, it is unsurprising that bloggers have been characterized as everything from ignorant partisans (Rall, 2005), to "ego-gratifying rabble" (Parker, 2005), to reformers of the news industry (Bennett, 2005), to "the future of journalism" (Drummond, 2005).

Prior chapters have detailed various sorts of media criticism which have appeared in the blogosphere, that is, criticism of the mainstream media contained in blogs. As might be expected, corresponding criticism of blogs and bloggers has appeared in mainstream outlets. It would be tempting to dismiss this exchange as a shouting match between two competing sectors of the media industry, but that would gloss the possibility that the entry of blogs into the media mix has actually made reporting of events and commentary on issues less trustworthy, on the whole, or that blogs are untrustworthy, in general — which is what some observers have charged. Here again, the question of media bias predates the appearance of blogs; there is no reason to think blogs caused the issue to arise, when it was not a concern before. Again, the question here is whether blogs have contributed to any existing media bias, or whether they might have — contrary to emphatic pronouncements in some quarters — actually mitigated existing media bias.

Perhaps the most productive way to approach that question is to first consider the degree to which the traditional news media can be considered objective, that is, to be free of the distortion or slant which has come to be called media bias. In a sense, this gives a baseline indicator against which any change induced by blogs can be observed. As an indicator of how far from consensus even this limited question is, scholarly opinion of media bias — prior to the emergence of the blogosphere in the media mix — ranges from an assessment of the traditional media as leaning rightward (e.g., Herman & Chomsky, 1988) to leaning leftward (Kuypers, 2002); indeed, there is not even a modest degree of concurrence, among the folks who make a living studying media or commenting on them, about what facts might constitute relevant evidence in weighing the answer to the question (see Cooper, 2006b; Cooper, 1994).

That said, we will take as axiomatic the impossibility of any journalism, in any channel, being universally acclaimed as objective — in the sense of being perceived as a perfectly transparent vehicle by which reality is conveyed across distance and time. This is not to say that the issue is irrelevant; clearly, the degree of coloration in the mediated accounts of reality matters, as does the political or economic interests such coloration may favor or disfavor. But just as it seems a vain hope that a perfect discourse on a contentious issue will lead, in the end, to a universally-shared sense of the best ideas about it, it likewise seems vain to expect any single news outlet to attain an ideal of objectivity, if we take objectivity to mean irreproachable fidelity of its products to reality.

A more modest, ostensibly attainable, goal is that journalism might be balanced, in the sense of neutral to all parties engaged in an issue and perceived by at least most of the readers as being fair to all parties. As a vision of ideal journalism this makes good sense, but there are also good reasons not to expect any single news outlet to actually exhibit this trait, and, indeed, few seem to. A given news outlet does tend to gravitate toward a certain point of view or consistency in perspective — regardless of the merits of the competing positions in any given issue — if only for the sake of coherence in its content or style. This is to be expected, for two reasons. One is that a news outlet needs to attract and retain an audience, for the sake of maintaining a stable source of funding for its operations. This is a need which applies to both commercial and non-commercial outlets, such as National Public Radio. Just as the producers of other goods in a free marketplace establish their brand names, so do news outlets, in practice, develop an identity of their own in a crowded marketplace of news and commentary. To put this point quite bluntly, regarding the need to attract and retain a stable segment of the consumer market, there is no real difference between a private-for-profit media outlet and a so-called "public" media outlet.

A second reason has to do with organizational culture. For the sake of its own cohesion as a functioning organization, a news outlet will evolve a culture, in the sense of some degree of uniformity in values, attitudes, and practices among the organizational members. This shared viewpoint will manifest itself in the subtle, taken-for-granted value judgments embedded in the news content distributed by the outlet. By no means does this necessarily reflect a professional shortcoming on the part of newsworkers; rather, it is an unavoidable trait of real news content created by normal human beings working collaboratively in organizations, content intended to be consumed by a greatly heterogeneous public.

So if even the very highest quality news outlets tend to develop bias, in the sense of a coloration in their depiction of reality — a point which the former public editor of *The New York Times* acknowledged about his own newspaper (Okrent, 2004c) — we ought look to the marketplace as a whole for the desired balance of viewpoints and perspectives, rather than any particular outlet or sector of the marketplace. In short, the chronic problem with the media bias debate has been a mismatch between its comparatively narrow scope and the actual breadth of the social phenomenon it attempts to encompass.

What to make, then, of the bloggers, with their overtly personalized content, their often-irreverent style, and their overtly viewpoint-centered ethos? Some have argued that despite the mainstream media's professed standard of objectivity, as a professional value of journalism, there often seems to be preferential treatment of certain causes, ideas, or actors (e.g., Kuypers, 2002), perhaps attributable to the socialization process journalists experience. In contrast, bloggers as a population are wildly heterogeneous with regard to the practices, assumptions, and world views which tend to be relatively uniform among professional journalists (see Lichter, Rothman, & Lichter, 1990). While many bloggers say explicitly that they are only expressing their individual viewpoints, across the entire blogosphere there is a very broad and deep heterogeneity of perspectives, arguably far greater than that found among the traditional media outlets. Paradoxically, the subjective viewpoints of individual bloggers accumulate into a social object enacting the kind of multi-perspective objectivity promised, but not actually delivered, by the mainstream media.

If this author is correct in thinking that any process of writing an account of events or in suggesting interpretations of an event is inherently viewpoint-centered and any depiction of reality is inherently shaped by the finite awareness and predispositions of the author (see Kuypers & Cooper, 2005, for an example), the idea that any single account can attain objectivity, or that the objectivity of any single news outlet be beyond question, is a vain hope. The key idea in considering the effect blogs might have on the public discourse is that the free-for-all they generate is more likely to cancel out biases in the news marketplace than induce them. To the extent that the addition of blogs to the media mix have moved the public sphere away from an oligopoly and in the direction of a more strongly competitive marketplace of ideas, they have helped neutralize whatever media bias is attributable to the previously limited number of suppliers in that marketplace. In short, deficiencies in the quality of products available in the marketplace of news information goods — in this case, deficiencies in the form of bias in the content of those products — tend to be corrected by the entry of competing products from new suppliers to that market.

An alternative way of approaching the media bias question would be to use system theory as the analytical framework (see Demers, 1996, ch. 4 for an overview of system theory applied to the mass media). We would then think of the media system as a subsystem of the complete social system. Media dependency would be a condition apparent at a number of levels in the complex social system (see Demers, 1996, p. 83 for a concise illustration): individuals would be dependent on the media system for gratification of their information needs; journalists would be dependent on various power centers for the raw materials from which to make their news products; those power centers would be dependent on the media for maintaining the social stability which permits the continuance of their power.

The introduction of a new component into the media system — in this case, the blogosphere — would clearly have the potential to reduce the rigidity of all those existing interdependencies. This is not to say that the blogosphere in itself would necessarily remain a permanent outsider to the web of interdependencies; that would seem quite unlikely, since as the blogosphere matures into a social object it will, by definition, become an established part of the social structure. But what the blogosphere may indeed do, long term, is to mitigate the severity of those dependencies throughout the entire social system, simply by offering alternative means of gratifying the various information needs of the various social actors.

In short, we might expect the increase in the complexity of the media system brought about by the introduction of the blogosphere to precipitate a corresponding reduction in the strength of media dependencies across the entire social system — at both the individual and institutional levels. And in turn, we might expect the degree of bias in media content attributable to the dependency of any social actors on any other actors to be attenuated, over time.

Quantity and Quality, Both

So we can break the issue of the beneficence of the blogosphere, with regard to the social system, into two parts: the quantity of participation, and the quality of the participation. Regarding quantity, the question would be, is the blogosphere providing a new level of support for entry into the discourse? This author's answer is, yes — decisively. It is easier now than it ever has been, for ordinary people to take part in the interpretation of events or debates over public policy. They can easily raise their questions, make their assertions, or express their concerns about any question in the public sphere. They can easily expose themselves to the unfiltered opinions of their peers, without the gatekeeping or intervention of a professional elite.

Regarding the quality of the discourse, the question would be, are those new viewpoints being brought into the discourse constructive additions to it? This author's answer is, yes, overall. This is not to say that every post or every blog is a constructive addition, but rather to say that the blogosphere as a social object is a constructive addition. Earlier chapters described many examples of substantive and thoughtful contributions, in the form of constructive criticism of the mainstream media, or alternative media products. Moreover, the public discourse is simply a more competitive marketplace of ideas for the new entrants into it; we have taken another step closer to that vigorous and free-ranging process of argumentation envisioned as an ideal.

Clearly the emergence of the blogosphere as a social feature has made that argumentation more raucous! It also seems clear that the outcome of the argumentation is more often a reasoned — if sometimes sullen — disagreement than a consensus. But if the quintessential critical question is "Whom does this discourse serve?" (Foucault, 1981, p. 115; Moore, 1997), the key point is that the blogosphere has opened up the discourse, apparently contrary to the preferences of some of the current actors, to newcomers with heterodox viewpoints. In that light, the discourse is the better for the emergence of the blogosphere.

Quite simply, the blogosphere exists because it fills a need. It was not brought into being by fiat; it evolved through the accumulation of individual acts. The many people who find it worth their investment in time and effort to create blog content surely do it because they find it fills a need for expression, for giving voice to their thoughts, in a way the previous outlets available to them did not. So, too, does the blogosphere fill a need for those who read the content, and participate in discussion by adding their comments. In this sense, then, the blogosphere represents a *vox populi* the technology did not determine, but did, instead, facilitate. This is clearly a free market perspective on the blogosphere; the author finds it the most satisfying understanding of it.

Probably the critical theorists, as a school of thought, would be discomfited by the notion that a blatantly commercial marketplace in communication technology has facilitated the evolution of a genre of computer-mediated communication (*viz.*, blogs) with such a relentlessly individualist ethos, yet having such a clear public benefit.

Probably they would not have expected that a genre with such inconsequential roots (*viz.*, personal web pages) could have opened up public discourse to a collective level only considered a theoretical ideal. Probably they would have assumed that even an approximation of that ideal discourse could come into being only through some sort of concerted political action, not through the accumulation of voluntary interactions in a decentralized, unmanaged virtual space. Yet, that is precisely what has happened.

This author is inclined to think that social structures which evolve through the voluntary interactions and exchanges among people — such as the blogosphere — tend in general to be more beneficial than structures created through the deliberate exercise of power, however well-intentioned — such as regulatory bureaucracies. That idea cannot be fully explored here. For our purposes, we can simply note that the blogosphere would seem to be a near-perfect instantiation of the ideal discourse.

Real life can often be a pleasant surprise. And that is a good thing about it.

Endnotes

1. AP Bias Strikes Again (2004, September 03)
   http://spinswimming.blogspot.com/2004/09/ap-bias-strikes-again.html
   AP Retracts "Boo" Story; Left Not Convinced (2004, September 04)
   http://powerlineblog.com/archives/2004_09.php
   The Associated Press Makes It Up (2004, September 03)
   http://powerlineblog.com/archives/2004_09.php
   Let's Open a Dialogue (2004, September 05)
   http://powerlineblog.com/archives/2004_09.php
   We Hear From Mr. Borenstein (2004, September 7)
   http://powerlineblog.com/archives/2004_09.php
   Waiting for Mr. Hayes (2004, September 7)
   http://powerlineblog.com/archives/2004_09.php
2. *L.A. Times* Needs a New Fact-checker for Those Editorials (2005, July 2)
   http://patterico.com/2005/07/02/3276/la-times-needs-a-new-fact-checker-for-those-editorials
3. Small Party and Great Hopes (2004, June 29)
   http://iraqthemodel.blogspot.com/2004_06_01_iraqthemodel_archive.html
   From Um Mushtaq to Abu Haider (2004, July 1)
   http://iraqthemodel.blogspot.com/2004_07_01_iraqthemodel_archive.html
   Speechless (2004, July 1)
   http://timblair.spleenville.com/archives/007071.php
   Yet Another Falsehood on the Front Page of the *Los Angeles Times* (2004, July 4)
   http://www.patterico.com/2004/07/04/yet-another-falsehood-on-the-front-page-of-the-los-angeles-times
   The LA *Times* Reporter Responds! (2004, July 4)
   http://iraqnow.blogspot.com/2004/07/la-times-reporter-responds.html
   The Mysterious Bremer Farewell Speech (2004, July 7)
   http://deadparrots.net/archives/current_events/0407the_mysterious_bremer_farewell_speech.html
   Los Angeles Times Corrects False Statement Regarding Bremer Farewell Speech (2004, July 8)
   http://patterico.com/2004/07/08/ilos-angeles-timesi-corrects-false-statement-regarding-bremer-farewell-speech/
   Washington Post Issues Correction on Bremer Farewell Speech (2004, July 9)
   http://patterico.com/2004/07/09/1687/iwashington-posti-issues-correction-on-bremer-farewell-speech/

4. Geez, Paul Krugman Lies a Lot (2005, August 18)
   http://thechiefbrief.blogspot.com/2005/08/geez-paul-krugman-lies-lot.html
   Krugman Tries To Pull a Fast One (2005, August 19)
   http://corner.nationalreview.com/05_08_14_corner-archive.asp#073602
   More Krugmania on the 2000 Recounts (2005, August 19)
   http://corner.nationalreview.com/05_08_14_corner-archive.asp#073659
   Paul Krugman: Liar, or Just Sloppy? (2005, August 19)
   http://brainster.blogspot.com/2005_08_14_brainster_archive.html#1124470
   07208455651
   Krugmania (2005, August 20)
   http://powerlineblog.com/archives/011407.php
   The Krugman Correction (2005, August 26)
   http://michellemalkin.com/archives/003406.htm
   Paul Krugman Just Can't Get It Right (2005, August 26)
   http://patterico.com/2005/08/26/3512/paul-krugman-just-cant-get-it-right/
   Krugman Officially Corrects His Florida 2000 Lies (2005, August 26)
   http://www.poorandstupid.com/2005_08_21_chronArchive.asp#112503484
   243947813
5. AP Puts Words in Ariel Sharon's Mouth (2005, April 13)
   http://www.brendanloy.com/archives/017560.html
6. Introducing Washington Post Reporter Terry Neal to Google, and the Dangers
   of Relying on Ralph Neas Talking Points (2005, May 3)
   http://www.hughhewitt.com/old_site/cgi-bin/calendar.pl?month=5&year=2
   005&view=Event&event_id=746#postid1588
   Misreporting the Filibuster (2005, May 3)
   http://powerlineblog.com/archives/010353.php
7. The Evolution of the Maureen Dowd Ellipsis-Distortion Story (n.d.)
   http://www.thenationaldebate.com/blogger/articles/dowd1.htm
   President Visits Arkansas (2003, May 5)
   http://www.whitehouse.gov/news/ releases/2003/05/print/20030505-4.html
   Not Sure Who to Send This E-mail To (2003, May 14)
   http://www.thenationaldebate.com/blogger/articles/original.htm
   Maureen Dowd's Dishonest Deletion (2003, May 14)
   http://www.timeswatch.org/articles/2003/0514.asp#3
   Dowd's Distortion (2003, May 14)
   http://andrewsullivan.com/index.php?dish_inc=archives/2003_05_11_dish_
   archive.html#200290689
   Dowd Spawns Bush Media Myth (2003, May 22)
   http://www.spinsanity.org/columns/20030522.html
   Dowd's Dots and the Non-correction Correction (2003, June 4)
   http://www.thenationaldebate.com/blogger/articles/dowd2.htm
   Maureen Won't Come Clean So (2003, May 28)
   http://www.belgraviadispatch.com/archives/003160.html
   Dowdification (n.d.)
   http://www.samizdata.net/blog/ glossary_archives/003822.html
8. The Sixty-first Minute (2004, September 9)
   http://powerlineblog.com/archives/007760.php

Bush Guard Documents: Forged (2004, September 9)
    http://littlegreenfootballs.com/weblog/?entry=12526&only=yes
The Smoking Memo (2004, September 14)
    http://littlegreenfootballs.com/weblog/?entry=12615&only
An Officer Weighs In (2004, September 9)
    http://powerlineblog.com/archives/007765.php
Another Officer Speaks (2004, September 9)
    http://powerlineblog.com/archives/007767.php
Rather Puts Neck on Chopping Block (2004, September 10)
    http://powerlineblog.com/archives/007778.php
TANG Typewriter Follies; Wingnuts Wrong (2004, September 10)
    http://www.dailykos.com/story/2004/9/10/34914/1603
The Daily Kos Strikes Out (2004, September 10)
    http://powerlineblog.com/archives/007779.php
Dr. Bouffard Speaks About *Boston Globe*! (2004, September 11)
    http://www.indcjournal.com/archives/000859.php
The Bush "Guard Memos" are Forgeries (2004, September 11)
    http://www.flounder.com/bush2.htm
The Real Robert Strong (2004, September 12)
    http://powerlineblog.com/archives/007814.php
CBS Keeps Digging (2004, September 13)
    http://powerlineblog.com/archives/007821.php
Naked (2004, September 14)
    http://powerlineblog.com/archives/007831.php
Last Nail in the Coffin (2004, September 14)
    http://powerlineblog.com/archives/007837.php
Catch-22 (2004, September 18)
    http://powerlineblog.com/archives/007885.php
The Post Recaps Rathergate (2004, September 19)
    http://powerlineblog.com/archives/007894.php
9. New Doc: Fake, But Accurate! (2005, March 19)
    http://fishkite.com/2005/03/19/693/
Is This the Biggest Hoax Since the Sixty Minutes Story? (2005, March 21)
    http://powerlineblog.com/archives/009929.php
Show Us the Memo (2005, March 22)
    http://powerlineblog.com/archives/009937.php
So: Where Did It Come From? (2005, March 22)
    http://powerlineblog.com/archives/009940.php
Senate "Talking Points" Update and Timeline (2005, March 22)
    http://fishkite.com/2005/03/22/701/
Show Us the Source (2005, March 23)
    http://powerlineblog.com/archives/009943.php
A Fishy Story Gets Fishier (2005, March 23)
    http://powerlineblog.com/archives/009953.php
What Exactly Did the *Post* Say About That Memo? (2005, March 31)
    http://michellemalkin.com/archives/001935.htm

Mystery Solved? (2005, April 6)
   http://powerlineblog.com/archives/010093.php
Real Memo, Fake Story (2005, April 8)
   http://powerlineblog.com/archives/ 010105.php

10. Department of Awful Statistics (2005, June 8)
   http://www.janegalt.net/blog/archives/005356.html

11. Choke on that Cinnabon (2005, April 24)
   http://www.unfogged.com/archives/wee_2005_04_24.html
   Their Worst Nightmare (2005, April 24).
   http://justoneminute.typepad.com/main/2005/04/their_worst_nig.html

12. Shiller Shills for the Left on Social Security (2005, March 21)
   http://www.poorandstupid.com/2005_03_20chronArchive.asp#1111388279
   50153042

13. More Bad Poll Data (2005, April 26)
   http://powerlineblog.com/archives/010281.php

14. Persistent, Pervasive and Pernicious: The "100,000 Civilians Dead" Canard
   (2005, March 18)
   http://www.thatliberalmedia.com/archives/003999.html
   FAIR Hypes Shaky Estimate of Iraqi Casualties (2005, March 21)
   http://www.brendan-nyhan.com/blog/2005/03/fair_hypes_shak.html
   That Liberal Media (2005, March 18)
   http://instapundit.com/archives/021873.php
   Lancet Post Number 41 (2005, March 21)
   http://timlambert.org/2005/03/lancet24/
   That Lancet Study! The One About 100,000 Dead Iraqis (2005, March 20)
   http://sacredcowgraveyard.blogspot.com/2005/03/that-lancet-study-one-abo
   ut-100000.html
   More On Those Dead Iraqis (2005, March 22)
   http://sacredcowgraveyard.blogspot.com/2005/03/more-on-those-dead-iraqi
   s.html

15. Out-and-out Dishonesty at the *New York Times* (2005, April 27)
   http://instapundit.com/archives/022681.php
   More Historical Revisionism (2005, April 14)
   http://instapundit.com/archives/022447.php

16. Middle Class Blues (2005, July 10)
   http://vodkapundit.com/archives/007943.php
   "They Were Good Muslims" (2005, July 13)
   http://www.rantingprofs.com/rantingprofs/2005/07/they_were_good_.html

17. Cuban Mythology (2005, March 12)
   http://www.babalublog.com/archives/001470.html
   The Mythology of Cuban Medical Care (2005, March 14)
   http://www.captainsquartersblog.com/mt/archives/004070.php

18. Bold, Aggressive Attack! (2005, March 21)
   http://www.rantingprofs.com/rantingprofs/2005/03/bold_aggressive.html
   Another Frame (2005, March 22)
   http://www.rantingprofs.com/rantingprofs/2005/03/another_frame.html

AP's Version of Events (2005, March 22)
http://www.rantingprofs.com/rantingprofs/2005/03/aps_version_of_.html
Don't Be Afraid to Call It or Anything (2005, April 21)
http://www.rantingprofs.com/rantingprofs/2005/04/dont_be_afraid_.html

19. *The Washington Post's* New Aversion to the F-Word (2005, May 27)
http://www.nationalreview.com/benchmemos/064619.asp

20. SS Reform is Dead; Long Live SS Reform (2005, March 15)
http://www.qando.net/details.aspx?Entry=1394

21. Well, What Would You Suggest? (2005, February 5)
http://www.rantingprofs.com/rantingprofs/2005/02/well_what_would.html
Compare and Contrast (2005, April 5)
http://www.rantingprofs.com/rantingprofs/2005/04/compare_and_con.html

22. The Person Next to You is Nuts (2005, June 7)
http://www.buzzmachine.com/archives/2005_06_07.html
Angry Young Men (2005, July 16)
http://www.buzzmachine.com/archives/2005_07_16.html

23. The Fox Hunting Standard: Why No Demonstrations Against Terror? (2005, July 15)
http://www.rantingprofs.com/rantingprofs/2005/07/why_no_demonstr.html
Here Comes the Party Line (2005, July 20)
http://powerlineblog.com/archives/011089.php

24. That was Then, This is Now (2005, April 12)
http://powerlineblog.com/archives/010145.php
Amber Alert: Another Missing Headline (2005, March 30)
http://iraqnow.blogspot.com/2005/03/amber-alert-another-missing-headline.html
New York Times Master's [sic] Coverage Takes Balls (2005, April 6)
http://www.thenationaldebate.com/blog/archives/2005/04/new_york_times_18.html.

25. Yeah, That's a Winning Strategy (2005, May 3)
http://www.rantingprofs.com/rantingprofs/2005/05/yeah_thats_a_wi.html
Oh, *That* Liberal Media (2005, April 22)
http://vodkapundit.com/archives/007801.php
No Coverage of Soldier Capturing His Would-be Murderer and Saving His Life! (2005, July 15)
http://treyjackson.typepad.com/junction/2005/07/ no_coveraage_of.html
Given How Interesting This Story Is (2005, July 16)
http://instapundit.com/archives/024306.php
But Hey, You Didn't Hear It From Me (2005, August 26)
http://www.rantingprofs.com/rantingprofs/2005/08/but_hey_you_did.html

26. Don't Show It (2005, June 26) http://atrios.blogspot.com/
2005_06_26_atrios_archive.html#111988861896618157
No Reason for Networks to Show Bush's Iraq Speech? (2005, June 27)
http://www.davidcorn.com/2005/06/no_reason_for_n.php

The TV Networks Shouldn't Broadcast Bush's Propaganda Speech (2005, June 27)
http://americablog.blogspot.com/2005/06/tv-networks-shouldnt-broadcast-bushs.html

27. Don't Let Me Interrupt (2005, July 15)
http://www.rantingprofs.com/rantingprofs/2005/07/dont_let_me_int.html

28. The Senate Resolution You Didn't Hear About (March 16, 2005)
http://www.poorandstupid.com/2005_03_chronArchive.asp#111099604476114640

Where's the Follow-Up? (2005, April 28)
http://www.rantingprofs.com/rantingprofs/2005/04/wheres_the_foll.html

The Beat Goes On (2005, September 22)
http://rantingprofs.com/rantingprofs/2005/09/the_beat-goes_o.html

29. Have the *New York Times* and *Washington Post* Become Junk Food for War Opponents? (2005, February 22)
http://tks.nationalreview.com/post/?q=MWNjNTA4OWQwN2QwZTZjNTA

Taliban Giving Up in Afghanistan? (2005, February 21)
http://www.captainsquartersblog.com/mt/archives/003896.php

30. Good News from Iraq, Part 23 (2005, March 14)
http://chrenkoff.blogspot.com/2005/03/good-news-from-iraq-part-23.html

Good News from Afghanistan, Part 14 (2005, July 11)
http://chrenkoff.blogspot.com/2005/07/good-news-from-afghanistan-part-14.html

Good News from Iraq, Part III; Bigger and Better Than Ever (2004, June 10)
http://chrenkoff.blogspot.com/2004/06/good-news-from-iraq-part-iii-bigger.html

31. Stonewalling on 46th Street (2004, February 9)
http://rogerlsimon.com/archives/00000683.htm

Enron on the East River (2004, February 25)
http://rogerlsimon.com/archives/00000717.htm

Kojo, Kofi & Kerry (2004, March 10)
http://rogerlsimon.com/archives/00000755.htm

"Oil-for-Food!" Get Yer Hot "Oil-for-Food"...READ ALL ABOUDIT! (2004, March 29)
http://rogerlsimon.com/archives/00000814.htm

Trouble at the UN — Opposing Papers on Same Side (2004, April 7)
http://rogerlsimon.com/00000840.htm

A Tale of Two Hearings (2004, April 19)
http://rogerlsimon.com/archives/00000877.htm

UNSCAM Should Not Be Ideological (2004, April 29)
http://rogerlsimon.com/archives/00000908.htm

Blame Canada! (2004, April 30)
http://rogerlsimon.com/archives/00000910.htm

Important Oil-for-Food Update (2004, October 24)
http://www.rogerlsimon.com/mt-archives/2004/10/important_oilfo.php

Important Oil-for-Food Breakthrough (2004, November 17)
http://www.rogerlsimon.com/mt-archives/2004/11/important_oilfo.php
Annan Family Values (2004, November 29)
http://www.rogerlsimon.com/mt-archives/2004/11/annan_family_va.php
Special Report #1 — Oil-for-Food Investigation (2005, March 27)
http://www.rogerlsimon.com/mt-archives/2005/03/special_report.php
Special Report #2 — The Case of the "Main Mentor" (2005, March 30)
http://www.rogerlsimon.com/mt-archives/2005/03/special_report_1.php
[sic]
Special Report #3 — "Corruption in the Palace of Justice" (2005, April 1)
http://www.rogerlsimon.com/mt-archives/2005/04/special_report_2.php
[sic]
Special Investigation #4 — The Big Shame (2005, April 3)
http://www.rogerlsimon.com/mt-archives/2005/04/special_investi.php
Uncovering the Coverup — More Mouselli On the Way (2005, April 12)
http://www.rogerlsimon.com/mt-archives/2005/04/uncovering_the.php
Trouble in (Volcker) Paradise? (2005, April 19)
http://www.rogerlsimon.com/mt-archives/2005/04/trouble_in_volc.php
Your Foreign Relations Committee at Work! (2005, April 20)
http://www.rogerlsimon.com/mt-archives/2005/04/your_foreign_re.php
Pinocchios of the Volcker Committee (2005, April 20)
http://www.rogerlsimon.com/mt-archives/2005/04/pinocchios_of_t.php
UPDATE: Oil-for-Resignations (2005, April 23)
http://www.rogerlsimon.com/mt-archives/2005/04/update_oilforre.php
32. Several Readers Have Written (2005, July 14)
http://instapundit.com/archives/024254.php
33. Rathergate Update (2004, November 21)
http://instapundit.com/archives/019380.php
Fox News and ABC Radio are Reporting (2004, November 23)
http://instapundit.com/archives/019400.php
First Thoughts on Rather's Departure (2004, November 23)
http://www.nationalreview.com/kerry/kerry200411231234.asp
CBS' Spin Control (2004, November 23)
http://andrewsullivan.com/index.php?dish_inc=archives/2004_11_21_dish_
archive.html
Rather Resigned (2004, November 23)
http://www.captainsquartersblog.com/mt/archives/003150.php
34. http://www.powerlineblognews.com/
http://www.memeorandum.com/
Q: Who's Included? (2005, September 22)
http://blog.memeorandum.com/050922/whos-included
http://pajamasmedia.com/index_html
35. Let Us Not Speak Ill of the Dead (2005, April 17)
http://www.rantingprofs.com/rantingprofs/2005/04/let_us_not_spea.html
What's Coming Out Now (2005, April 19)
http://www.rantingprofs.com/rantingprofs/2005/04/whats_coming_ou.html

36. There are Benefits to Embedding (2005, April 21)
    http://www.rantingprofs.com/rantingprofs/2005/04/there_are_benef.html
    Give the *Times* Its Due (2005, August 21)
    http://www.rantingprofs.com/rantingprofs/2005/08/give_the_times_.html
    Meanwhile, Back at the Hotel (2005, February 28)
    http://www.rantingprofs.com/rantingprofs/2005/02/meanwhile_back_.html
    The Jaws of Victory (2005, March 1)
    http://www.mudvillegazette.com/archives/002276.html
37. A New Video: Question the Provenance (2005, May 2)
    http://www.rantingprofs.com/rantingprofs/2005/05/a_new_video_que.html
    Shame on NBC (2005, December 4)
    http://www.rantingprofs.com/rantingprofs/2005/12/shame_on_nbc.html
    Disinformation Alert (n.d.)
    http://www.iimefpublic.usmc.mil/public/iimefpublic.nsf/all/B787AD0EBA
    C79A0B88257008004E35A6
38. The Odds Against (2004, December 20)
    http://belmontclub.blogspot.com/2004/12/odds-against-associated-press-arti
    cle.html
    Follman, M. (2004, December 22). The Associated Press "insurgency."
    http://www.salon.com/opinion/feature/2004/12/22/executions/
    Sixty Four Dollars (2004, December 23)
    http://belmontclub.blogspot.com/2004/12/sixty-four-dollars-salon-claims-th
    at.html
    Haifa Street (2004, December 23)
    http://belmontclub.blogspot.com/2004/12/haifa-street-execution-of-iraqi.ht
    ml
    Incident on Haifa Street (2004, December 24)
    http://littlegreenfootballs.com/weblog/?entry=14077_Incident_on_Haifa_St
    reet
    Stokes, J. (2004, December 23). AP on its Iraqi photographers and insurgents.
    http://www.poynter.org/forum/view_post.asp?id=8533
    "Insurgents Want Their Stories Told" (2004, December 24)
    http://belmontclub.blogspot.com/2004/12/photographer-become-aware-that
    -story.html
    On the AP and the Murders (2004, December 24)
    http://powerlineblog.com/archives/009018.php
    AP Admits Relationship With Terrorists (2004, December 25)
    http://powerlineblog.com/archives/009026.php
    Media Critics: Haifa Street Execution Photo Edition (2005, January 1)
    http://www.deadparrots.net/archives/media/0501media_critics_haifa_street
    _execution_photo_edition.html
    Breaking News Photography (n.d.)
    http://www.pulitzer.org/year/2005/breaking-news-photography/works/warz
    one20.html
    The Pulitzer Prize for Felony Murder... (2005, April 5)
    http://powerlineblog.com/archives/010066.php

Haifa Street Critics Are Back (2005, April 8)
http://www.deadparrots.net/archives/media/0504haifa_street_critics_are_back.html

Murder on Haifa Street: An Update (2005, April 10)
http://powerlineblog.com/archives/010128.php

Lyon, S. (2005, April 4). The story behind the photo.
http://www.ap.org/pages/about/whatsnew/wn_040505b.html

A Postscript From D. Gorton (2005, April 10)
http://powerlineblog.com/archives/010132.php

Haifa Street Update III: Sunday Developments (2005, April 10)
http://www.deadparrots.net/archives/blogging/0504haifa_street_update_iii_sunday_developments.html

39. Unprofessional — *WaPo*'s Rathergate (2005, September 12)
http://www.dailykos.com/story/2005/9/12/124433/197

WaPo Follies (2005, September 12)
http://atrios.blogspot.com/2005_09_11_atrios_archive.html#112654608631375564

Period (2005, September 12)
http://atrios.blogspot.com/2005_09_11_atrios_archive.html#112653667287335870

40. *NY Times* = Suckers (2005, July 15)
http://www.liberaloasis.com/archives/071005.htm#071505

Ridiculous *New York Times* Anonymous Source of the Day (2005, July 15)
http://atrios.blogspot.com/2005_07_10_atrios_archive.html#112142973339466074

41. The Sunnis (2005, October 14)
http://www.rantingprofs.com/rantingprofs/2005/10/the_sunnis.html

No Gloom or Doom (2005, November 4)
http://www.rantingprofs.com/rantingprofs/2005/11/no_gloom_or_doo.html

42. Cpl. Jeffrey B. Starr: What the *NY Times* Left Out (2005, October 28)
http://michellemalkin.com/archives/003793.htm

43. *New York Times* Blows One — BIG TIME! (2005, July 6)
http://markinmexico.blogspot.com/2005/07/new-york-times-blows-one-big-time.html

Carter, P. (2005a, July 6). The quiet man.
http://www.nytimes.com/2005/07/06/opinion/06carter.html?ex=1278302400&en=10a4e4dbb71ca9fa&ei=5090&partner=rssuserland&emc=rss.

NYT Caught Lying Again (2005, July 6)
http://www.dailypundit.com/newarchives/002791.php

Oops... (2005, July 6)
http://www.washingtonmonthly.com/archives/individual/2005_07/006658.php

44. Astroturf Alert: Another MoveOn.org Mail Blitz (2005, April 18)
http://michellemalkin.com/archives/002133.htm

Stupid Papers and GOP Astroturf (2004, August 17)
http://www.dailykos.com/story/2004/8/17/17029/2550

45. Pravda-Media Regresses to Sand Box Mentality (2005, October 7)
     http://polipundit.com/index.php?p=10363
    Is It Parody? I Can't Tell (2005, March 20)
     http://powerlineblog.com/archives/009916.php
    Deborah Solomon is Harsh (2005, March 29)
     http://www.brendan-nyhan.com/blog/2005/03/deborah_solomon.html
    Becker, E., & Sanger, D. E. (2005, March 16). Bush chooses a top Pentagon
     aide to head the World Bank.
     http://www.nytimes.com/2005/03/16/international/16cnd-bank.html?ex=12
     68629200&en=895a29cb9304e205&ei=5090&partner=rssuserland
    "Elisabeth" (2005, March 16)
     http://instapundit.com/archives/021828.php
    Just the Story (2006, January 2)
     http://www.rantingprofs.com/rantingprofs/2006/01/just_the_story.html
46. Finally (2005, October 6)
     http://hoystory.blogspot.com/2005/10/finally-todays-new-york-times-finall
     y.html
    All the Good Stuff Gets Buried (2005, December 10)
     http://www.rantingprofs.com/rantingprofs/2005/12/all_the_good_st.html
47. The Return of the Restaurant Story (2005, January 23)
     http://www.rantingprofs.com/rantingprofs/2005/01/the_return_of_t.html
    What to Do When the Polls Don't Go Your Way (2005, March 17)
     http://www.rantingprofs.com/rantingprofs/2005/03/what_to_do_when.html
48. Here We Go Again: More Koran Desecration (2005, November 1)
     http://www.rantingprofs.com/rantingprofs/2005/11/here_we_go_agai.html
    When the Story Gets in the Way of the Truth (2005, May 15)
     http://www.buzzmachine.com/archives/2005_05_15.html#009685
    Newsweek Apologizes for Riot-sparking Koran Story (2005, May 15)
     http://www.themoderatevoice.com/posts/1116199979.shtml
    Newsweek Uses "R" Word and Retracts Koran Desecration Story (2005, May
     16) http://www.themoderatevoice.com/posts/1116280793.shtml
    Why Do They Hate Us? (2005, May 16)
     http://www.rantingprofs.com/rantingprofs/2005/05/why_do_they_hat.html
    Newsweek Has Retracted Its Koran-flushing Story (2005, May 16)
     http://instapundit.com/archives/023026.php
    Newsweek Lied, People Died (2005, May 16)
     http://semirandomramblings.blogspot.com/2005/05/newsweek-lied-people-
     died.html
    Lesson Eighteen: Prisons and Detention Centers (n.d.)
     http://www.usdoj.gov/ag/manualpart1_4.pdf
49. Resolving Competing Claims (2005, October 18)
     http://www.rantingprofs.com/rantingprofs/2005/10/resolving_compe.html
    The *Post* Has Decided Who to Believe (2005, December 2)
     http://www.rantingprofs.com/rantingprofs/2005/12/the_post_has_de.html
50. The Coverage of Civilian Casualties in Iraq (2004, January 26)
     http://rantingprofs.typepad.com/rantingprofs/2004/01/the_coverage_of.html

The *New York Times* Responds to Criticism of its Coverage on Civilian Casualties (2004, March 1) http://rantingprofs.typepad.com/rantingprofs/2004/03/the_new_york_ti.html

51. Squeeze Play (2004, June 21)
http://rantingprofs.typepad.com/rantingprofs/2004/06/squeeze_play.html

52. Wilson-Lied Media Spin Update (2004, July 18)
http://instapundit.com/archives/016608.php
What I Didn't Find in the *NY Times* (2004, July 18)
http://justoneminute.typepad.com/main/2004/07/what_i_didnt_fi.html

53. The Rowback of All Rowbacks (2004, July 14)
http://www.rantingprofs.com/rantingprofs/2004/07/the_rowback_of_.html

54. An Anti-War Smear Artist Exposed (2005, November 6)
http://michellemalkin.com/archives/003841.htm
Jimmy Massey: A Slanderer and His MSM Enablers (2005, November 7)
http://michellemalkin.com/archives/003844.htm
The Media and the Unhinged Marine (2005, November 9)
http://michellemalkin.com/archives/003861.htm
Jimmy Massey's Lies: The AP Finally Wakes Up (2005, December 14)
http://michellemalkin.com/archives/004073.htm

55. Lt. Gen. David Petraeus Speaks at Princeton (2005, October 2)
http://tigerhawk.blogspot.com/2005/10/lt-gen-david-petraeus-speaks-at.html
Pictures From the Air of Gulfport and Biloxi Areas (2005, September 10)
http://www.murdoconline.net/archives/002772.html
Gulf Coast Photos (2006, January 30)
http://www.murdoconline.net/archives/003394.html

56. The Safest City in Iraq (2006, February 21)
http://www.michaeltotten.com/archives/001061.html
The Utah of the Middle East (2006, February 28)
http://www.michaeltotten.com/archives/001066.html
"The Head of the Snake" (2006, March 3)
http://www.michaeltotten.com/archives/001068.html

57. The Hounds of Husaybah (2005, November 28)
http://billroggio.com/archives/2005/11/the_hounds_of_husayb.php

58. Prelude (2005, August 1)
http://www.michaelyon-online.com/wp/prelude.htm
Gates of Fire (2005, August 31)
http://www.michaelyon-online.com/wp/gates-of-fire.htm

59. Iraqi Tribes in Anbar Arrest 270 Arab and Foreign al-Qaeda Members! (2006, January 27)
http://iraqthemodel.blogspot.com/2006/01/iraqi-tribes-in-anbar-arrest-270-arab.html
On the Mosque Bombing (2006, February 24)
http://powerlineblog.com/archives/013235.php
We Are All Misinformed! (2006, February 23)
http://twentyfourstepstoliberty.blogspot.com/2006/02/we-are-all-misinformed-you-guys-always_23.html

60. Shame, Guilt, the Muslim Psyche, and the Danish Cartoons (2006, February 6)
http://drsanity.blogspot.com/2006/02/shame-guilt-muslim-psyche-and-dani
sh.html
The Information War (2006, February 27)
http://shrinkwrapped.blogs.com/blog/2006/02/the_information.html

61. Picture of the Day: Do I Offend? (2006, February 21)
http://elephantsinacademia.blogspot.com/2006_02_01_elephantsinacademi
a_archive.html#114052718853139177#links
Case Studies on the Minimum Wage (2005, March 29)
http://www.coyoteblog.com/coyote_blog/2005/03/case_studies_on.html

62. A Mind is a Difficult Thing to Change: Interlude (2005, March 30)
http://neo-neocon.blogspot.com/2005/03/mind-is-difficult-thing-to-change.
html
What Independence Means For Me (2005, July 5)
http://afreeiraqi.blogspot.com/2005/07/what-independence-means-for-me.ht
ml

References

Abrams et al. v. United States (1919). 250 U.S. 616.

A Fishy Story Gets Fishier (2005, March 23). Retrieved 7/22/05 from http://powerlineblog.com/archives/009953.php.

Alexy, R. (1990). A theory of practical discourse (D. Frisby, Trans.) In *The Communicative Ethics Controversy* (S. Benhabib & F. Dallmayr, Eds.). Cambridge, MA: MIT Press.

Allen, M., & Roig-Franzia, M. (2005, March 20). Congress steps in on Schiavo case. *The Washington Post*. Retrieved 7/21/05 from LexisNexis Academic.

Allen, M. (2005a, March 22). Congress and the Schiavo case. *The Washington Post*. Retrieved 7/22/05 from http://washingtonpost.com/wp-dyn/articles/A54766-2005Mar21.html.

Allen, M. (2005b, April 7). Counsel to GOP senator wrote memo on Schiavo. *The Washington Post*. Retrieved 7/24/05 from LexisNexis Academic.

All the Good Stuff Gets Buried (2005, December 10). Retrieved 12/10/05 from http://www.rantingprofs.com/rantingprofs/2005/12/all_the_good_st.html.

Amber Alert: Another Missing Headline (2005, March 30). Retrieved 3/31/05 from http://iraqnow.blogspot.com/2005/03/amber-alert-another-missing-headline.html.

A Mind is a Difficult Thing to Change: Interlude (2005, March 30). Retrieved 3/14/06 from http://neo-neocon.blogspot.com/2005/03/mind-is-difficult-thing-to-change.html.

An Anti-War Smear Artist Exposed (2005, November 6). Retrieved 1/9/06 from http://michellemalkin.com/archives/003841.htm.

A New Video: Question the Provenance (2005, May 2). Retrieved 5/2/05 from http://www.rantingprofs.com/rantingprofs/2005/05/a_new_video_que.html.

Angry Young Men (2005, July 16). Retrieved 7/17/05 from http://www.buzzmachine.com/archives/2005_07_16.html.

Annan "Disappointed and Surprised" Over Oil-for-Food Payments (2004, November 30). *The Frontrunner*. Retrieved 12/29/05 from LexisNexis Academic.

Annan Family Values (2004, November 29). Retrieved 7/14/05 from http://www.rogerlsimon.com/mt-archives/2004/11/annan_family_va.php.

An Officer Weighs In (2004, September 9). Retrieved 7/25/05 from http://powerlineblog.com/archives/007765.php.

Another Frame (2005, March 22). Retrieved 3/23/05 from http://www.rantingprofs.com/rantingprofs/2005/03/another_frame.html.

Another Officer Speaks (2004, September 9). Retrieved 7/25/05 from http://powerlineblog.com/archives/007767.php.

AP Admits Relationship With Terrorists (2004, December 25). Retrieved 11/18/05 from http://powerlineblog.com/archives/009026.php.

AP Bias Strikes Again (2004, September 03). Retrieved 3/23/05 from http://spinswimming.blogspot.com/2004/09/ap-bias-strikes-again.html.

AP Changes "Boos" to "Ooohs" in Report on Bush and Clinton (2004, September 03). *Editor & Publisher*. Retrieved 3/23/05 from http://www.mediainfo.com/eandp/news/article_display.jsp?vnu_content_id=1000624935.

AP Puts Words in Ariel Sharon's Mouth (2005, April 13). Retrieved 4/14/05 from http://www.brendanloy.com/archives/017560.html.

AP Retracts "Boo" Story; Left Not Convinced (2004, September 04). Retrieved 3/23/05 from http://powerlineblog.com/archives/2004_09.php.

AP's Version of Events (2005, March 22). Retrieved 3/23/05 from http://www.rantingprofs.com/rantingprofs/2005/03/aps_version_of_.html.

A Postscript From D. Gorton (2005, April 10). Retrieved 11/21/05 from http://powerlineblog.com/archives/010132.php.

Are Bush Memos Authentic? (2004, September 10). "The O'Reilly Factor." Fox News Network. Retrieved 2/24/06 from LexisNexis Academic.

Art — An Unintentional Manifesto (2001, July 26). Retrieved 3/6/06 from http://denbeste.nu/essays/art.shtml.

Astroturf Alert: Another MoveOn.org Mail Blitz (2005, April 18). Retrieved 9/5/05 from http://michellemalkin.com/archives/002133.htm.

A Tale of Two Hearings (2004, April 19). Retrieved 7/13/05 from http://rogerlsimon.com/archives/00000877.htm.

Audience Boos as Bush Offers Best Wishes for Clinton's Recovery (2004, September 3). Associated Press. Retrieved 6/6/05 from LexisNexis Academic.

Babbie, E. (1990). *Survey Research Methods*. Belmont, CA: Wadsworth.

Babington, C. (2005, May 27). Democrats extend debate on Bolton. *The Washington Post*. Retrieved 6/22/05 from LexisNexis Academic.

Becker, E., & Sanger, D. E. (2005a, March 16). Bush chooses a top Pentagon aide to head the World Bank. Retrieved 1/16/06 from http://www.nytimes.com/2005/03/16/international/16cnd-bank.html?ex=1268629200&en=895a29cb9304e205&ei=5090&partner=rssuserland.

Becker, E. & Sanger, D. E. (2005b, March 17). Wolfowitz gets Bush nomination for World Bank. *The New York Times*. Retrieved 1/16/06 from LexisNexis Academic.

Benac, N. (2005, October 7). Cheney throwing stones at Democrats. Associated Press. Retrieved 10/7/05 from LexisNexis Academic.

Bennett, R. K. (2005). The best thing that has ever happened to journalism. Retrieved 3/4/05 from http://www.techcentralstation.com/030405B.html.

Blackmore, S. (2000, October). The power of memes. *Scientific American, 283*(4). Retrieved 6/6/05 from Academic Search Premier.

Blackmore, S. (1999). *The Meme Machine*. Oxford, England: Oxford University Press.

Blame Canada! (2004, April 30). Retrieved 7/13/05 from http://rogerlsimon.com/archives/00000910.htm.

Blitzer, W. (2004). Dan Rather's stand. CNN. Retrieved 7/30/05 from LexisNexis Academic.

Blog (n.d.). Retrieved 8/21/05 from http://www.samizdata.net/blog/glossary_archives/001959.html.

Blog Readers are Shockingly Influential (2005, March 17). Retrieved 3/23/05 from http://weblog.blogads.com/comments/P1002_0_1_0/.

Blogroll (n.d.). Retrieved 2/13/06 from http://www.samizdata.net/blog/glossary_archives/002030.html.

Bold, Aggressive Attack! (2005, March 21). Retrieved 3/21/05 from http://www.rantingprofs.com/rantingprofs/2005/03/bold_aggressive.html.

Breaking News Photography (n.d.). Retrieved 11/18/05 from http://www.pulitzer.org/year/2005/breaking-news-photography/works/warzone20.html.

Brooks, D. (2005, April 24). Living longer is the best revenge. *The New York Times*. Retrieved 6/9/05 from LexisNexis Academic.

Brown, S., Jr. (2005, April 14). Anyone can deal with Republicans who shoot straight. *St. Louis Post-Dispatch*. Retrieved 6/12/05 from LexisNexis Academic.

Burying the Better News (2005, March 21). Retrieved 3/21/05 from http://chrenkoff.blogspot.com/2005/03/burying-better-news.html.

Bush Guard Documents: Forged (2004, September 9). Retrieved 7/25/05 from http://littlegreenfootballs.com/weblog/?entry=12526&only=yes.

Bush Offers Best Wishes for Clinton (2004, September 3). Associated Press. Retrieved 6/6/05 from LexisNexis Academic.

But Hey, You Didn't Hear It From Me (2005, August 26). Retrieved 10/27/05 from http://www.rantingprofs.com/rantingprofs/2005/08/but_hey_you_did.html.

Butler, D. (2004, October 23). Iraqis reveal in secret interviews how Saddam manipulated oil-for-food program. Associated Press. Retrieved 12/29/05 from LexisNexis Academic.

Butler, D. (2005, April 23). Investigator decries Oil-for-Food probe. Associated Press. Retrieved 12/29/05 from LexisNexis Academic.

Butler, D. O., & Wadhams, N. (2005, April 20). Two oil-for-food investigators resign, saying probe too soft on Kofi Annan. Associated Press. Retrieved 1/4/06 from LexisNexis Academic.

But Who Checks the Bloggers? (2004, September 21). Retrieved 8/4/05 from http://powerlineblog.com/archives/007916.php.

By the Book (2002, February 20). CBS News Transcripts. Retrieved 1/27/06 from LexisNexis Academic.

Calame, B. (2005, July 17). When an explanation doesn't explain enough. *The New York Times*. Retrieved 1/16/06 from LexisNexis Academic.

Carey, B. (2005, June 7). Most will be mentally ill at some point, study says. *The New York Times*. Retrieved 6/22/05 from LexisNexis Academic.

Carl, T. (2005, March 21). Iraq sees largest militant toll in months. Associated Press. Retrieved 6/12/05 from LexisNexis Academic.

Carlyle, T. (1993). *On Heroes, Hero-Worship, & the Heroic in History* (M. K. Goldber, J. J. Brattin, & M. Engel, Eds.). Berkeley, CA: University of California Press.

Carter, P. (2005a, July 6). The quiet man. Retrieved 7/9/05 from
http://www.nytimes.com/2005/07/06/opinion/06carter.html?ex=1278302400&e
n=10a4e4dbb71ca9fa&ei=5090&partner=rssuserland&emc=rss.

Carter, P. (2005b, July 6). The quiet man. *The New York Times*. Retrieved 7/12/05
from LexisNexis Academic.

Case Studies on the Minimum Wage (2005, March 29). Retrieved 3/30/05 from
http://www.coyoteblog.com/coyote_blog/2005/03/case_studies_on.html.

Catch-22 (2004, September 18). Retrieved 7/28/05 from
http://powerlineblog.com/archives/007885.php.

Cauchon, D. (2001, April 4). Newspapers' recount show Bush prevailed in Fla.
vote. *USA Today*. Retrieved 8/24/05 from LexisNexis Academic.

Cauchon, D., & Drinkard, J. (2001, May 11). Florida voter errors cost Gore the
election. *USA Today*. Retrieved 8/30/05 from LexisNexis Academic.

Caves, R. E., & Williamson, P. J. (1985). What is product differentiation, really?
The Journal of Industrial Economics, 34(2), 113-132.

CBS Keeps Digging (2004, September 13). Retrieved 7/28/05 from
http://powerlineblog.com/archives/007821.php.

CBS Ousts 4 for Bush Guard Story (2005, January 10). Retrieved 7/28/05 from
http://www.cbsnews.com/stories/2005/01/10/national/main665727.shtml.

CBS'[s] Spin Control (2004, November 23). Retrieved 7/16/05 from
http://andrewsullivan.com/index.php?dish_inc=archives/2004_11_21_dish_arc
hive.html.

CBS Statement on Bush Memos (2004, September 20). CBS News. Retrieved
7/28/05 from
http://www.cbsnews.com/stories/2004/09/20/politics/main644539.shtml.

Chandresekaran, R. (2004, June 29). A grand mission ends quietly. *The Washington
Post*. Retrieved 7/7/05 from LexisNexis Academic.

Children "Starving" in New Iraq (2005, March 30). BBC News World Edition.
Retrieved 6/03/05 from http://news.bbc.co.uk/2/hi/middle_east/4395525.stm.

Choke on that Cinnabon (2005, April 24). Retrieved 4/25/05 from
http://www.unfogged.com/archives/wee_2005_04_24.html.

CNN Wolf Blitzer Reports (2004, September 10). CNN. Retrieved 7/30/05 from
LexisNexis Academic.

Cohen, B. C. (1963). *The Press and Foreign Policy*. Princeton, NJ: Princeton
University Press.

Compare and Contrast (2005, April 5). Retrieved 4/5/05 from
http://www.rantingprofs.com/rantingprofs/2005/04/compare_and_con.html.

Condescension and Leaving the Political Fold (2005, March 28). Retrieved 3/31/05
from http://neo-neocon.blogspot.com/2005/03/condescension-and-leaving-
political.html.

Congressman: Blame Iraq for Sanctions, But World Can Do More (2000, April 25).
CNN.com. Retrieved 6/12/05 from http://archives.cnn.com/2000/WORLD/
meast/04/25/iraq.sanctions/.

Constable, P. (2005, April 19). A disarming presence in a dangerous world. *The
Washington Post*. Retrieved 9/24/05 from LexisNexis Academic.

Cooper, S. (1994). News media objectivity: How do we ask the questions? *New
Jersey Journal of Communication*, 2(2), 91-106.

Cooper, S. D. (2006a). Journalistic ethics. In *Social Issues in America* (J. Ciment, Ed.). Armonk, NY: M. E. Sharpe.

Cooper, S. D. (2006b). Media bias. In *Social Issues in America* (J. Ciment, Ed.). Armonk, NY: M. E. Sharpe.

Cooper, S. D. (2003). Press controls in wartime: The legal, historical, and institutional context. *The American Communication Journal,* 6(4).

Cooper, S. D., & Kuypers, J. A. (2004). Embedded versus behind-the-lines reporting on the 2003 Iraq war. In *Global Media Go to War* (R. D. Berenger, Ed.). Spokane, WA: Marquette Books.

Corrections (2004, July 9). *The Washington Post.* Retrieved 7/7/05 from LexisNexis Academic.

Counting the Iraqi Dead (2005, March 21). Fairness and Accuracy in Reporting. Retrieved 6/13/05 from http://fair.org/index.php?page=2472.

Cpl. Jeffrey B. Starr: What the NY Times Left Out (2005, October 28). Retrieved 11/2/05 from http://michellemalkin.com/archives/003793.htm.

Crary, D. (2004, May 11). Some suggest post-Sept. 11 quest for vengeance created atmosphere conducive to abuse of Iraqis. Associated Press. Retrieved 1/30/06 from LexisNexis Academic.

Crumbs for Africa (2005, June 8). *The New York Times.* Retrieved 7/1/05 from LexisNexis Academic.

Cuban Mythology (2005, March 12). Retrieved 6/12/05 from http://www.babalublog.com/archives/001470.html.

Dao, J. (2005, October 26). 2,000 dead: As Iraq tours stretch on, a grim mark. *The New York Times.* Retrieved 11/10/05 from LexisNexis Academic.

Davey, M. (2006). Iraq, once so distant, suddenly looms close for a private recruited in wartime. *The New York Times.* Retrieved 1/16/06 from LexisNexis Academic.

Dawkins, R. (1989). *The Selfish Gene.* Oxford, England: Oxford University Press.

Deborah Solomon is Harsh (2005, March 29). Retrieved 9/24/05 from http://www.brendan-nyhan.com/blog/2005/03/deborah_solomon.html.

DeLay Says He's Not Giving Up Schiavo Fight (2005, March 19). Retrieved 8/1/05 from http://abcnews.go.com/GMA/Schiavo/story?id=595905&page=2.

Demers, D. P. (1996). *The Menace of the Corporate Newspaper: Fact or Fiction?* Ames, IA: Iowa State University Press.

Department of Awful Statistics (2005, June 8). Retrieved 6/23/05 from http://www.janegalt.net/blog/archives/005356.html.

Diderich, J. (2005, October 7). Former Marine in Iraq claims in book that he and his platoon committed atrocities. Associated Press. Retrieved 1/30/06 from LexisNexis Academic.

DiMaggio, P. J., & Powell, W. W. (1983). The iron cage revisited: Institutional isomorphism and collective rationality in organizational fields. *American Sociological Review,* 48(2), 147-160.

Disinformation Alert (n.d.). Retrieved 12/24/05 from http://www.iimefpublic.usmc.mil/public/iimefpublic.nsf/all/B787AD0EBAC79A0B88257008004E35A6.

Dobbs, M., & Kurtz, H. (2004, September 14). Expert cited by CBS says he didn't authenticate papers. *The Washington Post*. Retrieved 7/30/05 from LexisNexis Academic.

Documents Suggest Special Treatment for Bush in Guard (2004, September 8). Retrieved 3/20/06 from http://www.freerepublic.com/focus/f-news/1210662/posts.

Don't Be Afraid to Call It or Anything (2005, April 21). Retrieved 4/21/05 from http://www.rantingprofs.com/rantingprofs/2005/04/dont_be_afraid_.html.

Don't Let Me Interrupt (2005, July 15). Retrieved 7/16/05 from http://www.rantingprofs.com/rantingprofs/2005/07/dont_let_me_int.html.

Don't Show It (2005, June 26). Retrieved 3/20/06 from http://atrios.blogspot.com/2005_06_26_atrios_archive.html#111988861896618157.

Dowdification (n.d.). Retrieved 8/21/05 from http://www.samizdata.net/blog/glossary_archives/003822.html.

Dowd, M. (2003a, May 14). Osama's offspring. *The New York Times*. Retrieved 8/14/05 from LexisNexis Academic.

Dowd, M. (2003b, May 28). In-a-gadda da-vida we trust. *The New York Times*. Retrieved 8/15/05 from LexisNexis Academic.

Dowd's Distortion (2003, May 14). Retrieved 8/14/05 from http://andrewsullivan.com/index.php?dish_inc=archives/2003_05_11_dish_archive.html#200290689.

Dowd's Dots and the Non-correction Correction (2003, June 4). Retrieved 8/14/05 from http://www.thenationaldebate.com/blogger/articles/dowd2.htm.

Dowd Spawns Bush Media Myth (2003, May 22). Retrieved 8/14/05 from http://www.spinsanity.org/columns/20030522.html.

Dr. Bouffard Speaks About *Boston Globe*! (2004, September 11). Retrieved 7/25/05 from http://www.indcjournal.com/archives/000859.php.

Drummond, D. J. (2005, December 29). Hypocrisy Does Not Befit You, Madam. Retrieved 12/29/05 from http://polipundit.com/index.php?p=11751.

Duff-Brown, B. (2004, December 8). Former Marine in Iraq: We fired on unarmed civilians, wounded combatants. Associated Press. Retrieved 1/30/06 from LexisNexis Academic.

Dumb Edwards Statistic on Poverty (2005, March 22). Retrieved 3/23/05 from http://www.brendan-nyhan.com/blog/2005/03/dumb_edwards_st.html.

"Elisabeth" (2005, March 16). Retrieved 1/16/06 from http://instapundit.com/archives/021828.php.

End Sanctions on Iraq (n.d.). Peace Action Education Fund. Retrieved 6/13/05 from http://www.peace-action.org/camp/justice/iraqfs.pdf.

Engberg, E. (2004). Blogging as typing, not journalism. Retrieved 3/4/05 from http://www.cbsnews.com/stories/2004/11/08/opinion/main654285.shtml.

Enron on the East River (2004, February 25). Retrieved 7/13/05 from http://rogerlsimon.com/archives/00000717.htm.

Fainaru, S., & Shadid, A. (2005, October 14). In Iraqi swing city, hope vs. defiance. *The Washington Post*. Retrieved 10/17/05 from LexisNexis Academic.

FAIR Hypes Shaky Estimate of Iraqi Casualties (2005, March 21). Retrieved
3/23/05 from
http://www.brendan-nyhan.com/blog/2005/03/fair_hypes_shak.html.

Farrell, T. B. (1993). *Norms of Rhetorical Culture*. New Haven, CT: Yale
University Press.

Fattah, H. M. (2005, July 16). Anger burns on the fringe of Britain's Muslims. *The
New York Times*. Retrieved 7/18/05 from LexisNexis Academic.

Fessenden, F., & Broder, J. M. (2001, November 12). Study of disputed Florida
ballots finds Justices did not cast the deciding vote. *The New York Times*.
Retrieved 8/24/05 from LexisNexis Academic.

Finally (2005, October 6). Retrieved 10/6/05 from http://hoystory.blogspot.com/
2005/10/finally-todays-new-york-times-finally.html.

Finer, J. (2005, September 22). Iraqi forces show signs of progress in offensive. *The
Washington Post*. Retrieved 9/23/05 from LexisNexis Academic.

First Thoughts on Rather's Departure (2004, November 23). Retrieved 7/16/05 from
http://www.nationalreview.com/kerry/kerry200411231234.asp.

Fisk (n.d.). Retrieved 8/21/05 from http://www.samizdata.net/blog/
glossary_archives/001961.html.

Follman, M. (2004, December 22). The Associated Press "insurgency." *Salon*.
Retrieved 11/18/05 from http://www.salon.com/opinion/feature/2004/
12/22/executions/.

Foucault, M. (1981). *Power/Knowledge* (C. Gordon, Ed.). New York, NY: Pantheon
Books.

Fox News and ABC Radio are Reporting (2004, November 23). Retrieved 7/16/05
from http://instapundit.com/archives/019400.php.

Friedman, M. (2002). *Capitalism and freedom*. Chicago, IL: University of Chicago.

From Um Mushtaq to Abu Haider (2004, July 1). Retrieved 7/15/05 from
http://iraqthemodel.blogspot.com/2004_07_01_iraqthemodel_archive.html.

Fund, J. (2004, September 14). We'd rather be blogging. *New York Sun*. Retrieved
6/3/05 from LexisNexis Academic.

Gall, C. (2005, August 21). A nomad campaigns to serve her people in Afghanistan.
The New York Times. Retrieved 10/27/05 from LexisNexis Academic.

Gamson, W. A. (1989). News as framing: Comments on Graber. *American
Behavioral Scientist, 33*(2), pp. 157-161.

Gates of Fire (2005, August 31). Retrieved 3/6/06 from
http://www.michaelyon-online.com/wp/gates-of-fire.htm.

Geez, Paul Krugman Lies a Lot (2005, August 18). Retrieved 8/29/05 from
http://thechiefbrief.blogspot.com/2005/08/geez-paul-krugman-lies-lot.html.

Gettleman, J. (2005, January 23). Iraq remains sharply split over election. Retrieved
9/23/05 from LexisNexis Academic.

Giddens, A. (1984). *The Constitution of Society*. Berkeley, CA: University of
California Press.

Given How Interesting This Story Is (2005, July 16). Retrieved 7/16/05 from
http://instapundit.com/archives/024306.php.

Give the *Times* Its Due (2005, August 21). Retrieved 8/21/05 from
http://www.rantingprofs.com/rantingprofs/2005/08/give_the_times_.html.

Glassman, M. (2005, April 11). Blogs incensed over Pulitzer photo award. *The New York Times*. Retrieved 12/20/05 from LexisNexis Academic.

Goldberg, B. (2003). *Bias*. New York, NY: HarperCollins.

Good News from Afghanistan, Part 14 (2005, July 11). Retrieved 7/11/05 from http://chrenkoff.blogspot.com/2005/07/good-news-from-afghanistan-part-14.html.

Good News from Iraq, Part III; Bigger and Better Than Ever (2004, June 10). Retrieved 7/11/05 from http://chrenkoff.blogspot.com/2004/06/good-news-from-iraq-part-iii-bigger.html.

Good News from Iraq, Part 23 (2005, March 14). Retrieved 7/11/05 from http://chrenkoff.blogspot.com/2005/03/good-news-from-iraq-part-23.html.

Goodnight, G. T. (1992). Habermas, the public sphere, and controversy. *International Journal of Public Opinion Research, 4*(3), 243-255.

Graham, S. (2005, April 21). U.S. military: more than 12 insurgents killed in battle in southeastern Afghanistan. Associated Press. Retrieved 7/11/05 from LexisNexis Academic.

Grant, K. (2005, February 28). A blinkered view from the Baghdad Hilton. *The Scotsman*. Retrieved 11/15/05 from http://thescotsman.scotsman.com/opinion.cfm?id=222062005.

Group blog (n.d.). Retrieved 2/18/06 from http://www.samizdata.net/blog/glossary_archives/001972.html.

Gulf Coast Photos (2006, January 30). Retrieved 2/10/06 from http://www.murdoconline.net/archives/003394.html.

Habermas, J. (1975). *Legitimation Crisis* (T. McCarthy, Trans.). Boston, MA: Beacon Press.

Habermas, J. (1990). *Moral Consciousness and Communicative Action* (C. Lenhart & S. W. Nicholsen, Trans.). Cambridge, MA: MIT Press.

Habermas, J. (2001). *On the Pragmatics of Social Interaction* (B. Fultner, Trans.). Cambridge, MA: MIT Press.

Hack, D. (2005, April 5). What's missing at Augusta? Controversy. *The New York Times*. Retrieved 6/13/05 from LexisNexis Academic.

Haifa Street (2004, December 23). Retrieved 11/15/05 from http://belmontclub.blogspot.com/2004/12/haifa-street-execution-of-iraqi.html.

Haifa Street Critics Are Back (2005, April 8). Retrieved 7/14/05 from http://www.deadparrots.net/archives/media/0504haifa_street_critics_are_back.html.

Haifa Street Update III: Sunday Developments (2005, April 10). Retrieved 11/21/05 from http://www.deadparrots.net/archives/blogging/0504haifa_street_update_iii_sunday_developments.html.

Hampson, R. (2005, March 21). Recruiter-turned-peacenik hits nerve in N.C. *USA Today*. Retrieved 1/29/06 from LexisNexis Academic.

Harris, R. (2005a, November 6). Is Jimmy Massey telling the truth about Iraq? *St. Louis Post-Dispatch*. Retrieved 1/16/06 from LexisNexis Academic.

Harris, R. (2005b, November 6). Why did the press fail to check Massey's stories? *St. Louis Post-Dispatch*. Retrieved 1/16/06 from LexisNexis Academic.

Hauser, C. (2005, February 5). Iraqi police use kidnappers' videos to fight crime. *The New York Times*. Retrieved 6/11/05 from LexisNexis Academic.

Have the *New York Times* and *Washington Post* Become Junk Food for War
   Opponents? (2005, February 22). Retrieved 6/18/06 from
   http://tks.nationalreview.com/post/?q=MWNjNTA40WQwZTZjNTA2ODYwM
   zkxNmUyYzIxZmM=

Here Comes the Party Line (2005, July 20). Retrieved 7/21/05 from
   http://powerlineblog.com/archives/011089.php.

Here We Go Again: More Koran Desecration (2005, November 1). Retrieved
   11/1/05 from http://www.rantingprofs.com/rantingprofs/2005/11/
   here_we_go_agai.html.

Herman, E. S., & Chomsky, N. (1988). *Manufacturing Consent.* New York, NY:
   Pantheon Books.

Hernandez, E. (2005, April 23). Kennedy relative tied to financing case. *The New
   York Times.* Retrieved 7/11/05 from LexisNexis Academic.

Hernandez, R. (2005, October 5). Democrats are on defensive in Maryland Senate
   race. *The New York Times.* Retrieved 10/6/05 from LexisNexis Academic.

Hewitt, H. (2005). *Blog.* Nashville, TN: Nelson Books.

Ibbitson, J. (2004, April 30). PM hopes to extricate Canada from UN box. *Globe
   and Mail*, p. A4.

Important Oil-for-Food Breakthrough (2004, November 17). Retrieved 7/14/05
   from http://www.rogerlsimon.com/mt-archives/2004/11/important_oilfo.php.

Important Oil-for-Food Update (2004, October 24). Retrieved 7/14/05 from
   http://www.rogerlsimon.com/mt-archives/2004/10/important_oilfo.php.

Incident on Haifa Street (2004, December 24). Retrieved 11/15/05 from
   http://littlegreenfootballs.com/weblog/?entry=14077_Incident_on_Haifa_Street.

Inside Air America Extra: Lizz Winstead Case (2005, August 20). Retrieved
   2/20/06 from http://radioequalizer.blogspot.com/2005/08/
   inside-air-america-extra-winstead.html.

Inside Air America, Part 1: A Trail of Debts (2005, August 17). Retrieved 2/20/06
   from http://michellemalkin.com/archives/003282.htm.

Inside Air America, Part 2: Beyond Evan — More Shell Games? (2005, August 18).
   Retrieved 2/20/06 from http://radioequalizer.blogspot.com/2005/08/
   inside-air-america-investigative-blog.html.

"Insurgents Want Their Stories Told" (2004, December 24). Retrieved 11/18/05
   from http://belmontclub.blogspot.com/2004/12/
   photographer-become-aware-that-story.html.

Interview With Scott Johnson (2004, September 14). "Special Report With Brit
   Hume." Fox News Network. Retrieved 2/24/06 from LexisNexis Academic.

Introducing Washington Post Reporter Terry Neal to Google, and the Dangers of
   Relying on Ralph Neas Talking Points (2005, May 3). Retrieved 3/20/06 from
   http://www.hughhewitt.com/old_site/cgi-bin/calendar.pl?month=5&year=2005
   &view=Event&event_id=746#postid1588.

I Propose a Name (2001, December 30). Retrieved 7/21/05 from
   http://www.iw3p.com/DailyPundit/2001_12_30_dailypundit_archive.php.

Iraqi Tribes in Anbar Arrest 270 Arab and Foreign al-Qaeda Members! (2006,
   January 27). Retrieved 3/6/06 from http://iraqthemodel.blogspot.com/2006/
   01/iraqi-tribes-in-anbar-arrest-270-arab.html.

Iraq Needs a Credible U.N. (2004, April 7). *The New York Times*. Retrieved 12/29/05 from LexisNexis Academic.

Isikoff, M., & Barry, J. (2005, May 9). Guantanamo: A scandal spreads. *Newsweek* (Periscope section). Retrieved 1/23/06 from LexisNexis Academic.

Is It Healthier to Be a Little Overweight? (2005, October). *Consumer Reports on Health*, 17(10), 8-9.

Is It Parody? I Can't Tell (2005, March 20). Retrieved 9/5/05 from http://powerlineblog.com/archives/009916.php.

Islamic Extremism: Common Concern for Muslim and Western Publics (2005, July 14). Pew Global Attitudes Project. Retrieved 7/16/05 from http://pewglobal.org/reports/display.php?ReportID=248.

Is This the Biggest Hoax Since the Sixty Minutes Story? (2005, March 21). Retrieved 7/21/05 from http://powerlineblog.com/archives/009929.php.

Jimmy Massey: A Slanderer and His MSM Enablers (2005, November 7). Retrieved 1/9/06 from http://michellemalkin.com/archives/003844.htm.

Jimmy Massey's Lies: The AP Finally Wakes Up (2005, December 14). Retrieved 12/14/05 from http://michellemalkin.com/archives/004073.htm.

Johnston, D., & Stevenson, R. W. (2005, July 15). Rove reportedly held phone talk on C.I.A. officer. *The New York Times*. Retrieved 10/3/05 from LexisNexis Academic.

Just the Story (2006, January 2). Retrieved 1/3/06 from http://www.rantingprofs.com/rantingprofs/2006/01/just_the_story.html.

Kaplan, F. (2004, October 29). 100,000 Dead — or 8,000. *Slate*. Retrieved 6/20/05 from http://slate.msn/id/2108887/.

Katz, E., Blumler, J. G., & Gurevitch, M. (1974). Uses and gratifications research. *Public Opinion Quarterly*, 37(4), 509-523.

Katz, E., & Lazarsfeld, P. F. (1955). *Personal Influence: The Part Played by People in the Flow of Mass Communications*. Glencoe, IL: Free Press.

Keller, S. J. (2004, June 21). 9/11 panel members debate Qaeda-Iraq "tie." *The New York Times*. Retrieved 1/29/06 from LexisNexis Academic.

Kirkpatrick, D. D., & Stolberg, S. G. (2005, March 22). How family's cause reached the halls of Congress. *The New York Times*. Retrieved 7/22/05 from LexisNexis Academic.

Knickmeyer, E. (2005a, October 18). Iraqis say civilians killed in U.S. raids. *The Washington Post*. Retrieved 10/18/05 from LexisNexis Academic.

Knickmeyer, E. (2005b, December 2). Ramadi insurgents flaunt threat. *The Washington Post*. Retrieved 12/24/05 from LexisNexis Academic.

Knickmeyer, E. (2005c, December 10). Iraq's mosques rock the vote as election nears. *The Washington Post*. Retrieved 12/12/05 from LexisNexis Academic.

Kojo, Kofi & Kerry (2004, March 10). Retrieved 7/13/05 from http://rogerlsimon.com/archives/00000755.htm.

Kristof, N. D. (2003, June 13). White House in denial. *The New York Times*. Retrieved 2/7/06 from LexisNexis Academic.

Krugmania (2005, August 20). Retrieved 8/21/05 from http://powerlineblog.com/archives/011407.php.

Krugman, P. (2005a, August 19). What they did last fall. *The New York Times*. Retrieved 8/27/05 from LexisNexis Academic.

Krugman, P. (2005b, August 22). Don't prettify our history. *The New York Times.* Retrieved 9/1/05 from LexisNexis Academic.

Krugman, P. (2005c, August 26). Summer of our discontent. *The New York Times.* Retrieved 8/27/05 from LexisNexis Academic.

Krugman Officially Corrects His Florida 2000 Lies (2005, August 26). Retrieved 8/27/05 from http://www.poorandstupid.com/ 2005_08_21_chronArchive.asp#112503484243947813.

Krugman Tries To Pull a Fast One (2005, August 19). Retrieved 8/29/05 from http://corner.nationalreview.com/05_08_14_corner-archive.asp#073602.

Kurtz, H. (2005). Hearings tempest downgraded to tropical storm. *The Washington Post.* Retrieved 9/13/05 from LexisNexis Academic.

Kurtz, H. (2004a, September 22). CBS, sitting between fiasco and fallout. *The Washington Post.* Retrieved 7/19/05 from LexisNexis Academic.

Kurtz, H. (2004b, November 24). Dan Rather to step down at CBS. *The Washington Post.* Retrieved 7/19/05 from LexisNexis Academic.

Kurtz, H., Dobbs, M., & Grimaldi, J. V. (2004, September 19). In rush to air, CBS quashed memo worries. *The Washington Post.* Retrieved 7/28/05 from LexisNexis Academic.

Kurtz, H., & Milbank, D. (2005, January 11). A setback for a network, and the mainstream media. *The Washington Post.* Retrieved 7/19/05 from LexisNexis Academic.

Kuypers, J. A. (2002). *Press Bias and Politics.* Westport, CT: Praeger Publishers.

Kuypers, J. A. & Cooper, S. D. (2005). A comparative framing analysis of embedded and behind-the-lines-reporting on the 2003 Iraq war. *Qualitative Research Reports in Communication,* 6(1), 1-10.

Lancet Post Number 41 (2005, March 21). Retrieved 6/18/06 from http://timlambert.org/2005/03/lancet24.

Last Nail in the Coffin (2004, September 14). Retrieved 7/25/05 from http://powerlineblog.com/archives/007837.php.

Lathem, N. (2004, March 29). Eye on 'spy' in U.N. oil scandal. *New York Post.* Retrieved 12/29/05 from LexisNexis Academic.

L.A. Times Needs a New Fact-checker for Those Editorials (2005, July 2). Retrieved 7/6/05 from http://patterico.com/2005/07/02/3276/ la-times-needs-a-new-fact-checker-for-those-editorials.

Latour, F., & Rezendes, M. (2004, September 11). Authenticity backed on Bush documents. *Boston Globe.* Retrieved 7/30/05 from LexisNexis Academic.

Laurence, C., & Samuel, H. (2005, April 24). Investigators resigned over oil for food inquiry "cover-up." *London Telegraph.* Retrieved 1/4/06 from LexisNexis Academic.

Lavie, M. (2005, April 13). Sharon rules out attacking Iran over nukes. Associated Press. Retrieved 6/6/05 from LexisNexis Academic.

Lazarsfeld, P. F., Berelson, B., & Gaudet, H. (1968). *The People's Choice,* 3rd edition. New York, NY: Columbia University Press.

Lekic, S. (2004, December 19). Photo sequence shows rebels executing electoral workers. Associated Press. Retrieved 11/17/05 from LexisNexis Academic.

Leo, J. (2004). Blogging the watchdogs. *U.S. News and World Report.* Retrieved 7/14/04 from http://www.usnews.com/usnews/issue/040719/opinion/19john.htm.

Leopold, E. (2004, November 29). Annan "disappointed" in son's lack of disclosure. Reuters News. Retrieved 1/9/06 via e-mail from Reuters group archivist.

Lesson Eighteen: Prisons and Detention Centers (n.d.). Retrieved 1/27/06 from http://www.usdoj.gov/ag/manualpart1_4.pdf.

LeSure, E. (2005, April 4). *L.A. Times, WSJ* Win Two Pulitzers Apiece. Associated Press. Retrieved 12/20/05 from LexisNexis Academic.

Let's Open a Dialogue (2004, September 05). Retrieved 3/23/05 from http://powerlineblog.com/archives/2004_09.php.

Let Us Not Speak Ill of the Dead (2005, April 17). Retrieved 10/26/05 from http://www.rantingprofs.com/rantingprofs/2005/04/let_us_not_spea.html.

Lewin, K. (1947). Frontiers in group dynamics, II: Channels of group life. *Human Relations,* 1, pp. 143-153.

Lichter, S. R., Rothman, S., & Lichter, L. S. (1990). *The Media Elite.* New York, NY: Hastings House.

Los Angeles Times Corrects False Statement Regarding Bremer Farewell Speech (2004, July 8). Retrieved 7/7/05 from http://patterico.com/2004/07/08/ilos-angeles-timesi-corrects-false-statement-regarding-bremer-farewell-speech/.

Losing Ground in Iraq (2005, April 27). *The New York Times.* Retrieved 6/12/05 from LexisNexis Academic.

Lt. Gen. David Petraeus Speaks at Princeton (2005, October 2). Retrieved 10/4/05 from http://tigerhawk.blogspot.com/2005/10/lt-gen-david-petraeus-speaks-at.html.

Lyon, S. (2005, April 4). The story behind the photo. Retrieved 11/21/05 from http://www.ap.org/pages/about/whatsnew/wn_040505b.html.

Maloney, B, & Malkin, M. (2005, August 22). Money pit. *New York Post Online.* Retrieved 2/20/06 from http://www.nypost.com/postopinion/opedcolumnists/51519.htm.

Marine's Tales of Iraq Atrocities Debunked (2005, November 7). CNN. Retrieved 1/16/06 from LexisNexis Academic.

Massing, M. (2002, September/October). A run with the pack. *Columbia Journalism Review.* Retrieved 10/26/05 from LexisNexis Academic.

Maureen Dowd's Dishonest Deletion (2003, May 14). Retrieved 8/14/05 from http://www.timeswatch.org/articles/2003/0514.asp#3.

Maureen Won't Come Clean So (2003, May 28). Retrieved 8/21/05 from http://www.belgraviadispatch.com/archives/003160.html.

McClam, E. (2005, December 10). A Marine confronts nightmares of Iraq — but are they real? Associated Press. Retrieved 1/30/06 from LexisNexis Academic.

McCombs, M. E., & Shaw, D. L. (1972). The agenda-setting function of mass media. *Public Opinion Quarterly,* 36, pp. 176-187.

Meanwhile, Back at the Hotel (2005, February 28). Retrieved 11/15/05 from http://www.rantingprofs.com/rantingprofs/2005/02/meanwhile_back_.html.

Media Critics: Haifa Street Execution Photo Edition (2005, January 1). Retrieved 11/18/05 from http://www.deadparrots.net/archives/media/0501media_critics_haifa_street_execution_photo_edition.html.

Meme (n.d.). Retrieved 6/22/05 from http://www.samizdata.net/blog/glossary_archives/002143.html.

Mencher, M. (1991). *News Reporting and Writing*. Dubuque, IA: Wm. C. Brown Publishers.

Middle Class Blues (2005, July 10). Retrieved 7/13/05 from http://vodkapundit.com/archives/007943.php.

Misreporting the Filibuster (2005, May 3). Retrieved 5/4/05 from http://powerlineblog.com/archives/010353.php.

Moore, S. (1997). "Whom does this discourse serve?": Some requirements for communication suggested by Foucault's analysis of power. *New Jersey Journal of Communication, 5*(2), 150-166.

More Bad Poll Data (2005, April 26). Retrieved 4/26/05 from http://powerlineblog.com/archives/010281.php.

More Historical Revisionism (2005, April 14). Retrieved 4/14/05 and 4/27/05 from http://instapundit.com/archives/022447.php.

More Krugmania on the 2000 Recounts (2005, August 19). Retrieved 8/29/05 from http://corner.nationalreview.com/05_08_14_corner-archive.asp#073659.

More On Those Dead Iraqis (2005, March 22). Retrieved 6/20/05 from http://sacredcowgraveyard.blogspot.com/2005/03/more-on-those-dead-iraqis.html.

Morin, R., & Balz, D. (2005, April 26). Filibuster rule change opposed. *The Washington Post*. Retrieved 6/9/05 from LexisNexis Academic.

Morley, J. (2004, April 29). From a Baghdad weekly, a global scandal. Retrieved 12/29/05 from http://www.washingtonpost.com/wp-dyn/articles/A52438-2004Apr29.html.

Murder on Haifa Street: An Update (2005, April 10). Retrieved 11/21/05 from http://powerlineblog.com/archives/010128.php.

Murphy, C., & Saffar, K. (2005, April 5). Actors in the insurgency are reluctant TV stars. *The Washington Post*. Retrieved 6/12/05 from LexisNexis Academic.

My Second "Outside the Tent" Piece in the *L.A. Times* (2005, August 21). Retrieved 8/21/05 from http://patterico.com/2005/08/21/3495/my-second-outside-the-tent-piece-in-the-la-times/.

Mystery Solved? (2005, April 6). Retrieved 7/21/05 from http://powerlineblog.com/archives/010093.php.

Naked (2004, September 14). Retrieved 7/28/05 from http://powerlineblog.com/archives/007831.php.

Neal, T. M. (2005a, May 2). Attitudes toward filibuster are about power, not partisanship. *The Washington Post*. Retrieved 6/3/05 from LexisNexis Academic.

Neal, T. M. (2005b, May 4). Attitudes toward filibuster are about power, not partisanship (correction appended). *The Washington Post*. Retrieved 6/3/05 from LexisNexis Academic.

New Doc: Fake, But Accurate! (2005, March 19). Retrieved 8/1/05 from http://fishkite.com/2005/03/19/693/.

New Questions on Bush Guard Duty (2004, September 8). CBS News. Retrieved 7/25/05 from http://www.cbsnews.com/stories/2004/09/08/60II/main641984.shtml.

News Style (n.d.). Retrieved 1/24/06 from http://en.wikipedia.org/wiki/News_style.

Newsweek Apologizes for Riot-sparking Koran Story (2005, May 15). Retrieved 1/23/06 from http://www.themoderatevoice.com/posts/1116199979.shtml.

Newsweek Backs Off Quran Desecration Story (2005, May 15). CNN.com. Retrieved 1/23/06 from LexisNexis Academic.

Newsweek Has Retracted Its Koran-flushing Story (2005, May 16). Retrieved 1/27/06 from http://instapundit.com/archives/023026.php.

Newsweek Lied, People Died (2005, May 16). Retrieved 1/27/06 from http://semirandomramblings.blogspot.com/2005/05/newsweek-lied-people-died.html.

Newsweek Statement on Qur'an Story from Editor Mark Whitaker (2005, May 16). *PR Newswire*. Retrieved 1/23/06 from LexisNexis Academic.

Newsweek Uses "R" Word and Retracts Koran Desecration Story (2005, May 16). Retrieved 1/23/06 from http://www.themoderatevoice.com/posts/1116280793.shtml.

New York Times Blows One — BIG TIME! (2005, July 6). Retrieved 7/9/05 from http://markinmexico.blogspot.com/2005/07/new-york-times-blows-one-big-time.html.

New York Times Co. v. Sullivan (1964). 376 U.S. 254.

New York Times Master's [sic] Coverage Takes Balls (2005, April 6). Retrieved 3/21/06 from http://www.thenationaldebate.com/blog/archives/2005/04/new_york_times_18.html.

No Coverage of Soldier Capturing His Would-be Murderer and Saving His Life! (2005, July 15). Retrieved 7/16/05 from http://treyjackson.typepad.com/junction/2005/07/no_coveraage_of.html.

Noelle-Neumann, E. (1993). *The Spiral of Silence* (2nd ed.). Chicago, IL: University of Chicago Press.

No Gloom or Doom (2005, November 4). Retrieved 11/4/05 from http://www.rantingprofs.com/rantingprofs/2005/11/no_gloom_or_doo.html.

No Reason for Networks to Show Bush's Iraq Speech? (2005, June 27). Retrieved 7/17/05 from http://www.davidcorn.com/2005/06/no_reason_for_n.php.

Norfolk, A., & Jenkins, R. (2005, July 13, 2005). A laughing lad from the chippie and his wild mate. *Times of London*. Retrieved 7/13/05 from LexisNexis Academic.

Not Sure Who to Send This E-mail To (2003, May 14). Retrieved 8/21/05 from http://www.thenationaldebate.com/blogger/articles/original.htm.

NYT Caught Lying Again (2005, July 6). Retrieved 7/8/05 from http://www.dailypundit.com/newarchives/002791.php.

NY Times = Suckers (2005, July 15). Retrieved 9/14/05 from http://www.liberaloasis.com/archives/071005.htm#071505.

O'Connor Leaves... (2005, July 2). *Los Angeles Times*. Retrieved 7/11/05 from LexisNexis Academic.

O'Connor Leaves...Correction Appended (2005, July 7). *Los Angeles Times*. Retrieved 7/11/05 from LexisNexis Academic.

Oh, *That* Liberal Media (2005, April 22). Retrieved 5/3/05 from http://vodkapundit.com/archives/007801.php.

"Oil-for-Food!" Get Yer Hot "Oil-for-Food"...READ ALL ABOUDIT! (2004, March 29). Retrieved 7/13/05 from http://rogerlsimon.com/archives/00000814.htm.

Okrent, D. (2004a, March 14). Setting the Record Straight (But Who Can Find the Record?). *The New York Times.* Retrieved 1/31/06 from LexisNexis Academic.

Okrent, D. (2004b, March 28). The Privileges of Opinion, the Obligations of Fact. *The New York Times.* Retrieved 1/31/06 from LexisNexis Academic.

Okrent, D. (2004c, July 25). Is the *New York Times* a Liberal Newspaper? *The New York Times.* Retrieved 3/7/2005 from LexisNexis Academic.

On the AP and the Murders (2004, December 24). Retrieved 11/21/05 from http://powerlineblog.com/archives/009018.php.

On the Mosque Bombing (2006, February 24). Retrieved 2/24/06 from http://powerlineblog.com/archives/013235.php.

Oops... (2005, July 6). Retrieved 7/9/05 from http://www.washingtonmonthly.com/archives/individual/2005_07/006658.php.

Out-and-Out Dishonesty at the *New York Times* (2005, April 27). Retrieved 4/27/05 from http://instapundit.com/archives/022681.php.

Outing, S. (2005, June 15). The 11 layers of citizen journalism. *Poynteronline.* Retrieved 3/3/06 from http://www.poynter.org/content/content_view.asp?id=83126.

Oxfeld, J. (2005, March 1). Letting the blogs out. *Editor & Publisher.* Retrieved 7/11/05 from LexisNexis Academic.

Parker, K. (2005, December 28). Lord of the Blogs. Retrieved 12/31/05 from http://www.townhall.com/opinion/columns/kathleenparker/2005/12/28/180480.html.

Paul Krugman Just Can't Get It Right (2005, August 26). Retrieved 8/27/05 from http://patterico.com/2005/08/26/3512/paul-krugman-just-cant-get-it-right/.

Paul Krugman: Liar, or Just Sloppy? (2005, August 19). Retrieved 8/31/05 from http://brainster.blogspot.com/2005_08_14_brainster_archive.html#1124470072 08455651.

Period (2005, September 12). Retrieved 9/13/05 from http://atrios.blogspot.com/2005_09_11_atrios_archive.html#112653667287335870.

Permalink (n.d.). Retrieved 2/13/06 from http://www.samizdata.net/blog/glossary_archives/002034.html.

Persistent, Pervasive and Pernicious: The "100,000 Civilians Dead" Canard (2005, March 18). Retrieved 6/03/05 from http://www.thatliberalmedia.com/archives/003999.html.

Picture of the Day: Do I Offend? (2006, February 21). Retrieved 2/28/06 from http://elephantsinacademia.blogspot.com/2006_02_01_elephantsinacademia_archive.html#114052718853139177#links.

Pictures From the Air of Gulfport and Biloxi Areas (2005, September 10). Retrieved 2/10/06 from http://www.murdoconline.net/archives/002772.html.

Pinocchios of the Volcker Committee (2005, April 20). Retrieved 7/13/05 from http://www.rogerlsimon.com/mt-archives/2005/04/pinocchios_of_t.php.

Porter, B., & Ferris, T. (1988). *The Practice of Journalism*. Englewood Cliffs, NJ: Prentice Hall.

Pravda-Media Regresses to Sand Box Mentality (2005, October 7). Retrieved 10/7/05 from http://polipundit.com/index.php?p=10363.

Prelude (2005, August 1). Retrieved 3/6/06 from http://www.michaelyon-online.com/wp/prelude.htm.

President Visits Arkansas (2003, May 5). Retrieved 8/14/05 from http://www.whitehouse.gov/news/releases/2003/05/print/20030505-4.html.

Q: Who's Included? (2005, September 22). Retrieved 12/24/05 from http://blog.memeorandum.com/050922/whos-included.

Rall, T. (2005, February 22). Bloggers and the new McCarthyism. Retrieved 2/13/06 from http://www.uexpress.com/tedrall/index.html?uc_full_date=20050222.

Raphael, T. (2004, February 9). Saddam's global payroll. *Opinion Journal*. Retrieved 12/29/05 from http://www.opinionjournal.com/extra/?id=110004667.

Rathergate Update (2004, November 21). Retrieved 7/16/05 from http://instapundit.com/archives/019380.php.

Rather Puts Neck on Chopping Block (2004, September 10). Retrieved 7/25/05 from http://powerlineblog.com/archives/007778.php.

Rather Resigned (2004, November 23). Retrieved 7/16/05 from http://www.captainsquartersblog.com/mt/archives/003150.php.

Real Memo, Fake Story (2005, April 8). Retrieved 7/24/05 from http://powerlineblog.com/archives/010105.php.

Resolving Competing Claims (2005, October 18). Retrieved 10/18/05 from http://www.rantingprofs.com/rantingprofs/2005/10/resolving_compe.html.

Ridiculous *New York Times* Anonymous Source of the Day (2005, July 15). Retrieved 9/14/05 from http://atrios.blogspot.com/2005_07_10_atrios_archive.html#112142973339466074.

Risen, J. (2004, July 14). How Niger uranium story defied wide skepticism. *The New York Times*. Retrieved 1/29/06 from LexisNexis Academic.

Roberts, L., Lafta, R., Garfield, R., Khudhairi, J., & Burnham, G. (2004). Mortality before and after the 2003 invasion of Iraq: Cluster sample survey. *The Lancet*. Retrieved 6/13/05 from http://image.thelancet.com/extras/04art10342web.pdf.

Robinson, W. V., & Latour, F. (2004, September 9). Bid cited to boost Bush in Guard. *Boston Globe*. Retrieved 7/28/05 from Lexis/Nexis Academic.

Rockwell, P. (2004, May 16). "I killed innocent people for our government." *Sacramento Bee*. Retrieved 1/29/06 from LexisNexis Academic.

Rogers, E. M. (1995). *Diffusion of innovations* (4th ed.). New York, NY: Free Press.

Roig-Franzia, M., & Hsu, S. (2005, September 3). Many evacuated, but thousands still waiting; White House shifts blame to state and local officials. *The Washington Post*. Retrieved 9/14/05 from LexisNexis Academic.

Rosen, J. (2005, February 11). Eason Jordan resigns. Retrieved 3/24/05 from http://journalism.nyu.edu/pubzone/weblogs/pressthink/2005/02/11/esn_res.html

Rubin, A. J. (2004a, June 29). Before leaving, Bremer visits a welcome place. *Los Angeles Times*, p. A6.

Rubin, A. J. (2004b, July 4). Premier gets off to strong start. *Los Angeles Times*, pp. A1 & A9.

Saddam's U.N. Financiers (2004, April 7). Opinion Journal. Retrieved 12/29/05 from http://www.opinionjournal.com/editorial/feature.html?id=110004919.

Schmerker, J. (2005, March 30). One year later, Marine's story marches on. *The Mountaineer*. Retrieved 2/9/06 from http://www.themountaineer.com/archives/2005/03/30/topstories_oneyearlatermariness.html.

Seelye, K. Q. (2005, May 16). *Newsweek* apologizes for report of Koran insult. *The New York Times*. Retrieved 1/23/06 from LexisNexis Academic.

Seelye, K. Q., & Blumenthal, R. (2004, September 9). Documents suggest Guard gave Bush special treatment. *The New York Times*. Retrieved 7/28/05 from Lexis/Nexis Academic.

Senate "Talking Points" Update and Timeline (2005, March 22). Retrieved 8/1/05 from http://fishkite.com/2005/03/22/701/.

Several Readers Have Written (2005, July 14). Retrieved 7/14/05 from http://instapundit.com/archives/024254.php.

Shame, Guilt, the Muslim Psyche, and the Danish Cartoons (2006, February 6). Retrieved 3/3/06 from http://drsanity.blogspot.com/2006/02/shame-guilt-muslim-psyche-and-danish.html.

Shame on NBC (2005, December 4). Retrieved 12/24/05 from http://www.rantingprofs.com/rantingprofs/2005/12/shame_on_nbc.html.

Shearer, E. (2004, October/November). Rooting out rowback. *American Journalism Review*, 26(5), p. 10.

Shiller Shills for the Left on Social Security (2005, March 21) Retrieved 6/18/06 from http://www.poorandstupid.com/2005_03_20chronArchive.asp#111138827950153042

Show Us the Memo (2005, March 22). Retrieved 7/21/05 from http://powerlineblog.com/archives/009937.php.

Show Us the Source (2005, March 23). Retrieved 7/22/05 from http://powerlineblog.com/archives/009943.php.

Sixty Four Dollars (2004, December 23). Retrieved 11/21/05 from http://belmontclub.blogspot.com/2004/12/sixty-four-dollars-salon-claims-that.html.

Slavin, B. (2005, March 16). Most Iraqis say future looks brighter. *USA Today*. Retrieved 1/24/06 from LexisNexis Academic.

Slover, P. (2004, September 15). Ex-aide disavows Bush Guard memos. *The Dallas Morning News*. Retrieved 7/30/05 from http://www.dallasnews.com/sharedcontent/dws/dn/latestnews/stories/091504dnpolnatguard.1185eb4ae.html.

Small Party and Great Hopes (2004, June 29). Retrieved 7/11/05 from http://iraqthemodel.blogspot.com/2004_06_01_iraqthemodel_archive.html.

Smith, D. (2005, April 14). The enemy on our airwaves. *The Wall Street Journal*, A14.

Smolkin, R. (2003, March). Howell much is too much? *American Journalism Review*. Retrieved 6/13/05 from LexisNexis Academic.

Society of Professional Journalists (1996). Code of ethics. Retrieved 9/6/05 from http://www.spj.org/ethics_code.asp.

Soldier Survives Attack; Captures, Medically Treats Sniper (2005, July 15). Retrieved 7/17/05 from http://www.armytimes.com/ story.php?f=1-292925-976420.php.

Solomon, D. (2005, March 20). Blogged down. *The New York Times*. Retrieved 9/5/05 from LexisNexis Academic.

So: Where Did It Come From? (2005, March 22). Retrieved 7/21/05 from http://powerlineblog.com/archives/009940.php.

Special Investigation #4 — The Big Shame (2005, April 3). Retrieved 7/13/05 from http://www.rogerlsimon.com/mt-archives/2005/04/special_investi.php.

Special Report #1 — Oil-for-Food Investigation (2005, March 27). Retrieved 12/29/05 from http://www.rogerlsimon.com/mt-archives/ 2005/03/special_report.php.

Special Report #2 — The Case of the "Main Mentor" (2005, March 30). Retrieved 12/29/05 from http://www.rogerlsimon.com/mt-archives/2005/ 03/special_report_1.php [sic].

Special Report #3 — "Corruption in the Palace of Justice" (2005, April 1). Retrieved 12/29/05 from http://www.rogerlsimon.com/mt-archives/2005/ 04/special_report_2.php [sic].

Speechless (2004, July 1). Retrieved 7/15/05 from http://timblair.spleenville.com/ archives/007071.php.

Spinner, J., & Sebti, B. (2005, November 4). In and around Iraq, gloom takes a holiday. *The Washington Post*. Retrieved 11/4/05 from LexisNexis Academic.

Squeeze Play (2004, June 21). Retrieved 1/29/06 from http://rantingprofs.typepad.com/rantingprofs/2004/06/squeeze_play.html.

SS Reform is Dead; Long Live SS Reform (2005, March 15). Retrieved 6/22/05 from http://www.qando.net/details.aspx?Entry=1394.

Stevenson, R. W., & Johnston, D. (2004, July 18). New reports reopen debate over whether Iraq sought uranium in Niger. *The New York Times*. Retrieved 1/29/06 from LexisNexis Academic.

Stokes, J. (2004, December 23). AP on its Iraqi photographers and insurgents. Retrieved 11/18/05 from http://www.poynter.org/forum/ view_post.asp?id=8533.

Stolberg, S. G. (2005, March 16). Senate splits in test vote on Social Security. *The New York Times*. Retrieved 7/11/05 from LexisNexis Academic.

Stonewalling on 46th Street (2004, February 9). Retrieved 7/13/05 from http://rogerlsimon.com/archives/00000683.htm.

Strengthening Social Security for the 21st Century (2005, February). Retrieved 6/30/05 from http://www.whitehouse.gov/infocus/social-security/ 200501/socialsecurity.pdf.

Struck, D. (2004, December 8). Former Marine testifies to atrocities in Iraq. *The Washington Post*. Retrieved 1/29/06 from LexisNexis Academic.

Stupid Papers and GOP Astroturf (2004, August 17). Retrieved 1/10/06 from http://www.dailykos.com/story/2004/8/17/17029/2550.

Sullivan, A. (2004, September 14). Retorting 101. *The New Republic Online*. Retrieved 2/27/06 from http://www.tnr.com/ doc.mhtml?pt=ojT4kAHMxYif0J12sUAH8B==.

Sunnstein, C. R. (2002). The law of group polarization. *The Journal of Political Philosophy,* 10(2), 175-195.

Taliban Giving Up in Afghanistan? (2005, February 21). Retrieved 7/9/05 from http://www.captainsquartersblog.com/mt/archives/003896.php.

TANG Typewriter Follies; Wingnuts Wrong (2004, September 10). Retrieved 3/22/05 from http://www.dailykos.com/story/2004/9/10/34914/1603.

That Lancet Study! The One About 100,000 Dead Iraqis (2005, March 20). Retrieved 6/20/05 from http://sacredcowgraveyard.blogspot.com/2005/03/that-lancet-study-one-about-100000.html.

That Liberal Media (2005, March 18). Retrieved 3/23/05 from http://instapundit.com/archives/021873.php.

That Was Then, This Is Now (2005, April 12). Retrieved 4/12/05 from http://powerlineblog.com/archives/010145.php.

The Associated Press Makes It Up (2004, September 03). Retrieved 3/23/05 from http://powerlineblog.com/archives/2004_09.php.

The Beat Goes On (2005, September 22). Retrieved 9/23/05 from http://rantingprofs.com/rantingprofs/2005/09/the_beat-goes_o.html.

The Bush "Guard Memos" are Forgeries (2004, September 11). Retrieved 7/25/05 from http://www.flounder.com/bush2.htm.

The Coverage of Civilian Casualties in Iraq (2004, January 26). Retrieved 1/29/06 from http://rantingprofs.typepad.com/rantingprofs/2004/01/the_coverage_of.html.

The Daily Kos Strikes Out (2004, September 10). Retrieved 7/25/05 from http://powerlineblog.com/archives/007779.php.

The Evolution of the Maureen Dowd Ellipsis-Distortion Story (n.d.). Retrieved 8/14/05 from http://www.thenationaldebate.com/blogger/articles/dowd1.htm.

The Fox Hunting Standard: Why No Demonstrations Against Terror? (2005, July 15). Retrieved 7/17/05 from http://www.rantingprofs.com/rantingprofs/2005/07/why_no_demonstr.html.

"The Head of the Snake" (2006, March 3). Retrieved 3/6/06 from http://www.michaeltotten.com/archives/001068.html.

The Hounds of Husaybah (2005, November 28). Retrieved 3/6/06 from http://billroggio.com/archives/2005/11/the_hounds_of_husayb.php.

The Information War (2006, February 27). Retrieved 3/3/06 from http://shrinkwrapped.blogs.com/blog/2006/02/the_information.html.

Their Worst Nightmare (2005, April 24). Retrieved 4/25/05 from http://justoneminute.typepad.com/main/2005/04/their_worst_nig.html.

The Jaws of Victory (2005, March 1). Retrieved 11/15/05 from http://www.mudvillegazette.com/archives/002276.html.

The Krugman Correction (2005, August 26). Retrieved 8/27/05 from http://michellemalkin.com/archives/003406.htm.

The *LA Times* Reporter Responds! (2004, July 4). Retrieved 7/7/05 from http://iraqnow.blogspot.com/2004/07/la-times-reporter-responds.html.

The Media and the Unhinged Marine (2005, November 9). Retrieved 1/9/06 from http://michellemalkin.com/archives/003861.htm.

The Mysterious Bremer Farewell Speech (2004, July 7). Retrieved 7/7/05 from http://deadparrots.net/archives/current_events/0407the_mysterious_bremer_fare well_speech.html.

The Mythology of Cuban Medical Care (2005, March 14). Retrieved 3/20/06 from http://www.captainsquartersblog.com/mt/archives/004070.php.

The *New York Times* Responds to Criticism of its Coverage on Civilian Casualties (2004, March 1). Retrieved 1/29/06 from http://rantingprofs.typepad.com/ rantingprofs/2004/03/the_new_york_ti.html.

The Odds Against (2004, December 20). Retrieved 11/15/05 from http://belmontclub.blogspot.com/2004/12/odds-against-associated-press-article. html.

The Person Next to You is Nuts (2005, June 7). Retrieved 6/22/05 from http://www.buzzmachine.com/archives/2005_06_07.html.

The *Post* Has Decided Who to Believe (2005, December 2). Retrieved 12/2/05 from http://www.rantingprofs.com/rantingprofs/2005/12/the_post_has_de.html.

The *Post* Recaps Rathergate (2004, September 19). Retrieved 7/28/05 from http://powerlineblog.com/archives/007894.php.

The Pulitzer Prize for Felony Murder... (2005, April 5). Retrieved 11/18/05 from http://powerlineblog.com/archives/010066.php.

The Real Robert Strong (2004, September 12). Retrieved 8/4/05 from http://powerlineblog.com/archives/007814.php.

There are Benefits to Embedding (2005, April 21). Retrieved 4/21/05 from http://www.rantingprofs.com/rantingprofs/2005/04/there_are_benef.html.

The Return of the Restaurant Story (2005, January 23). Retrieved 9/23/05 from http://www.rantingprofs.com/rantingprofs/2005/01/the_return_of_t.html.

The Rowback of All Rowbacks (2004, July 14). Retrieved 1/29/06 from http://www.rantingprofs.com/rantingprofs/2004/07/the_rowback_of_.html.

The Safest City in Iraq (2006, February 21). Retrieved 2/28/06 from http://www.michaeltotten.com/archives/001061.html.

The Senate Resolution You Didn't Hear About (March 16, 2005). Retrieved 3/24/05 from http://www.poorandstupid.com/2005_03_chronArchive.asp# 111099604476114640

The Smoking Memo (2004, September 14). Retrieved 7/25/05 from http://littlegreenfootballs.com/weblog/?entry=12615&only.

The Sixty-first Minute (2004, September 9). Retrieved 7/25/05 from http://powerlineblog.com/archives/007760.php.

The Sunnis (2005, October 14). Retrieved 10/14/05 from http://www.rantingprofs.com/rantingprofs/2005/10/the_sunnis.html.

The TV Networks Shouldn't Broadcast Bush's Propaganda Speech (2005, June 27). Retrieved 7/17/05 from http://americablog.blogspot.com/2005/06/ tv-networks-shouldnt-broadcast-bushs.html.

The UN's Coalition of the Bribed (2004, November 17). *Chicago Tribune*, p. 24.

The Utah of the Middle East (2006, February 28). Retrieved 3/6/06 from http://www.michaeltotten.com/archives/001066.html.

The *Washington Post's* New Aversion to the F-Word (2005, May 27). Retrieved 6/3/05 from http://www.nationalreview.com/benchmemos/064619.asp.

"They Were Good Muslims" (2005, July 13). Retrieved 7/13/05 from
    http://www.rantingprofs.com/rantingprofs/2005/07/they_were_good_.html.
To Our Readers (2004, September 15). Retrieved 7/28/05 from
    http://powerlineblog.com/archives/007851.php.
To Witness (2005, July 18). Retrieved 2/10/06 from
    http://www.buzzmachine.com/index.php/2005/07/18/to-witness/.
Trackback (n.d.). Retrieved 2/13/06 from
    http://www.samizdata.net/blog/glossary_archives/003617.html.
Trouble at the UN — Opposing Papers on Same Side (2004, April 7). Retrieved
    7/13/05 from http://rogerlsimon.com/00000840.htm.
Trouble in (Volcker) Paradise? (2005, April 19). Retrieved 12/29/05 from
    http://www.rogerlsimon.com/mt-archives/2005/04/trouble_in_volc.php.
Tyson, A. S. (2005, April 21). Horror glimpsed from the inside of a Humvee in Iraq.
    The Washington Post. Retrieved 9/23/05 from LexisNexis Academic.
Uncovering the Coverup — More Mouselli On the Way (2005, April 12). Retrieved
    7/13/05 from http://www.rogerlsimon.com/mt-archives/2005/04/
    uncovering_the.php.
Unprofessional — *WaPo*'s Rathergate (2005, September 12). Retrieved 9/14/05
    from http://www.dailykos.com/story/2005/9/12/124433/197.
UNSCAM Should Not Be Ideological (2004, April 29). Retrieved 7/13/05 from
    http://rogerlsimon.com/archives/00000908.htm.
UPDATE: Oil-for-Resignations (2005, April 23). Retrieved 7/13/05 from
    http://www.rogerlsimon.com/mt-archives/2005/04/update_oilforre.php.
U.S. Military Says Airstrikes Destroyed Suspected Terror Base in Western Iraq
    (2005, August 26). The Associated Press. Retrieved 10/27/05 from LexisNexis
    Academic.
VandeHei, J. (2005, June 16). Bush is expected to address specifics on Iraq. *The
    Washington Post.* Retrieved 7/17/05 from LexisNexis Academic.
Waiting for Mr. Hayes (2004, September 7). Retrieved 3/22/05 from
    http://powerlineblog.com/archives/2004_09.php.
WaPo Follies (2005, September 12). Retrieved 9/13/05 from
    http://atrios.blogspot.com/2005_09_11_atrios_archive.html#112654608631375
    564.
Washington Post Issues Correction on Bremer Farewell Speech (2004, July 9).
    Retrieved 7/7/05 from http://patterico.com/2004/07/09/1687/
    iwashington-posti-issues-correction-on-bremer-farewell-speech/.
We Are All Misinformed! (2006, February 23). Retrieved 3/10/06 from
    http://twentyfourstepstoliberty.blogspot.com/2006/02/we-are-all-misinformed-y
    ou-guys-always_23.html.
We Hear From Mr. Borenstein (2004, September 7). Retrieved 3/23/05 from
    http://powerlineblog.com/archives/2004_09.php.
Weisman, J. (2004, October 12). Senate passes corporate tax bill. *The Washington
    Post.* Retrieved 7/1/05 from LexisNexis Academic.
Weisman, J. (2005a, March 15). Skepticism of Bush's Social Security plan is
    growing. *The Washington Post.* Retrieved 6/12/05 from LexisNexis Academic.

Weisman, J. (2005b, March 19). Retirement accounts questioned; Paper challenges expected benefits. *The Washington Post*. Retrieved 6/9/05 from LexisNexis Academic.

Well, What Would You Suggest? (2005, February 5). Retrieved 4/5/05 from http://www.rantingprofs.com/rantingprofs/2005/02/well_what_would.html.

What Exactly Did the *Post* Say About That Memo? (2005, March 31). Retrieved 9/19/05 from http://michellemalkin.com/archives/001935.htm.

What I Didn't Find in the *NY Times* (2004, July 18). Retrieved 1/29/06 from http://justoneminute.typepad.com/main/2004/07/what_i_didnt_fi.html.

What Independence Means For Me (2005, July 5). Retrieved 7/11/05 from http://afreeiraqi.blogspot.com/2005/07/what-independence-means-for-me.html.

What's Coming Out Now (2005, April 19). Retrieved 4/19/05 from http://www.rantingprofs.com/rantingprofs/2005/04/whats_coming_ou.html.

What to Do When the Polls Don't Go Your Way (2005, March 17). Retrieved 1/24/06 from http://www.rantingprofs.com/rantingprofs/2005/03/what_to_do_when.html.

When the Story Gets in the Way of the Truth (2005, May 15). Retrieved 1/23/06 from http://www.buzzmachine.com/archives/2005_05_15.html#009685.

Where's the Follow-Up? (2005, April 28). Retrieved 4/28/05 from http://www.rantingprofs.com/rantingprofs/2005/04/wheres_the_foll.html.

Whitaker, M. (2005, May 23). The editor's desk. *Newsweek*. Retrieved 1/23/06 from LexisNexis Academic.

White, D. M. (1950). The "gatekeeper": A case study in the selection of news. *Journalism Quarterly, 27*(4), 383-390.

White, J. (2005, November 1). Guantanamo desperation seen in suicide attempts. *The Washington Post*. Retrieved 11/3/05 from LexisNexis Academic.

Why Do They Hate Us? (2005, May 16). Retrieved 1/23/06 from http://www.rantingprofs.com/rantingprofs/2005/05/why_do_they_hat.html.

Wilson, J. C. IV (2003, July 6). What I didn't find in Africa. *The New York Times*. Retrieved 2/7/06 from LexisNexis Academic.

Wilson-Lied Media Spin Update (2004, July 18). Retrieved 1/29/06 from http://instapundit.com/archives/016608.php.

Winnett, R. (2005, April 3). "Cover-up" row on report clearing Annan. *Times of London*. Retrieved 1/3/06 from LexisNexis Academic.

Winnett, R., & Leppard, D. (2005, July 10). Leaked no. 10 dossier reveals Al-Qaeda's British recruits. *Times of London*. Retrieved 7/13/05 from LexisNexis Academic.

Wong, E. (2004a, January 13). G.I.'s fire on family in car, killing 2, witnesses say. *The New York Times*. Retrieved 1/29/06 from LexisNexis Academic.

Wong, E. (2004b, January 14). Army copter downed west of Baghdad in hotbed of anti-U.S. sentiment. *The New York Times*. Retrieved 2/7/06 from LexisNexis Academic.

Wong, E. (2005, March 21). 24 Insurgents die in attack near Bagdad. *The New York Times*. Retrieved 6/9/05 from LexisNexis Academic.

Worth, R. F. (2005, March 17). Many Iraqis losing hope that politics will yield real change. *The New York Times*. Retrieved 1/24/06 from LexisNexis Academic.

Wright, R. (2005, July 15). Support for Bin Laden, violence down among Muslims, poll says. *The Washington Post*. Retrieved 8/15/05 from LexisNexis Academic.

Yancey, M. (2005, April 6). Sen. Martinez's office source of Schiavo politics memo. Associated Press. Retrieved 7/24/05 from LexisNexis Academic.

Yeah, That's a Winning Strategy (2005, May 3). Retrieved 5/3/05 from http://www.rantingprofs.com/rantingprofs/2005/05/yeah_thats_a_wi.html.

Yet Another Falsehood on the Front Page of the *Los Angeles Times* (2004, July 4). Retrieved 7/7/05 from http://www.patterico.com/2004/07/04/yet-another-falsehood-on-the-front-page-of-the-los-angeles-times.

Yost, P. (2005, July 20). Roberts has backed administration policies. Associated Press. Retrieved 7/21/05 from LexisNexis Academic.

Your Foreign Relations Committee at Work! (2005, April 20). Retrieved 12/29/05 from http://www.rogerlsimon.com/mt-archives/2005/04/your_foreign_re.php.

Zerbisias, A. (2004, November 25). The pajamahadeens are digging their own graves. *Toronto Star,* sec. A, p. 27. Retrieved 3/22/05 from LexisNexis Academic.

Index

B

D

E

F

G

H

I

J

K

L

M

N

O

P

Q

R

S

T

Y

Z